Explore th

NELLES

GW00342473

PORTUGAL

Authors:
Gabriel Calvo, Sabine Tzschaschel

An Up-to-date travel guide with 150 color photos
and 14 maps

First Edition
1996

Dear Reader,

Being up-to-date is the main goal of the Nelles series. To achieve it, we have a network of far-flung correspondents who keep us abreast of the latest developments in the travel scene, and our cartographers always make sure that maps and texts are adjusted to each other.

Each travel chapter ends with its own list of useful tips, accommodations, restaurants, tourist offices, sights. At the end of the book you will find practical information from A to Z. But the travel world is fast moving, and we cannot guarantee that all the contents are always valid. Should you come across a discrepancy, please write us at: Nelles Verlag GmbH, Schleissheimer Str. 371 b, D-80935 München, Germany, Tel: (089) 3515084, Fax: (089) 3542544.

LEGEND

✳ Place of Interest	National Border	Expressway
▪ Public or Significant Building	Sesimbra — Place Mentioned in Text	Multi-Lane Highway
■ Hotel	⇥ ⇥ Airport, Airfield	Principal Highway
● Restaurant		National Road
■ ○ Shopping Center, Market	♣ National Park, Nature Reserve	Important Main Road
✝ Church	Torre 1993 Mountain Summit (Height in Meters)	Main Road
—●— Subway	9 IP1 Route Number	Secondary Road
〜 Beach	25 Distance in Kilometers	Track
		Railway

PORTUGAL
© Nelles Verlag GmbH, 80935 München
All rights reserved

First Edition 1996
ISBN 3-88618-417-X
Printed in Slovenia

Publisher:	Günter Nelles	**Photo Editor:**	K. Bärmann-Thümmel
Editor in Chief:	Berthold Schwarz	**Lithos:**	Schimann, Karlskron
Project Editors:	Dr. Gabriel Calvo	**Cartography:**	Nelles Verlag GmbH,
	Dr. Sabine Tzschaschel		München,
Editors: Susanne Braun, Andrea Russ			by courtesy of
English Editor:	Anne Midgette		RV-Verlag, München
Translation:	Marton Radkai	**Printed by:**	Gorenjski Tisk

TABLE OF CONTENTS

TRAVEL INFORMATION

MAP LIST

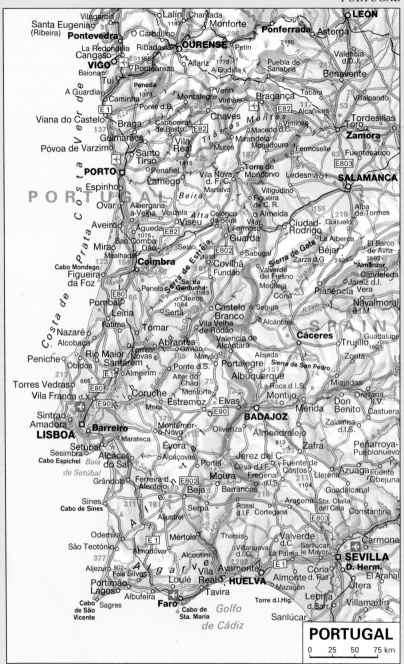

PORTUGAL

0   25   50   75 km

HISTORY

In 1995, Portugal's electric company EDP was forced to interrupt construction of the Côa dam in the Tras-os-Montes region. A young archaeologist had discovered a 12.5-mile-long (20 km) stretch of cliff with rock carvings depicting animals, estimated at 20,000 years of age.

This is not, however, the only evidence of Portugal's dense settlement before and during the Bronze Age: megalithic tombs, cultic sites, and dolmens (*antas*) are scattered throughout the country. In more recent history, some of these have been integrated into newer buildings or turned into chapels, such as those in Pavía or Alcoperta. A great number of cromlechs, large flat stones supported by four other stones, have also been discovered, such as the one in Herdade dos Almendros near Évora; so, too, have proud and phallic menhirs, such as those of Abeilhoa or Outeiro.

During the second millenium B.C., Phoenicians reached the Atlantic coast of Portugal, and true to their mercantile tradition, established several trading posts in what became Lisbon, Nazaré and Aveiro. They were followed by the Carthaginians, who began settling the Algarve coast from the 4th century B.C. onwards. At the time the southern inland region of the Iberian Peninsula was populated by tribes of Ibero-Celts, descendants of Berber tribes who had migrated from North Africa and mixed with the Celts coming southward around 600 B.C. In the north of Portugal, archaeologists discovered the remains of Celtic round houses and mighty fortified walls known

Preceding pages: The colorful roosters of Barcelos – Portugal's national symbol. Fishing is a main source of income. A handsome couple. Left: The menhir of Telheiro.

as *castro* or *citânia*, such as those in Póvoa de Lanhoso and Briteiros near Guimarães. The boars and bulls of stone, cultic figures endowed with magic power, also date from this period. In fact the "boar of Murça" gave its name to the wine produced in the region.

At the beginning of the Christian Era, Portugal was on the edge of the known world. The Greek geographer Strabo described the Lusitanians as a people that could not be compared to the other Mediterraneans; they drank a kind of beer instead of wine, used suet instead of oil, ate acorns and lived up in the mountains subsisting as husbandmen or bandits.

Viriato Against the Romans

The Romans arrived on the Iberian Peninsula in 218 B.C. during the second Punic War. Having defeated the Carthaginians, they turned their attention to the Iberian Celts. The shepherd Viriato, who hailed from the Serra da Estrêla, made history with his ferocious resistance against the colonizers. By means of guerilla tactics, he was able to trounce the Romans several times before being murdered by a traitor. A monument has been erected to him in Viseu.

The Romans were particularly interested in exploiting the agricultural possibilities of their new province. They introduced such staples as olives, wheat, grapes and cultivated plants, and established villages in the plains. Farms, known as *vila rustica*, were strategically located on rivers or in ports to facilitate the transport of produce back to Rome. The owners, or *domini*, were Romans; their workers were local slaves.

Remains of the old Roman communities are sprinkled all over Portugal. Some lie hidden under modern cities. Some finds have been neatly integrated into modern buildings, as in the basements of the museums in Coimbra and Mértola. There are excavation sites in,

among others, Milreu and Vilamoura on the Algarve, in Pisões near Beja, in Torre de Palma near Monforte, in Miróbriga near Santiago do Cacém, near Torres Novas, and in Conímbriga near Condeixa. In addition, you can find a number of bridges, roads, and the remains of aqueducts throughout the country.

While Pliny the Elder served as an official in Iberia from 69 to 73 A.D., Portugal was part of the province of Lusitania. Its capital was Augusta Emerita (now Mérida), and it was divided into three administrative districts, *Pacensis* (Beja), *Scalabitanus* (Santarém) and *Bracarensis* (Braga). The province encompassed 45 towns, including five colonies, the three free cities of Évora, Beja and Alcácer do Sal, and the port citiy of Olisipo, a *Municipium* of Roman citizens that later became Lisbon. The other 36 had to pay taxes (*stipendia*) to Rome.

Above: A Roman mosaic in Conímbriga.
Right: The temple of Diana in Évora, an-
other Roman relic.

Barbarians from the North

When the Huns invaded Central Europe during the 4th century, the Germanic peoples fled to the west. Alans and Swabians settled in the northwest of the Iberian Pensinsula and made Braga their capital. They were not a large people and their arrival did not cause any change in the administrative organization of the existing Hispano-Roman society that was by and large based on the clergy.

In 416, the Visigoths took over Iberia as allies of Rome, and made Toledo their capital. They were Arians and until the Council of 586, avoided mixing with the Roman Catholic inhabitants of the pensinsula. The Swabians also maintained their predominance in the northwest until 586. The Bishops' Councils served as the legislative bodies of the Visigoths. Parishes served as the civilian administrative units, the parish priests assumed the role once held by the *domini*, and the church congregation, known as *freguesia*, became the smallest administrative unit, and remains so to this day. Another relic from the Visigoth era are the names of the days of the week; they were numbered in order to distinguish them from the heathen Roman system.

The culture of the Visigoths hardly deviated from that of the Romans. They adopted the same language and architectural styles, although they generally used wood in construction, reserving stone for their religious buildings. Only a few of these have survived the centuries: São Pedro da Balsemão near Lamego, Santo Amaro in Beja and São Frutuoso in Braga. These small, compact structures with elegant use of arches clearly show that the Visigoths, on their travels along the northern Mediterranean coast, had picked up an architectural tradition that somewhat resembled that of the Moors who later entered Europe from the south.

The Arabs

Since 640 A.D., the Moslems had been pressing westward from Syria. In 711, taking advantage of the Visigoths' weakness, Berbers and Arabs crossed the Mediterranean near Gibraltar and conquered the Iberian Peninsula in one fell swoop. Their advance was stopped in 732 by Charles Martell at the battle of Poitiers.

The Arabs were more interested in agriculture than in natural resources. They brought in cotton, rice and sugar cane. The climate north of the Tejo proved inhospitable for their purposes, so they confined themselves to planting large vegetable gardens in the southern part of the peninsula and watering them with ingenious irrigation systems. The *vilas* in the north were left more or less untouched, and continued operating under the auspices of the Romans' successors.

The influence and duration of Arab rule in Portugal varied considerably. To the north, beyond the Douro, it left virtually no trace whatsoever; Porto and Braga reverted to Christian hands as

early as 868. In Estremadura, however, Arab rule lasted 400 years. Coimbra was reconquered in 1064, Lisbon in 1147. The longest and most intense occupation was on the Algarve coast, which the Arabs only relinquished in the middle of the 12th century. Some of Lisbon's districts, such as Alfama and Mouraria, still exude the atmosphere of this Moorish past, as do towns like Alentejo, Mértola and Castelo de Vide. Also dating back to the Moors are most of the fortresses, great places of refuge with vast walled-in areas where the soldiers, who were nomads back home, could pitch their tents. Not until later did the Christians add residential towers and churches; but the mosques of the Islamic occupants have all vanished without a trace.

Portucale

The new Christian kingdoms grew out of the three centers of resistance from northern Europe against the Arab empire: Asturias-León, Navarra-Pyrenees and

Catalonia. By the time of Alfonso III of Asturias (866-910), the *Reconquista* had already reached Mondego. Portucale, a village on the estuary of the Douro, had been retaken by Count Vimara Peres, and formed the core of his territory, which stretched from Miño to the Douro. Mumadona, the young widow of one of his descendents, had the fortress of São Mamede built and made Guimarães the capital of the county. Her successors ruled fairly independently, and even had significant influence on the king of León.

Further south, another county, whose capital was Coimbra, arose under nobles from Portucale. However, it was quickly reconquered by the Almoravides, a group of Berber warriors from southern Morocco, headquartered in Seville. In 1064, the king of León chased the Moors out of Coimbra once and for all.

Above: Moorish arches in the museum of Évora. Right: Christian knights storm a Moorish stronghold (tile painting in Torres Novas).

Portugal's Independence

The king of Castile and León succeeded in taking back Toledo in 1085 thanks to the help of counts Raymond and Henri of Burgundy. As a gesture of gratitude, he gave them his daughters Uracca and Teresa in marriage. Raymond and Uracca inherited the county of Galicia, while Henri and Teresa received Portucale – which was in fact a dependency of Galicia – and settled in Guimarães, where their son Afonso Henriques was born. He was baptized in the Chapel of São Miguel, which still stands today. Henri of Burgundy died in 1114, and his wife Teresa took over the reins of government. Her son, who was three years old at the time, was put in the care of one Egas Moniz to be raised according to the laws of chivalry. Teresa meanwhile defended her possessions successfully against the Moors and greedy relatives. But she also fell in love with the Galician Pérez Travere, and had three children with him. When Afonso Henriques reached the age of 17, he fought the battle of São Mamede against his mother, fearing that his inheritance would revert to the king of León. Teresa was captured, and her son proclaimed himself king of Portugal in Coimbra. In 1179, after long and difficult negotiations, the Pope finally anointed him as the legitimate ruler.

Afonso Henriques died in Coimbra in 1185 and was buried in the Monastery of Santa Cruz. During his 57-year rule, he founded numerous Cistercian monasteries; took 17 cities back from the Moors, including Lisbon, Santarém, Évora and Beja; commissioned the cathedrals of Coimbra, Évora and Braga, and finally, by winning the famous battle of Ourique in lower Alentejo, gave the young nation an identity.

It was at this battle, on July 25, 1139, that the Apostle James (Santiago) is supposed to have personally ridden into battle on a white steed in the guise of a

matamauros (a Moor-killer), just as he had done three centuries earlier in northern Spain, and helped bring about a Christian victory. As the years went on, however, the anti-Spanish stance of the Portuguese gradually wore away the image of the patron saint. In the mid-14th century Santiago was deposed in favor of Saint George, and the miraculous force during the Battle of Ourique was ascribed to the Christ of Batalha. In the 19th century, the historian Herculano suggested that all reports of the battle were pure legend, sparking a hefty controversy.

The Burgundian Dynasty

Sancho I (1185-1211) willed the towns of Alenquer and Montemor-o-Velho to his two daughters Sancha and Urraca, much to the dismay of his successor Afonso II (1211-1223), who promptly took up arms against his two sisters. He was supported by the king of León and the Portuguese nobles, who felt that siding with their king would be better for the country's strength and unity. Castile, which at that time was separated from León, took up the cause of the two sisters. Ultimately, Pope Innocent III negotiated between the two parties. Afonso II died in excommunication and was buried without the benefit of Christian rites. Urraca and Sancha, on the other hand, were beatified and after their death were buried in the church of the Lorvão convent.

Sancho II (1223-1248) was still a child when his father died. The government passed into the hands of the nobles during his minority, but things got so out of hand that Pope Innocent IV decided to withdraw his confidence in the Portuguese monarch and place it with his brother Afonso. A two-year-long civil war broke out between the supporters of the two kings, a war whose legends are still alive today. One tells of the mayor of Coimbra who refused to surrender the fortress of his town to Afonso as long as Sancho was still alive; another suggests that the monk Gil de Santerém was personally commissioned by the devil to

19

hand over to Sancho the document bringing the news of his unthroning.

Afonso III ruled until 1279. During his reign, the Moors were finally chased off the coast of the Algarve coast (in 1253) and the border with Spain was drawn approximately as it is today. This Afonso had dry docks built in Lisbon, Lagos and Porto, made Lisbon the capital of the nation, and placed the defense of the country in the hands of the military orders. The Templars resided in Tomar, the Knights of St. John in Crato, and the Knights of St. James in Évora.

His successor was Dom Dinis (1279-1325), the first Portuguese king who did not have to deal with the Moors and could therefore spend time and money caring for the welfare of his realm. He supported agriculture; had vast pine forests planted between the Douro and Tejo Rivers to provide wood for a large

Above: Gothic frescoes in the church of Vila Marim. Right: The tomb of Pedro I in the Cistercian church of Alcobaça.

merchant fleet; subsidized fishing and had impressive tuna-catching devices built. Himself a poet, he was a generous sponsor of the arts. Portuguese replaced Latin as the official language during his reign, and in 1228 he founded the University of Lisbon.

Dom Dinis married the Princess of Aragon, Isabella, who was later canonized. Her charity and compassion have become the stuff of countless legends. One tells of how coins she gave incognito to poor people suddenly turned into roses when the king unexpectedly showed up; or of how roses given in gratitude to the masons who built the cloister of Santa Clara-o-Velha in Coimbra mysteriously turned to gold.

Dom Dinis died in 1324 and was buried in Odivelas near Lisbon. His son Afonso IV (1325-1357) participated in the battle on the Salado River as an ally of the Castilians in 1340, whence his surname "the Brave." This was the decisive battle that pushed the Moors all the way back to the kingdom of Granada.

The Legend of Inés de Castro

Crown Prince Pedro I was married to Constanza of Navarra. Among their retinue was a Galician noblewoman named Inés de Navarra. An affair started up between the young prince and this gentlewoman. Pedro's wife died while bearing a child, the future Fernão I; but the Pope did not allow the Crown Prince to marry his beloved, fearing the possible consequences of Spanish influence upon the Portuguese court. Finally, King Afonso IV had Inés de Castro murdered in Coimbra. When Pedro I (1357-1367) acceded to the throne, he condemned his father's counselors to death for sanctioning the murder of his beloved Inés. He also made public that he had married her secretly in the Church of São Vincente of Bragança, and had the tomb of Alcobaça built for himself and her, one of the most significant examples of Gothic reclining tombs in Portugal. That is where the two lovers now lie, opposite each other in the side wings of the transept, so that they can see each other when they arise on Judgment Day.

The legend of Inés de Castro lives on, and has grown a number of offshoots in the popular imagination. One literary embellishment has Pedro I exhuming his deceased beloved, decorating her with jewels and crowning her queen. A solemn stanza in the Lusiades of Camões, as well as Portuguese, Spanish and French plays have taken up the topic. At the beginning of the 20th century no fewer than 127 Italian tone poems were written based on this legend.

Leonor de Teles

Pedro I died in 1371. The rule of his son, Fernão I (1367-1383), was marked by a series of wars against Castile that pushed Portugal's economy to the brink of ruin. It was a love affair, however, that altered the course of the country's destiny. According to one of the treaties with Castile, Fernão was supposed to marry one of the daughters of the Castilian king.

Instead he decided to continue his affair with Leonor Teles, a divorcee and a commoner. The chronicler Fernão Lopes described the events that followed: When Fernão I died, he left the throne to his daughter Beatriz, who was married to the king of Castile. Dona Leonor was supposed to conduct the affairs of state until the princess bore a son and he reached the age of 14. But popular sentiment, in particular that of the cities' burghers, whose mercantilism had endowed them with considerable power, was dead set against the machinations of Dona Leonor and her new lover, and opposed the potential successor to the throne, because it could mean a merging of the two kingdoms. The people favored Fernão's half brother, Grandmaster of the Order of Avis, who later became João I. The battle of Alubarrota in 1385 pitched the Castilians backing Dona Leonor against the

Above: "Henry the Navigator," a 1940 portrait by A. de Sousa Lopes. Right: The monument to the discoveries in Belém.

Portuguese nobles on the side of João. His victory became a veritable symbol of Portuguese independence of Spain, made manifest in the Monastery of Batalha, which the new king had built not far from the site of the battle in gratitude for his success. João's enthroning signalled the beginning of the rule of the Avis dynasty, which lasted until the 16th century.

The Age of Discoveries

João I (1383-1433) took Filipa of Lancaster as his wife, which did a great deal to reinforce Portugal's ties with England. The queen actively patronized the fine arts. At the same time, this 50-year reign witnessed a Golden Age in terms of trade, crafts and science. Lisbon grew to become the most important port in Europe. The royal couple had five children, among them the future Duarte I and Prince Henry.

Prince Henry (1394-1460) was bent on deciphering the mysteries of the seas and the horizon. Although he only participated in the conquest of Ceutas in 1415, he was nevertheless known as "the Navigator" after he settled down in the southwestern part of the country, near Cape São Vicente in Sagres. He invited a host of astronomers, geographers and cartographers to study the tides, the winds and the stars as a means of orientation for mariners. He founded the first school for navigators in Lagos, and after his brother Pedro returned from Italy with Marco Polo's account of his travels, he vowed to find a new passage to the Far East. The caravel, a kind of three-masted sailing ship, was designed under his aegis especially for exploratory expeditions. His explorers discovered Madeira and the Azores and sailed around Cape Verde.

Two generations later, João II (1481-1495) continued the search for new horizons. During his reign Diogo Cão and Martin Behaim discovered Angola and the Congo; Bartolomeu Dias rounded the Cape of Good Hope in 1488; and Pedro de Covilhã pushed ahead all the way to Sudan. In 1494 a treaty was signed dividing up the as-yet uncharted territories of the world between Spain and Portugal along a line extending 100 miles west of the Cape Verde Islands; this was later extended to 370 miles.

From then on, every spring, great fleets carrying soldiers and cannon left the port of Lisbon. The East, from the Cape of Good Hope all the way to Japan and the Pacific archipelagos, was simply called India. The capital of this heterogenous empire was Goa, now known as Panaji, which was Portuguese until 1961. It became a center not only for all of the eastern trade, but also for a slew of missions led, for the most part, by the Jesuits.

Expeditions to the Far East brought the country silk and other luxury items, and valuable, exotic spices such as pepper, ginger, cinnamon, coriander, saffron, nutmeg, mustard, and others that were highly valued in a wide variety of areas including medicine, cooking, coloring

and cosmetics. The sea routes to India soon proved faster and safer than the land routes, which effectively broke the back of the long-standing trade cartel of the Arabs, the Genoese and the Venetians.

From about the mid-15th century, African slaves were being imported from Africa to work the sugar-cane, cotton and tobacco plantations in Portugal and Madeira, and later in Brazil. The first slave market can still be seen today in Lagos.

The Age of Manuel I

Manuel I (1495-1521) has gone down in history with the nickname "the Fortunate." At no time in her history has Portugal experienced such wealth and international recognition as during his rule. He married three Spanish princesses; two were daughters of the Catholic kings and the other a sister of Carlos V.

A renewed spate of exploratory journeys brought Portugal even more fame and wealth. In 1498, Vasco da Gama reached Calcutta. Now that the Spanish,

furthermore, were systematically subjugating Central and northern South America after Columbus's discovery of the New World, the Portuguese wanted a piece of the action: on March 8, 1500, a fleet of 13 ships, commanded by Pedro Alvares de Cabral, left the estuary of the Tejo River and followed Vasco da Gama's route to the Cape Verde Islands. From there, de Cabral began the search for a southern Atlantic passage westward. On April 22 the flotilla reached Monte Pascual, and anchored in Puerto Seguro, the "safe haven." The new territory was named after its most valuable product, brazil wood, which was very much in demand in the red dye industry and in cabinetmaking.

The great wealth produced by Brazil altered society in the home country. Nobles and members of the royal house left their forbidding fortresses and moved

Above: Vasco da Gama portrayed by G. Lopes in 1524. Right: Sebastião I, a modern monument in Lagos.

into Renaissance palaces that were built and decorated in the overly rich "Manuelistic" style, as it later came to be known. The new royal palace stood on a representative square which, like Saint-Mark's Square in Venice, opened up onto the water. Cultural reforms were introduced as well, schools were built, and new laws enacted. The *Ordenações Manuelinas*, later completed under Felipe I, formed the basic legal codex of the country for centuries to come.

Dona Leonor, the wife of João II and the sister of Manuel I, founded many hospitals for the poor around the country. Many of them are still standing. In the 16th and 17th centuries the Misericórdia churches, which can be seen in many places, were added to them.

The banishment of the Jews from the Iberian Peninsula also took place during the reigns of João II and Manuel I. They were chased out of Spain in 1492. Over 100,000 sought refuge in neighboring Portugal, even though they were required to pay high taxes for the privilege. Anyone who wanted to stay was also asked to get baptized. These forced converts were then referred to as "new Christians," and the Inquisition, introduced in the 16th century, kept a sharp eye out on their religious practices. In some of the more remote mountain regions, communities of false Jewish converts still lived up until the 19th century.

Sebastianism

João III (1521-1557) left the throne to his 3-year-old grandson Sebastião. His widow, Katharina of Austria, the sister of Carlos V, took hold of the affairs of state during the regency. In 1568, the 14-year-old successor assumed his rightful place, obsessed with the notion of combatting the enemies of Christianity. In 1572, he assembled a fleet to sally forth against the Turks, but it ran into bad weather before it even got out of the Tejo estuary. Six

years later, at the age of 24, he met his death, along with about 17,000 of his soldiers, at the battle of Ksar el Kebir in Morocco.

The death of Sebastião I coincided with a period of national insecurity that crested in a form of collective superstition, so-called Sebastianism. Nobody was ready to admit that the king had been killed, because according to the knights' code of honor, each knight had the duty of dying for the king. It would have therefore been a dishonor to have to give notice of his death and still be alive. Hence the persistent belief that Dom Sebastião would one day return and solve all the country's problems. In 1530 a simple shoemaker named Bandarra had written a somewhat fuzzy prophetic poem treating a vaguely similar topic. His verse, which spoke of a Portuguese Messiah, suddenly took on great significance with the death of the young king. 60 years later, João IV of the Bragança Dynasty had to swear a solemn oath that he would abdicate in the event that Dom Se-

bastião returned. The great public expectation naturally spawned a spate of mountebanks who pretended to be the long-dead king. Some even made their way into the nation's historiography. Various facets of this national Messianic neurosis are reflected in Portuguese literature right up into the 20th century.

The Philippine Era

After the disappearance of Sebastião, Philip II of Spain, the grandson of Manuel I, made good on his rights to the Portuguese throne. For 60 years Portugal belonged to Spain, ruled by kings Philip (Felipe) II, III, and IV of the House of Hapsburg, and known in Portugal as Filipe I, II, and III. In the year Filipe I ascended the Portuguese throne, the national poet Camões died with the dramatic last words: "I am dying at the same time as my country."

Filipe I (1580-1598) enacted certain political statutes granting Portugal a degree of autonomy and aiming at pacif-

ying the Portuguese aristocracy. These concessions were for the most part accepted, and at first the anti-Spanish movement remained relatively insignificant. Economic and administrative improvements were introduced, and work started on several major new religious buildings.

When Filipe III took over in 1621, however, the country was in the midst of a profound economic crisis. All protests were naturally directed at the absentee king. When various rebellions started shaking Catalonia, at the other end of the Iberian Pensinsula, the Portuguese took advantage of the temporary weakness of Spain and crowned the most powerful nobleman in the country, the Duke of Bragança, King João IV. The Spanish reacted with the so-called Wars of Restoration, which lasted until 1668, ending once and for all with a formal treaty and the cession of Ceutas. A monument on

Above: A 1547 engraving depicting ships returning to Lisbon laden with wares.

Restauradores Square in Lisbon commemorates those who fought for the independence of Portugal.

Absolutism and the House of Bragança

The economic woes of the country did not improve even under the rule of João IV (1640-1656). But several decades later, during the reign of Pedro II (1683-1706), there came a dramatic turnaround: gold was discovered in the Gerais mines in Brazil. The first shipment of 1,100 pounds (500 kg) was delivered to Lisbon in 1699; the quantity increased from year to year, reaching its peak in 1720 with a total of 55,000 pounds (25,000 kg). Rio de Janeiro, the export harbor, became the capital of Brazil. In 1730, diamond mines were opened; by the end of the century, they had produced more than 2 million carats.

These highly lucrative imports came in during the reign of João V (1706-1750), but because of inadequate investment policies, they failed to leave any lasting mark on the country. 20 percent of the income generated from the sale of gold, precious stones, brazil wood, tobacco, sugar, port wine, salt, and slaves went to the state; but the king spent everything on maintaining his luxurious court and constructing the monastery-palace of Mafra. Meanwhile, international trade was stagnating, and a large part of the population emigrated to Brazil to find new opportunities. A trade treaty with England, the Methuen Treaty of 1703, did stimulate the export of port wine, but it also furthered the import of British wool, which proved stiff competition for the local product. Portugal also missed its chance to introduce early on a process of industrialization that would have helped more productively to process the riches that were entering the country.

José I (1750-1777), the successor of João V, placed all foreign policy affairs in the hands of Sebastião José Carvalho e Melo, who became Duke of Oeiras in 1759 and Marquis de Pombal in 1770. He was the first Prime Minister in the modern sense of the word. While the king led a life of ease, the Marquês de Pombal attended to state business.

On All Saints' Day 1755, at 11 am, a violent earthquake shook Lisbon. Thousands died, and more than 10,000 buildings in the center of the city collapsed, including many churches which, at that hour, were filled with commoners attending Mass; the nobles usually went later. The Marquis' first step was to take action against thieves and plunderers. He then summoned the army from the entire country and forced the fleeing population back into the ruined city. Having dealt with the initial emergency, he ordered the reconstruction of Lisbon. Every landowner was ordered to rebuild his house on his parcel within five years and according to certain standards of design. Anyone who failed in this enterprise, for whatever reason, was to lose his rights to the land. Ironically, these stringent measures meant that many noble families simply sold their houses, which were subsequently turned into apartment blocks.

The reconstruction of Lisbon was directed by the architects Eugenio dos Santos, Manuel da Maia, and Carlos Mardel, who joined the first two a little later. The districts of Baixa and Bairro Alto were designed on a geometric ground plan and with classical façades. In order to preserve the integral look of the city, placing flower pots before one's windows was prohibited. The state officials were housed around the Praça de Comercio where the royal palace once stood, and businesses were allowed to settle in the arcade of the ground floor. The equestrian statue of José I, whose horse is stomping on the "Vipers of Reaction," was placed in the middle of the plaza.

In 1758, an unsuccessful attempt on the life of the king gave Pombal another opportunity to cut back the power of the aristocracy. More than 2,000 noblemen were arrested; a number of these were executed, and almost all were expropriated. As the father confessors of the aristocracy, the Jesuits were also accused of collaboration and expelled from the country; the real motivation behind this was the great power of the Order in the colonies, their strong influence on education, and their vast wealth. A formal indictment of the Jesuits, blaming them for causing all of Portugal's troubles, ulitmately led Pope Clement XIV to dissolve the order in 1773.

During his 20-year incumbency, Pombal modernized the state according to the ideas of the Enlightenment. He strengthened the economy by creating state monopolies, founded manufactures for wool, silk, cotton, glass and porcelain, and filled the vacuum in the country's educational system that had been left by the forced departure of the Jesuits.

Vorstellung und Beschreibung des ganz erschröcklichen Erdbebens, wodurch die Königl. Portugiesische
Residenz-Stadt Lissabon samt dem grösten Theil der Einwohnern zu grunde gegangen.

The Viradeira

Maria I (1777-1816), the daughter of José I, was married to her uncle, Prince Consort Pedro III. She was also one of Pombal's opponents, and worked assiduously to undo many of his reforms. This backlash, the *viradeira*, was not quite as radical as Pombal's adversaries had wanted; nevertheless, 800 noblemen were let out of prison, and the state's absolute control of political and economic matters was abolished. Free trade, especially with America, in the throes of its war of independence, and England, which came out against revolutionary France, finally brought about an economic upswing.

The architecture of this period reflects the wealth of the aristocracy. The Rococo castle of Queluz was built as a royal residence, after a fire destroyed the

Above: In 1755, two-thirds of Lisbon was destroyed by an earthquake. Right: Praça do Commercio after its reconstruction.

wooden barracks where king and consort had lived since the earthquake. At the same time work started on the royal castle of Ajuda, which was never finished. Theaters were built in Lisbon and Porto, and the Basilica de la Estrêla in Lisbon was erected to give thanks for the birth of an heir to the throne.

When his mother went insane, João VI was forced to take the reins of government at a very young age. Times were turbulent, to say the least, with conflicting reactions to the French Revolution and an attack by the Spanish army under Minister Godoy. This dispute was ultimately settled, but to this day the border between the two nations has not been defined to the satisfaction of both parties, and has been a continued source of much tension.

The French Invasion

In 1807 Napoleon's army, under the command of Junot, invaded Portugal to enforce the Continental Blockade against

28

England. The royal family fled to Brazil, and remained there until 1821.

Not until 1811 did France suffer its first setbacks along the well-fortified line of Torres Vedras; its armies were ultimately routed by British troops under the Duke of Wellington. But the English also overstayed their welcome, and liberal ressentiment soon made itself felt in the land. The expected revolution broke out in 1821, forcing elections, a Republican constitution, universal suffrage, and the abolition of the Inquisition. The episode was short-lived. Miguel, the king's youngest son, gathered an army together, overthrew the new government, and restored the rights and privileges of the clergy and aristocracy. João VI returned from his exile in Brazil, leaving his son Pedro behind in the office of Viceroy; a year later, Pedro suddenly declared Brazil's independence and proclaimed himself Emperor.

As a ruler, João VI was completely under the thumb of his wife Carlota Joaquina, sister of the Spanish king Fernando VI, who ruled his own country in quite a despotic manner. After João's death in 1825, Crown Prince Pedro returned from Brazil and passed a new constitution that had some appeal to both liberals and monarchists.

But Pedro had no intention of abandoning Brazil, so, before returning overseas, he married off his younger brother Miguel to his daughter Maria, and handed her the throne. Miguel, however, convinced his wife the Queen to revoke the constitution, which led to a civil war in the north of the country between the supporters of Miguel on the one side, and the liberals who vouched for Pedro on the other. The confrontation peaked in the siege of Porto, and finally ended, in 1834, with Miguel's banishment.

One side effect of the peace treaty of Évoramonte was the secularization of Portugal. The huge estates of the religious orders were sold off, and the buildings were used as administrative offices, barracks and schools. Most of the buyers came from the growing ranks of the bour-

geoisie and the landed gentry, which thus increased their holdings and power.

Social Change

Growing social unrest marked the following years under Maria II (1826-1853). During the Industrial Revolution, which began in Portugal around 1860, the cities of Porto and Lisbon grew incrementally. Industrial enterprises settled on the edges of the cities, and this gave rise to new city districts of residential housing planned (and owned) by the bourgeoisie for the working classes, interspersed with spreading slums. State building funds could barely keep up with the cost of new streets and railway lines.

In 1851, the first Parliament with moderate political parties started its work during a relatively stable phase. Luis I

Above: The mechanization of agriculture (depicted in the train station of Azambuja). Right: The Salazar years – the Bridge of April 25 and the Christo Rei Monument.

(1861-1889) introduced civil marriages. His successor, Carlos I (1889-1908) ran into political problems with Portugal's age-old treaty partner, England, over African possessions. England threatened to break off trade relations, at which point the King relented, provoking a renewed Republican upheaval. Carlos reacted with drastic measures. In 1908 he and the Crown Prince were assassinated on the Praça de Comercio. His brother, Manuel II, succeeded to the throne. His attempts to salvage the monarchy by giving in to liberal demands failed to pacify the country: after a military coup on October 5, 1910, Portugal was declared a republic. The King and his family spent that night in the monastery of Mafra and the next day went into exile in England.

Republic and Dictatorship

The new Republican government thoroughly transformed the country. Noble privileges were abolished, church and state were strictly separated, schooling,

the right to strike, divorce and other social measures were introduced. During World War I, in 1916, the Democratic Party managed to push through a motion allying Portugal to the victorious powers, against Germany, to protect its African holdings.

But the dissatisfaction of workers, both in industry and agriculture, was swelling the ranks of Communist and Anarchist movements in the country. And the turbulent post-war years saw no fewer than 44 changes of government, and a total of 15 military coups, one of which resulted in a military government that ran the country from 1926 to 1933.

In 1928 Oliveira Salazar was named Minister of the Economy in hopes that he could somehow pull Portugal out of its financial hole. Four years later he became Prime Minister, ushering in an autocratic rule that lasted 30 years. He abolished freedom of the press, cancelled the right to strike, reorganized the unions and Parliament, and created a secret police to keep the country dancing to his tune. In

1949 Portugal joined NATO thanks to British pressure.

Draconian measures failed to improve the situation, however. Agriculture could no longer adequately feed even the farming population, which resulted in a veritable exodus during the first half of the 20th century. More than 2 million Portuguese emigrated, mostly to Brazil and Canada. After World War II, during the economic boom of the 1950s, another 1.5 million workers went off to find jobs in other European nations. These emigrés are now returning to their homeland, bringing their hard-earned savings with them and building grandiose houses or opening businesses ranging from restaurants to taxi companies.

In 1968, Salazar resigned for reasons of health. Marcelo Caetano, a professor of law from the University of Lisbon, succeeded him. Salazar had maintained peace and quiet in the country by economic backwardness, poverty, ignorance and, of course, military oppression. Caetano, on the other hand, began the pro-

cess of thawing out the nation. The first resistance cells started operating underground, and the songs of José Afonso became very popular, with their gentle but very clear protest lyrics.

The Carnation Revolution

The president during the Caetano government was Américo Tomás, an admiral intent on keeping the colonies of Angola and Mozambique. However, he met with intense opposition to further military involvement in Africa within his own country, so much so that, in 1974, General Spinola felt he had enough support to conduct a military coup.

On August 25, 1974, his followers occupied strategically vital points throughout the nation. The people reacted with fear at first. Then, with some amazement,

Above: "Soldiers and Peasants United," a message of the Carnation Revolution. Right: Many people from the former colonies returned home to their "motherland."

they understood the intentions of the military when soldiers started distributing red carnations.

This "Carnation Revolution" took place on a platform of democratization, independence for the colonies, social reform, education, and land reform. Spinola's government only lasted five months, but until 1982, the military council kept a sharp eye on democratic progress, the nationalization of the banks and heavy industries, and the expropriation of large estates. Nevertheless, economic survival was virtually impossible: foreign investors boycotted Portugal, capital fled the country, and in addition the world economy during the 1970s was in poor shape thanks to several oil crises.

The first free elections for a constitutional congress gave the Socialists a majority. The Left, including the revolutionary council, was at odds with itself, however, so by the end of 1975 it was a conservative government that took power.

Portugal Today

By 1975, Portugal's colonies of Mozambique, Angola, Guinea-Bissau and the Cape Verde Islands had achieved independence. In 1976, the Indonesian army annexed Portuguese Timor. More than 800,000 citizens from the former colonies migrated back to the mother country, many Africans among them. The trip was free of charge, and a special office was set up to facilitate their acclimatization; nonetheless, the bulk of them landed in the slums of Lisbon.

In 1976 a democratic constitution went into effect. From 1975 to 1986 Portugal changed governments ten times, and gradually the revolutionary spirit of the constitution's original text was whittled away. The promising land reforms were by and large repealed, but the new democratic state did set up modern systems of education and health care, and basic welfare was guaranteed to the population.

Joining the European Union in 1986 gave the nation a chance to take part in Europe's prosperity more directly than through the earnings of legion laborers working in Germany and France. In fact, because wages in Portugal are lower than in other EU countries, many foreign companies have moved production there. Nevertheless, even though roads are constantly being improved, the country's system is not yet adequate for full integration into the European market. Other sectors are also below European standards. More than 15% of the workers live from agriculture, but they only bring in 5% of the national income. The fishing fleet consists mainly of small boats that cannot compete with the Spanish flotilla. Tourists and foreign workers still bring in more revenue than does export. Almost all the energy and half of the foodstuffs have to be imported. Traveling across the country by train is tantamount to a trip around the world. Child labor is still a practice, and finally, more than 15 % of all Portuguese can neither read nor write.

Until 1995, the Social Democrats, under Aníbal Cavaco Silva, were the leading government party; but in the October, 1995 elections, the Socialists, under Antonio Guterres, took over the majority; and in January, 1996, the Socialist Jorge Sampaio won the Presidential elections. A few years ago, this would have frightened conservatives; but nowadays foreign investors find that a stable government, right, left or center, is easier to deal with than an unstable coalition. Thus Portugal is moving into the next millenium with a semblance of stability.

In 1998 Lisbon will hold this century's last World Exhibition, and the entire country is preparing diligently for the event. Portugal is no longer a dreamy agricultural country, but is gearing up its industry and working hard on developing tourism as a source of income. With its historical heritage, it can speak of being a country with tradition and a future. And in 1999, when Macao is returned to China, Portugal will have finally closed the book on 500 years of colonial history.

33

LISBON –
THE WHITE CITY

CITY DISTRICTS
MUSEUMS AND CHURCHES
PARKS AND PALACES
SUBURBS
QUELUZ
BELÉM

Lisbon – the White City

It's fair to say that Lisbon is one of the most beautiful cities in the world. Seen from the battlements of the Castelo, it spreads out in a bright, glowing sea of houses, their red tile roofs bristling with a thicket of antennas. As you walk through the narrow, crooked streets of the old city, countless *miradouros*, or observation terraces, invite you to pause for a moment and survey the city extending over the area's rolling hills. A light sea breeze wafts through Lisbon, where the hustle and bustle of the Baixa district contrasts with the dreaminess of the alleyways in Lapa and Graça, while around midday the smell of grilled sardines makes its way up the steep alleys of Alfama.

A visit to Lisbon means *uma bica* (an espresso) in the Café Brasileira, *uma cerveja* (a beer) in the bars around the Rossio, a glass of port in the Solar da Porto, and *fado* music in one of the night spots in Chiado. Other recommended excursions include a round-trip ride on tram line 28 tramway, a stroll in the Estufa

Preceding pages: A beautiful view from the Miradouro de Santa Luzia, Lisbon. Night falls in the Bairro Alto. Left: They might be the future of the national soccer team.

Fria (the"cool" greenhouse), a visit to the Gulbenkian Foundation, or an excursion to the seaside resorts of Cascais and Estoril. Lisbon, however, also has other less photogenic sides – a dense jungle of high-rises in Amadora, poverty-stricken slums lining the highways, and the daily traffic jams that congest the main roads.

City History

According to one old legend, Ulysses founded Lisbon. The Phoenecians called it *Alis Ubo* (the gentle bay); theGreeks and Carthagenians *Olissipo*; Julius Caesar named his new Roman settlement *Felicitas Julia*; the Visigoths chose the name *Olissabona*, which the Moors turned into *Al-Usbuna*; and in 1147, after Afonso Henriques, Portugal's first king, plucked it from Arab hands, this already historic city finally got the name *Lisboa*. In 1256, it was granted capital status. For more than 3,000 years, the well-protected harbor on the estuary of the Tejo River has been the most important trading post on the Iberian Peninsula.

In the 13th century, King Dom Dinis had the Tejo drained all the way back to what is now the Rossio. He completed the building of the Cathedral and founded the University in 1290; the latter was moved to Coimbra a few years later

owing to tension between commoners and the privileged students. In 1344 an earthquake shook Lisbon for the first time. After reconstruction, the city grew so fast that it soon swelled beyond its original defensive wall. During the struggles with neighboring Castile that marked the second half of the 14th century, Fernão I had the so-called "Fernandine" city wall erected, a massive defensive system with 77 towers and 34 gates that surrounded an area of 250 acres (1 sq. km) between the fortress and the Cathedral.

Portugal became a world power during the rule of the Avis kings. Portuguese discoveries and conquests in Africa and India endowed the country with enormous wealth that generated a late-Gothic building spree. Manuel I had a new residence built for himself on the Tejo, and redesigned the harbor – which had

Above and right: The Cathedral of Lisbon (Sé Patriarcal), seen from the outside, and inside during a service.

thereto, because of the danger of flooding, been used only for markets and warehouses – to make it the new center of the city. This Golden Age of Portuguese history ended in 1580 when Philip II of Spain took power.

The country achieved independence again in 1640, which ushered in a new phase of growth, stimulated particularly by the arrival of gold and diamonds from the Brazilian mines after the mid-18th century. King João V (1706-1750) used this windfall to build the monastery of Mafra, among other architectural monuments; the aqueduct of Lisbon, however, was financed with the city's hard-earned tax money. The aristocracy went on its own spree, building palaces, theaters, and even an opera house.

After the Quake

On November 1, 1755, a massive earthquake, whose shocks were felt all the way to Dakar, destroyed much of the city. More than 60,000 people were killed, and 17,000 of Lisbon's 20,000 houses lay in ruins. King José I and his faithful Prime Minister, later the Marquis of Pombal, set about reconstructiing the city in the spirit of the Enlightenment, the prevailing current of European thought. On the spot where the royal palace had stood, they built the Baixa, a city district with a grid of regular streets. The square in front of the palace, on the Tejo, was revamped into the Praça do Comerçio; inspired by St. Mark's Square in Venice, this broad plaza opened onto the river, the city's most important trade artery. Pombal carried out other changes as well: he expropriated the aristocracy by forcing them either to rebuild their palaces in five years or lose their land; and he had the Jesuits expelled from the country.

Secularization and the abolition of the Inquisition in the 19th century gave the city a slew of new spaces to be used as public facilities. Cloister gardens were turned into parks, Lisbon expanded to the north, and new boulevards were carved through the city. Cultural life came alive, and elegant shops opened in the Baixa and Chiado districts. Industrialization set in on the edge of town; the country's first railway went into operation in 1856; and *vilas*, cheap tenement communities such as the Estrêla d'Ouro settlement in Graça, were erected to house the new proletariat.

The city's population trebled during the second half of the 19th century. By 1900 it numbered 400,000. Around the Avenida da República, the city's main north-south axis, appeared the *Avenidas Novas*, wide, airy boulevards; today, these are lined with banks and modern office complexes. A system of tramways was set up, and elevators and funiculars were installed to negotiate the differences in altitude; some are still running perfectly today.

Progress came to a standstill at the beginning of the 20th century when the state was shaken by political turmoil. A republic was proclaimed, and shortly thereafter Portugal entered World War I. The 45-year dictatorship of the Salazar and Caetano governments signalled stagnation for education and the economy, including, the construction sector. Among the few significant buildings from this period are the National Library and the Palace of Justice. The slums around the city, however, experienced considerable growth. Social problems were exacerbated when almost a million Portuguese returned from the newly independent colonies in the mid-1970s.

Modern Lisbon

Today Lisbon is a city of 2.5 million inhabitants, and the industrial, economic, administrative and service-sector capital of the nation as well. The problems it faces are, on the one hand, uncontrolled growth, and on the other, trying to renovate the old buildings of the inner-city

districts in order to give them a modern look. After democratization in the 1970s and joining the European Union in 1986, the country's economy took off on an upward course. The government started work on large low-income housing projects that filled many of the valleys and hills around Lisbon. The new suburbs also meant an incremental increase in the number of commuters. Public transportation can hardly cope with the load, and the streets are hopelessly overcrowded. The Tejo Bridge, which seemed so gigantic back in the 1960s, can no longer handle the daily traffic passing over it.

In 1988 a fire raged through the old district of Chiado; the disaster spurred many nations into helping Lisbon with financial investments and cultural projects. In 1994, Lisbon was chosen as Europe's cultural capital, and in 1998 it will host the millenium's last World Fair in the restored harbor area. But lots of water will have flowed under the Tejo Bridge by time the last of the damp houses in Alfama has been renovated.

CITY DISTRICTS

Sé Patriarcal and Castelo de São Jorge

The first medieval community huddled around the fortress and the Cathedral, at a safe distance from floods. The foundation walls of a mosque served as the base for a church built in the 12th century; in the mid-14th century, this was replaced in turn by the **Sé Patriarcal Cathedral**, Lisbon's oldest surviving church. It underwent numerous facelifts in the course of the centuries, but most recently its original Romanesque look was in large part restored. With its low nave and side aisles and the two crenellated towers that have adorned the west facade since 1380, the Cathedral suggests a fortress rather than a place of worship. To the left beyond the entrance is the font where Saint Anthony of Padua was baptised in 1195. A chapel opposite the Cathedral was also named after that saint, because he was allegedly born on this spot; inside, there's a small museum to him.

In the first side chapel on the left is the famous Baroque crèche with terra-cotta figurines, created in 1766 by Joaquim Machado de Castro. After the 1755 earthquake, Machado also redid the tomb of Afonso IV and his wife that is on display in the chancel. Gothic sarcophagi bearing reclining figures are laid out in the chapels behind the altar. Beyond the chancel is the two-story Gothic cloister. The church treasury in the sacristy boasts the famous reliquary shrine of Saint Vincent and the complete monstrance, which is studded with precious stones.

The 37 bus runs up the hill to **Castelo de São Jorge**, 360 feet (110 m) above sea level. In the mid-12th century, the Moors used an Visigoth foundation to build their protective fortress, which Christian kings later turned into a royal residence. One of the old rooms of the castle has been gloriously restored and now houses an elegant restaurant. In the park-like grounds sur-

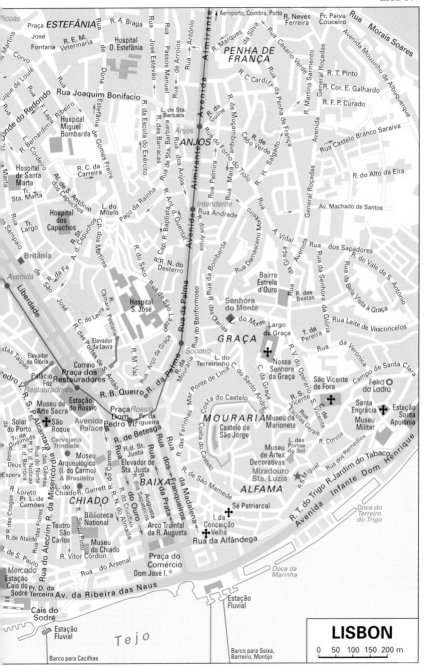

LISBON

0   50 100 150 200 m

rounding the fortress, peacocks proudly strut about, displaying the fans of their iridescent tail-feathers. The view of the city from here is one of the finest around.

Baixa

After the fateful earthquake of 1755, the Marquis de Pombal prohibited people from rebuilding their houses any way they liked. He had 15 streets laid out symmetrically in the old downtown area, and ordered buildings there to conform to uniform standards. Each had to be five stories high and equipped with a wooden inner structure to help reinforce it against future earthquakes; and the ground floors were to be used for shops.

Today, **Baixa** is a center for the city's shopping. At the lower end of Rua Augusta, a Triumphal Arch frames the view of the **Praça de Comerçio**, which was

Above: Pier, based on a Venetian model, on Praça do Comerçio. Right: Pedestrian zone on Rua Augusta.

redesigned after 1755, with, at its center, an equestrian statue of José I, king at the time of the earthquake and subsequent reconstruction of Lisbon. This large plaza, surrounded by government offices and arcades, serves as a major traffic hub (for ferries as well) and a parking lot. Directly on the Tejo, it appears to have been designed with an eye to the view from the sailing ships that used to moor here. "A wonderful dream apparition" is how Portugal's famous poet Fernando Pessoa (1888-1935) described the sight; you can still get a sense of it if you arrive in the city on the ferry from Cacilhas.

Not far from Praça de Comerçio, on Rua de Alfándega, the Manuelistic façade of the **Igreja da Conceiçao Velha** catches the eye in an otherwise uniform row of facades. Delicate ornamentation of windows and portals is all that remains of the Misericórdia church (1520), which stood here until the earthquake. The interior was rebuilt after 1755.

On the northern edge of Baixa are the three most lively squares of the city cen-

ter. Lisboners call the **Praça Dom Pedro IV** (with an equestrian statue of that king) simply the **Rossio**, after the adjacent train station that serves local traffic. Prior to the draining of the Tejo in the 13th century, the Rossio was on the banks of the river. For centuries it was used for tournaments, demonstrations and processions. It's still a hive of activity: cars and buses groan about it; cafés and tobacconists line it; and flower "girls" peddle their colorful bouquets at its center.

Next to the Rossio is **Praça de Figueira**, "fig tree square," with a monument to João I. A large marketplace stood here until 1950. Some distance to the north is **Praça dos Restauradores**, which commemorates the heroes who fought hard for Portugal's independence from Spain in 1640. Here begins the **Avenida da Liberdade**, a wide, majestic avenue lined with sycamores, which was laid out at the end of the 19th century. It ends at a round plaza, **Praça Marquês de Pombal**, where the great minister himself stands in effigy. Further on lies a pleasant spot of greenery, **Parque Eduardo VII**.

Chiado

The **Chiado** district, which lies off the western slope of Baixa, was named after the 16th-century writer António Ribeiro, who was nicknamed"Chiado." Rich in tradition, known as a neighborhood of writers and philosophers, painters, sculptors and book dealers, the district is not very big, but it did capture world attention after a fire destroyed 19 historic houses here, among them two department stores and a museum. The architect Alvaro Siza directed reconstruction efforts. Since then the façades have been redone, the apartment houses and office buildings restored, and the museum reopened. The department stores, however, have given way to a garage and a luxury hotel.

The most important street in Chiado is **Rua Garrett**, which ends at Praça Chiado. Here, you'll find fancy shops, well-stocked bookstores, and the famous

artists' café **A Brasileira**. Normally a statue of the poet Fernando Pessao stands in front of it, but because of work on the new underground, it has been temporarily removed until 1998. The quiet **Praça Largo de São Carlos**, which gave its name to the theater erected here at the end of the 18th century, lies just below Rua Garrett. House Nr. 4, the birthplace of Pessao, is open to the public, with a library, conference and exhibition rooms, and a restaurant. The house where he actually lived much of his life is in the Campo de Ourique district.

If you wish to avoid climbing the 100 feet (30 m) that separate the Baixa and Bairro Alto districts, you can use the **Elevador de Santa Justa**, built in 1902 by a student of Gustave Eiffel. At the end of it is a café and several platforms offering wonderful views of the city. A high bridge leads straight into Bairro Alto,

Above: The 100-foot (30 m) Elevador de Santa Justa connects Baixa to Bairro Alto.
Right: Ornate Baroque altar in São Roque.

passing by the ruins of the Gothic Carmo Monastery, **Igreja do Carmo**.

Bairro Alto

The influx of wealth from the new colonies and the rebuilding of the lower city districts around the new royal palace gave the aristocracy a reason to abandon their somewhat cramped city dwellings within Lisbon's defensive walls and settle on the hill opposite. After the earthquake, however, quite a few of these families could no longer afford to rebuild their houses in the **Bairro Alto**, especially considering the stringent five-year limit to do so imposed by Pombal, and were forced to sell off the land, which was soon occupied by apartments for the middle classes, built according to a specific, uniform design. Few of the opulent old villas still remain intact; but a few are grouped around the **Miradouro Santa Catarina** terrace or the **Parque Principe Real**, where some of Lisbon's most expensive residential housing is located.

This district is also the best spot to experience nightlife. Bars, restaurants, and fado places line the streets around the **Praça Luis de Camões** and **Chiado**, both named after poets. An absolute must is a visit to the small salon of the Port Institute in the **Casa Ludovice**, where the Mafra architect Ludwig once lived. Here, in a dignified ambience, you can sample some of its 200 different port wines.

The church of **São Roque** was designed by Italian architect Filipe Terzi. One of the side chapels is made entirely of Carrara marble and decorated with semiprecious stones. It was commissioned by João V, created in Italy (like the furnishings of the Mafra Monastery), blessed by Pope Benedict XIV, taken apart again, and reassembled on this spot in 1748. Adjacent to the church is the **Museu de São Roque**, devoted to religious art. The funicular **Elevador da Bica** leads from Bica down to sea level, tra-

versing a pretty residential district. Adjacent to the west is the district of Lapa.

Alfama

The **Alfama** district, which still exudes a medieval feeling, lies on the southern slope of the Castelo's hill. Its narrow, labyrinthine streets often end in cul-de-sacs, a typical feature of Arab urban planning. Originally outside the city wall, this was the Moorish quarter until Afonso Henriques allotted the Moors the district of Mouraria, to the north of the castle, in 1179. Alfama is the only district that survived the 1755 earthquake, which means that it boasts some of the city's oldest buildings.

The 28 tram runs straight through Alfama, offering visitors the option of riding to its highest point and then walking back down. At the top of the hill is a small park, **Santa Luiza**, with cafés and a panoramic view, and **Largo das Portas do Sol**, site of the 17th-century palace of the Count of Azurara. The latter now houses the **Museu-Escola de Artes Decorativas**, a Museum of Decorative Arts, where a wide selection of interior decorating styles from the 16th to the 20th centuries are presented in richly furnished rooms located on several floors.

Countless stairways connect a maze of pretty alleyways which only broaden out at the squares in front of churches. People here seem to live in front of rather than in their houses. Strolling around, one often has the feeling of walking straight through people's living rooms. During the late morning charcoal grills are kindled in the street to roast sardines or cutlets for lunch. And markets are also held in some of the streets.

This may all appear very quaint and romantic on the surface, but Alfama does have a negative side. The narrow streets make it very difficult to ventilate; everything, from handbag to shopping bag, has to be carried up the hill; delivery and construction vehicles have great difficulty reaching many of the houses; and finally, the apartments are very small and sanita-

tion, if at all available, usually leaves much to be desired. Efforts at restoring and modernizing the district are underway, but progress is slow at best.

Graça and Mouraria

These two districts are similar to Alfama in that they consist of a network of cramped and steeply sloping streets lined with small houses that are generally in need of repair and modernization. **Graça** lies to the northeast of the castle, and was named after **Nossa Senhora de Graça**, a pilgrimage church that crowns the top of the hill. It was rebuilt after the famous earthquake, and has been redone several times since. The generous esplanade stretching before it is a pleasant place to enjoy a rest and some people-watching at a café. A very long stairway with some

Above: A Nr. 28 trolley squeaks through an Alfama street. Above right: Life goes on in Alfama. The Cervejaria Trindade, a traditional meeting spot.

wonderful lookout terraces leads down to **Praça Largo do Terreirinho**, where you can start a tour of **Mouraria**, the old Moorish district to the northwest of the castle, which still has an Arabic feeling.

Night Life between the Rossio and the Harbor

Strolling around the Baixa district at night can be a lonely affair after a while. The area around the **Rossio** and the pedestrian **Rua das Portas de Santo Antão**, where there are several good restaurants, does stay alive a little while longer. In the **Bairro Alto**, in Rua São Pedro de Alcântara, Rua da Barroca, and Rua do Diario de Noticias, social life kicks into gear around 10 pm, thanks to a number of small restaurants and well-known places where one can hear fado, and a number of modern bars and discos. One must-see is the **Cervejaria** (beer hall) **Trindade**, its walls adorned with painted tiles, where a fine dark brew is on tap. In the past few years, the **harbor district** around **Cais**

de Sodré has become known for its seafood. Behind the train station complex, perched in boats or camped in makeshift harbor buildings, there are several truly excellent restaurants, but they are not cheap.

A bit farther on, around **Largo do Santos**, is the **Alcântara** tavern quarter, which stretches along Av. de 24 de Julho and the port. The area is so large that yuppies and business people drive from one place to the next in their sports cars. Indeed, one has to be fairly well-heeled to overcome the entrance fees of some of the exclusive discos, so "in" they don't even need signs to advertise their names. The only indication of their presence are the bouncers, guarding the doors against the masses. Farther on, around **Rua de São Bento**, there are places with music from Brazil and the Cape Verde Islands.

MUSEUMS

Like all European capitals, or at least large cities, Lisbon has a host of mu-seums covering a wide range of topics, be it the privately run puppet museum, or the one revealing the mysteries of the city's water supply system. The art collections are of an international caliber.

The **Museu Nacional de Arte Antiga** (National Museum of Ancient Art) is in a former convent and its adjacent palace. The convent chapel, ornamented with *talha dourada* (gilded woodcarvings), is used to display a particularly fine crèche by Machado de Castro. A part of the Gulbenkian collection and European art from the 15th to the 18th centuries has been hung on the second floor of the museum. Among the paintings on display here are works by Dürer, Velázquez, and Hieronymus Bosch, notably his *Temptation of Saint Anthony*.

The third floor illustrates oriental art from Portugal's erstwhile colonies, while the top storey is devoted to Portuguese artists. Here, you can view the country's most significant masterpiece, the wing altar of Saint Vincent, whose six panels were discovered in the Church of São

Vincente da Fora and restored in 1910. No one knows exactly when, why and by whom it was painted, nor, for that matter, how it originally stood. It has been attributed to Nuno Gonçalvez, a court painter of Afonso V in the mid-15th century, because the king, his son, and Henry the Navigator can be recognized. Depicting no fewer than 60 people, the panels illustrate a cross-section of society in a way wholly without precedent at that period. It should be noted that the seventh panel, which has never been found, may have provided the point of reference for the whole. But in any case, every social class is represented, all the way from the king and clergy to poor fishermen and beggars.

The **Museu Calouste Gulbenkian** (Gulbenkian Museum) is located in a newly-built complex in the north of the inner city. Gulbenkian, a billionaire of

Above: Modern Portuguese art in the new building of the Museu do Chiado. Right: In the Madre Deus convent church.

Armenian descent, was born in Istanbul in 1869. During World War I he organized the marketing of Middle Eastern crude oil, and in 1928 received a 5 percent commission for every deal made with one of the big oil companies, which led to his nickname, "Mr. 5 percent." In 1942, he retreated from the chaos of World War II into the seclusion of the Hotel Avis in Lisbon, where he died in 1955. One of his legacies was a foundation to support charities, culture and scientific research; another was a massive art collection, which was not sorted out enough to be exhibited until 1960, when it was finally put on display in the palace of the Marquis de Pombal in Oeiras. The 6,400 works of the collection are exhibited in 15 rooms. The first six focus on Classical and Oriental art. The rest cover European art from the 11th to the 19th centuries, and include works by Rubens, Rembrandt, Van Dyck, Ghirlandaio, Rodin and Turner. A separate room has been reserved for the glass creations and jewelry of the French Art-Nouveau

artist René Lalique, who was a personal friend of Gulbenkian.

During the Salazar era, the foundation concentrated its efforts on music, and since 1962 has had its own orchestra, chorus and ballet company. It also supports education in Portugal with 170 libraries and 59 book buses. University institutes, conferences and various publications are also part of the Gulbenkian program. Branch offices in foreign countries help Portuguese emigrants and members of the Armenian minority.

The foundation's complex in the center of Lisbon was inaugurated in 1969, on the 100th anniversary of the birth of Gulbenkian. As well as conference rooms, an auditorium, and a library with more than 60,000 volumes, the **Centro de Arte Moderna** (CAM, or Center of Modern Art) is also housed here, with an archive, a gallery, and a small art school.

The **Museu do Chiado** is situated in a former Franciscan monastery that has itself had a turbulent history. After the great quake of 1755, it remained closed until the 19th century. It then served in succession as a cookie factory, an academy of fine arts, and the national library, before finally becoming the National Museum of Contemporary Art in 1911. In 1988, after it burned down in the Chiado fire, the French architect Jean-Michel Wilmotte, who is best known for his work on the Louvre extension, was commissioned to give it a major facelift and restoration. It reopened in 1994, exhibiting its permanent collection of works by modern Portuguese painters, sculptors, and designers.

On the eastern edge of the city, quite a distance beyond Alfama, is the **Museu Nacional do Azulejo** (National Tile Museum), houseed in the former Madre Deus Convent. The latter was founded in the 15th century by Dona Leonor, the sister of Manuel I. The monastery's church, with Baroque *talha dourada* altars, and its refreshing, blue *azulejos*, has been incorporated into the museum, which displays Portuguese and foreign tiles. Exhibits in the rooms of the monastery trace

51

the development of tile painting in Portugal through the ages. One particularly fascinating item is the vast *azulejo* picture that occupies one entire side of the Renaissance cloister's upper level, depicting the city of Lisbon as it looked before the earthquake of 1755.

Two museums stand opposite one another on the congested northern part of the Campo Grande. The first is the City Museum (**Museu da Cidade**), in a palace which João V built for his lover, a nun in the convent of Odivelas, in 1739. Highlights here include the old kitchen and the extensive documentation of the city's history, which includes a model of prequake Lisbon. The other museum, in a villa built around the turn of the century, is devoted to **Rafael Bordalo Pinheiro** (1846-1905), a caricaturist and ceramics artist who brilliantly captured his fluctuating times in his pictures.

Above: A kindergarten class exploring Lisbon. Right: The King's Gallery in the garden of the Palace of the Counts of Fronteira.

CHURCHES

The two spires of the Church of Saint Vincent are visible from a great distance as they rise between the Alfama and Graça districts. The church's full name is **Igreja São Vincente Fora**, after a church that used to stand outside the city walls which the Spanish king Felipe II ordered to be torn down. He then had the Italian architect Filipe Terzi build the new one according to his own royal taste, that is, strictly late-Renaissance, uniform, simple, and using lots of marble. The adjacent Augustine monastery was organized around two cloisters whose tiled walls illustrate the fables of the French author Lafontaine. Behind it is the Pantheon of the Bragança Dynasty; Salazar commissioned the most recent sarcophagi here for Carlos I and his son, who were assassinated in 1908.

Very close by, the impressive dome of **Santa Egrencia** crowns the next hilltop. A local saying has it that waiting for construction on Santa Egrencia to make pro-

gress is equivalent to waiting for Doomsday. The cornerstone was laid in the 16th century and work actually ended in the 1960s when Salazar had the edifice completed as a kind of "National Pantheon." The **Feira da Ladra** flea market takes place around it every Saturday.

At the end of the 18th century, Maria I fulfilled a vow, and contracted Vincente and Manuel, two students of the great Mafra architect Ludovice, to build the **Basilica da Estrêla**. This large, airy church, with two towers on its western side and a voluminous crossing dome, displays a perfect mixture of Rococo and classicism. Of particular note are the marble sculptures that come from the Mafra school. Maria I herself lies buried to the south of the transept.

The **Igreja do Carmo** on Praça Carmo in the Bairro Alto district has remained a ruin since the earthquake of 1755. An archaeological museum has made its home here. It is difficult to say what is more attractive, the remains of the groined vaults that reach up to the sky, or the hodge-podge of Roman sarcophagi, Visigothic columns, and sculptures of Machado de Castro displayed on the ground. In summer, concerts are sometimes held here.

PARKS AND PALACES

The royal dynasties that once ruled Portugal left their mark on the cityscape of Lisbon, with their palaces, hunting parks and castles. After the earthquake, the kings had to take up residence in a temporary wooden construction until the new palace of Ajuda was inhabitable. But the latter was never completely finished; still, the apartments of the last Portuguese kings therein are open to the public. It was the Marquês de Pombal who had Ajuda's botanical gardens laid out.

The Ministry of Foreign Affairs is housed in the royal palace **Palácio Real das Necessidades** in the western part of the city. Like the monastery of Mafra, this great building was the result of a vow made by João V. In the 19th century it occasionally served as a royal residence.

The palace of **São Bento**, which houses the current Parliament of Portugal, is in fact a revamped Benedictine monastery that was secularized in 1834.

Lisbon's most beautiful parks are almost all outside the city center. The **Jardim da Estrêla**, with its idyllic ponds, giant cacti and tall trees, is in the district of Estrêla. The long and straight **Parque Eduardo VII** begins at the end of the Avenida da Liberdade, an austere complex. At its upper end, however, is the **Estufa Fria**, the "cool greenhouse," a separate garden promising refreshing air and an abundance of well-tended plants protected from the harsh Portuguese sun by bast mats and trellises.

Another attractive garden is the **Jardim Botânico**, the Botanical Garden, which lies to the west above Avenida da Liberdade. Also recommended is the **Zoo**, located in the northwest of the the city at the Sete Ríos subway station. Farther to the northwest is one of Lisbon's nearby recreational areas, the **Parque Florestal de Monsanto**, which consists of a large forest, crisscrossed by a few roads leading to a fort and the lookout **Miradouro das Montes Claros**.

About 7.5 miles (12 km) to the north of Lisbon, on the main road leading to Mafra, lies the **Parque do Monteiro-Mor**, an idyllic spot that seems light-years away from the hustle and bustle of the city. Gardens, fountains, statues and a luxurious restaurant surround an 18th-century palace housing the **Museu Nacional do Trajo** (the National Museum of Textiles and Fashion).

SUBURBS

Because of the cramped situation in the inner city, larger construction projects were often planned on the outskirts. The hospitals, for example, stand on the hill north of Baixa, and are accessible using the funicular from Praça Restauradores. The campus of the University was relo-

cated to the **Campo Grande**. The district of **Amoreiras** to the northwest of the inner city limits has become synonymous with the architect Taveira's colorful high-rise complex, visible from just about every point in Lisbon. Integrated herein are modern offices, apartments, various cinemas, international restaurants, boutiques and large shops.

Close by is the **Aqueduto das Aguas Livres**, a half-mile-long (1 km) aqueduct that reaches a height of 212 feet (65 m) over the Alcântara Valley on the western edge of the city. Since the 18th century, it has been bearing water to Lisbon from a reservoir 11 miles (18 km) away. The waterway itself is covered, with a footpath on either side. Lisbon's notorious

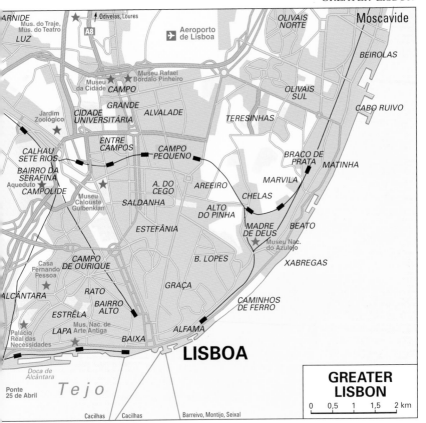

ARNIDE
Mus. do Traje,
Mus. do Teatro
LUZ

Odivelas, Loures

A8

Aeroporto
de Lisboa

OLIVAIS
NORTE

Moscavide

BEIROLAS

Museu Rafael
Bordalo Pinheiro

Museu
da Cidade CAMPO

GRANDE

CIDADE
UNIVERSITÁRIA ALVALADE

Jardim
Zoológico

ENTRE
CAMPOS

CALHAU
SETE RIOS

BAIRRO DA
SERAFINA
CAMPOLIDE

Aqueduto

CAMPO
PEQUENO

OLIVAIS
SUL

CABO RUIVO

TERESINHAS

Museu
Calouste
Gulbenkian

A. DO
CEGO

SALDANHA

AREEIRO

ALTO
DO PINHA

ESTEFÂNIA

BRACO DE
PRATA MATINHA

MARVILA

CHELAS

MADRE
DE DEUS

BEATO

Museu Nac.
do Azulejo

Casa
Fernando
Pessoa

CAMPO
DE OURIQUE

B. LOPES

XABREGAS

ALCÂNTARA

RATO

BAIRRO
ALTO

GRAÇA

ESTRÊLA

Palácio
Real das
Necessidades

LAPA Mus. Nac. de
Arte Antiga

BAIXA

CAMINHOS
DE FERRO

ALFAMA

LISBOA

Doca de
Alcântara

Ponte
25 de Abril

Tejo

GREATER
LISBON

0   0,5   1   1,5   2 km

Cacilhas   Cacilhas   Barreivo, Montijo, Seixal

lack of water led to demands for such a facility during the reign of João V. In spite of the royal house's ample funds, the project was financed by means of a tax hike on meat, wine and oil. When the job was completed in 1748, a plaque was hung at the point where the aqueduct crosses Rua das Amoreiras praising the construction as an achivement of the people of Lisbon and their privations. 25 years later, the Marquês de Pombal had another plaque hung exalting King João V as the best of all kings and the initiator of the aqueduct, which was in fact financed with public monies.

The satellite cities lie to the north of the town. The largest are **Amadora**, a kind of autonomous industrial metro-

polis, **Benefica**, **Pontinha**, **Odivelas**, **Loures** and **Cacém**. The old centers are often impossible to find, and it requires a veritable pioneer spirit to track down such worthy sights as the **Cistercian Monastery of Odivelas**. Nowadays it is a girls' boarding school. Some parts of the building were spared by the 1755 quake. One of the ladies of the school proudly shows off the tiled kitchen, the magnificent dining hall, and the church with its early Gothic chancel head. In the apsides are the tombs of King Dom Dinis and his daughter, who was murdered in the cloister.

In Benefica, at the edge of Monsanto Park near the Cruz da Pedra train station, is the **Palace of the Counts of Fron-**

55

teira, a Renaissance building still in private hands. The interiors are off-limits, but the gardens with their opulent *azulejo* paintings make an excursion worthwhile.

QUELUZ

Queluz has developed into a suburb of Lisbon, surrounded by high-rise complexes, industrial enterprises and highways. Contemplating it today, you might wonder how its name, which means "what light!", ever came about. Still, there is no denying the great charm of the **Palácio Nacional de Queluz**, a Rococo masterpiece that once served as a hunting and recreational lodge for the royal family. Work on it began in the middle of the 18th century during the reign of Pedro III according to plans drawn up by Vincente de Oliveiras. The palace was not yet fin-

Above: A view of the Rococo palace of Queluz. Right: The riding school of the palace of Belém has become a museum of grandiose carriages.

ished when the earthquake struck; later, the French architect Jean Baptiste Robillon completed it in 1790.

French influence is obvious in the interior decoration as well as the horse-shoe shaped gardens that are laid out in strictly geometrical patterns. Intricate stucco work and murals adorn the opulent throne room and hall of mirrors; crystal chandeliers, gracious furniture and tiles fill the other rooms; and in the king's sleeping quarters a cycle of paintings tells the story of Don Quixote. Tall windows, wall-size mirrors, and French doors opening out onto the garden make the place airy and light.

Considering that they're in the midst of a city suburb, the gardens are a veritable oasis. A graceful stairway flanked by lions, which cuts a corner in unusual fashion, leads to the west wing. The **Largo do Palácio** sprawls at the foot of the palace. An artificial brook, running in a bed tiled with *azulejo*, was once used for royal boat rides. Guests of the state reside in one part of the palace nowadays,

which is not always open for public tours. The servants' quarters opposite the main entrance is currently being turned into the newest Pousada hotel, and a luxury restaurant, the *Cozinha Velha*, has long been operating out of the palace's old kitchen.

BELÉM

After discovering the sea route to India, Vasco da Gama returned in 1499 and was joyously greeted by his king in the harbor of Belém. Manuel I intended to use 5 percent of the income from the India trade to build a monastery. Work on the **Mosteiro de Jerónimos** (Hieronymus Monastery), designed by Diogo Boytacas, lasted 60 years. This large building, with a limestone façade and two cloisters, illustrates the Manuelistic style, which made use of Gothic and Moorish elements. In the extensive west wing is the **Museu da Marinha** (Museum of Seafaring), with a special annex devoted to nautical instruments and several royal vessels, including the one in which the

last Portuguese king, Manuel II, fled the country in 1910. Next to the museum is the Gulbenkian Foundation's planetarium.

The most impressive section of the monastic complex is the **Igreja Santa Maria** (Church of Saint Mary), which stands at the southeast corner and runs along one of the cloisters. The monastery's donor, his wife, their patron saints and the four Evangelists are depicted on the portal of the western entrance. The representative portal, however, is on the south facade; it displays a Manuelistic ornateness, with saints under baldachins, foliation and turrets. The Virgin of Belém stands over the entrance, and Henry the Navigator has been given a spot on the central post of the double door.

The interior of the church is majestic, with a high groined vault supported by long and slender columns. It served as a mausoleum for the kings of the Avis dynasty and famous personalities. Behind the entrance are the sarcophagi of Vasco da Gama and Luis de Camões, though the

BELÉM

latter is empty: no one knows what happened to the corpse of Portugal's national poet, who died in 1580. In the transept is another empty coffin, belonging to King Sebastião, who died in battle. Opposite him lies his successor, King (and Cardinal) Henrique II. There are other tombs in the choir, including those of Manuel I and his wife, which are supported by elephants.

Adjoining the northern side of the church is the two-story **cloister**; grouped around this are the sacristy, the chapter's meeting room and the monastery's refectory, which is decorated with beautiful *azulejo* tiles. The grave of poet Fernando Pessoa, who died in 1935, is in one corner of the cloister. The adjacent sleeping quarters of the monks has been given over to the **Museu Nacional de Arqueología** (National Archeological Museum). It was revamped in 1990, and now dis-

Above: Slender columns support the vaulting of Sta. María in the Hieronymus Monastery of Belém.

plays finds excavated throughout the country.

The current presidential palace, **Paço Real de Belém** (Portuguese for Bethlehem), was the royal summer residence in the 18th century. José I survived the earthquake because he happened to be here at the time. The palace's riding school is the perfect background for the **Museu Nacional dos Coches** (Carriage Museum). The large plaza in front of the monastery, **Praça do Imperio**, was redesigned in 1940 for a World's Fair. A few years ago it was endowed with a new cultural center used for important international exhibitions.

Restelo harbor, the point of departure for the great exploratory voyages, once lay on the banks of the Tejo River in Belém. In 1960, the 177-foot (54 m) **Padrão dos Descobrimentos** (Discovery Monument) was inaugurated to honor the Portuguese mariners of the 15th century. Henry the Navigator stands on a stylized ship's bow; behind him are explorers, knights, and missionaries. In the bowels of the monument thematically relevant exhibitions are held; an elevator takes visitors up to a lookout platform. A giant compass and a map of the world have been set into the paving of the esplanade using pieces of differently colored marble.

A few steps farther on, beyond the **Museu de Etnologia** (Ethnological Museum), the massive **Torre de Belém** sticks out of the water. This tower, built in 1521 by Francisco de Arruda, not only defended the harbor, but was also used as a prison for a while. It was originally in the middle of the river, but various construction projects and the gradual silting up of the Tejo left it stranded near the bank. It's an amusing example of Manuelism, with little towers, merlons, coats-of-arms, and the Gothic loggia. The apartments of the governor, the king, and the commander are spread out over four floors, and there is even a fortress chapel.

LISBON
Area code for Lisbon: 01

Accommodation
LUXURY: **Hotel da Lapa**, Rua do Pau da Bandeira 4, Tel: 3950005, Fax: 3950665. A luxuriously renovated hold palace in a quiet setting, the most expensive and exclusive hotel in Lisbon. **Avenida Palace**, Rua 1 de Decembro 123, Tel: 3460151. In handsome turn-of-the-century style, right on the Rossio. **Tivoli**, Av. da Liberdade 185, Tel: 3530181. Classical fancy hotel. **Senhora do Monte**, Calçada do Monte 39, Tel: 8866002, Fax: 877783. Elegant new hotel with a nice view.

MODERATE: **Internacional**, Rua Bestega 3, Tel: 3466401, Fax: 3478635. An old-fashioned hotel, right on the Rossio. **Britânia**, Rua Rodrigues Sampaio 17, Tel: 3155016, Fax: 3155021. **Veneza**, Av. da Liberdade 189, Tel: 3522618, Fax: 3526678. An old palace whose modernization fails to pass muster. **Quinta Nova da Conceição**, Rua Cidade de Rabat, Tel: 7780091. Private rooms in an elegant palace, on the way to Benfica.

BUDGET: **Galicia**, Rua do Crucifixo 50, 4°. **Dom Afonso Henriques**, Rua Cristóvão Falcão, Tel: 8146574, Fax: 823375. **Dom João**, Rua José Estevão 43, Tel: 524171, Fax: 3524569. In the Estefanía district. **Dinastía**, Rua D. João V. 7, Tel: 3885067. Clean and good.

Restaurants and cafés
Michel, Largo da Igreja, Castelo. **Conventual**, Pr. das Flores 45, Tel: 609196. Traditional cuisine in romantic surroundings. **Estrêla d'Ouro**, Rua da Graça 22. **O Pardieiro**, Lg. da Graça 36, Tel: 8863486. **Cervejaria Portugalia**, Av. Almirante Reis 117. Large place with agreeable, folksy atmosphere. **Sua Exceléncia**, Rua do Conde 42, Tel: 603614. **O Vicentinho**, Rua da Voz do Operario 1B, Tel: 8881025. **Casa do Leão**, Castelo São Jorge, Tel: 875962. In the fortress, with a splendid view. Fish soup is the specialty. **Alcântara Café**, Rua Maria Luísa Holstein 15. A luxury restaurant with impressive old industrial interior decoration. **Casa Fernando Pessoa**, Rua Coelho da Rocha 16-18. In the house of the poet himself: coffee and meals until midnight. **Mercado do Peixe**, Est. Pedro Teixeira, Alto da Ajuda, Tel: 3636942. Excellent fish dishes.

VEGETARIAN: **Seleiro Dieta**, Rua 1 de Dezembro 65. **O Sol**, Calçado do Duque 23. **Espiral**, Pr. Ilha do Faial 14A. Saturdays with music. **O Tibetano**, Rua do Salitre 117. Excellent cuisine with a beautiful view of the fortress.

ALFAMA: **O Beco**, Rua São Miguel 87. **Mesa de Frades**, Rua dos Remedios 139A. **Costa do Castelo**, Calçada Marquês de Tancos. **Martelaldas**, Rua da Costa do Castelo 91, Tel: 8861271. Moderate

Prices, and the kitchen keeps working til 2 am. **Parreirinha de São Vicente**, Calçada de São Vicente 54, Tel: 8868893. Inexpensive and tasty standards. **Tolan**, Rua dos Remédios 134-136, Tel: 872234. Familial atmosphere, with one of the best *bacalhau*.

BAIRRO ALTO: **Carmo**, Largo do Carmo 16, Tel: 3423696. **Casal de Vinho**, Rua Diario de Noticias 72. Alentejo cuisine. **Fieis Ao Tacho**, Rua Fieis de Deus 29. **Sansão e Dalila**, Rua da Barroca 70. Designer establishment with *nouvelle cuisine*. **A Capela**, Rua da Atalaia 45. Jazz. **Camponesa**, Rua Marechal Saldanha 23. **Pintai**, Largo Trindade Coelho 22/23. Music. **Cataplana**, Rua Diario de Noticias 27, Tel: 3465919. Music. **Tavares Rico**, Rua da Misericórdia 35/37, Tel: 321112. **Tavares Pobre**, Trav. da Espera 20. The "rich" and the "poor" Tavares are both equally traditional, with good cooking, but in quite different price categories. **Pap d'Arçorda**, Rua da Atalaia 57, Tel: 3464811. Modern Portuguese cooking. **O Paço do Principe**, Pr. do Principe Real.

GRAÇA: **Via Graça**, Rua Damaseno Monteiro 9B, Tel: 870830. Modern designer establishment with a wonderful view.

CAIS DO SODRÉ: **Porto do Abrigo**, Rua dos Remolares 16. Guter Fisch. **Cais do Sodré**. Cais da Ribeira, Tel: 3423611. Wonderful, fresh crustaceans. **Bar do Río**, Tel: 3466727. **Bar & Co** - Rock-Disco on a boat with a special ambiente. **Zeta Pontão**, boat restaurant. **Gare Tejo**, Gare Marítima de Alcantara, Tel: 3976335.

FADO: **Painel do Fado**, Rua de São Pedro de Alcântara 65, Tel. 323966. **Adega Mesquita**, Rua Diario do Noticias 107. **A Severa**, Rua das Gáveas 51, Tel: 3464006. The most traditional fado establishment; The famous gypsy singer Maria Severa used to perform here; closed Thursdays. **Parreirinha de Alfama**, Beco do Espirito Santo 1, Tel: 8868209. **Fado Menor**, Rua das Praças 18, Tel: 671856. **A Guitarra da Bica**, Calçada da Bica 13, Tel: 3428309. Good atmosphere, and the music is not only for tourists. **Botequim**, Lg. da Graça, Tel: 871523. Founded by the poetess Natalia Correia. **Sr. Vinho**, Rua do Meio a Lapa 18, Tel: 3972681.Old tradition of fado, good singers. **Arcadas do Faia**, Rúa da Barroca 54, Tel: 3426742. **Adega do Ribatejo**, Rúa Diario de Notícias 23, Tel: 3648343. **Adega Machado**, Rua do Norte 91, Tel: 3160095.

CAFÉS: **Brasileira**, Rua Garret 120. An atmosphere charged with tradition: Fernando Pessoa used to drink his coffee here. **Nicola**, Rossio 27, is unfortunately being rebuilt (beginning 1996). **Costa do Castelo**, Calçada de Marquês de Tancos 1. **Café São Bento**, Rua de São Bento 212. Comfortable and quiet, open til 2 am. **As Vicentinas**, Rua de São Bento 700. A tea shop.

BARS AND DISCOS: Cerca Moura, Largo Portas do Sol 4. Terrace with a superb view. **Harry's Bar,** Rua de São Pedro de Alcântara 57. **Solar do Porto,** Rua de São Pedro de Alcântara 43. Dignified, quiet, worth a real bender. **La Folie,** Rua Diario do Noticias 122, Discothek. **Porão do Santos,** Santos. **A Chilena,** Lg. do Rato 12. **Acinox,** Santos. **Cervejaria Trindade,** Rua Nova da Trindade 20. A giant place for drinking beer and eating, open since 1836, with famous tile pictures on the walls. Excellent crustaceans. **Fox Trot,** Trav. de Sta. Teresa. **Procópio,** Altos São Francisco 2. **Targus,** Rua Diario de Noticias 40. **Tertulia,** Rua Diario de Noticias 60. **Ai-Ué,** Av. Ant. José de Almeida 5. Dancing to African music. **Lontra,** Rua de São Bento 157. **Pillon,** Rua do Alvito 10. Cape Verdian music. **Cinearte-Café,** Largo de Santos 2. **Alcool Puro,** Av. D. Carlos I 59.

ZONE ALCANTARA: **Kapital,** Av. 24 de Julho 68. The non plus ultra. Allegedly, one can only get in when one knows the name of the bouncer. **Kremlin,** Escandihas de Praia 5. Exzentrisch. Techno and acid rock. **Alcântara,** Rua M. Luísa Holstein 15. **Pavilhao Chinés,** Rua D. Pedro V 89. Several rooms designed quite differently. **Alcântara Mar,** Rua da Cozinha Económica 11. Unusual decoration with *talhas douradas*; it's the last to close for the night.

Sites and Museums

Casa Fernando Pessoa, Rua Coelho da Rocha 16, open from 10am to 6pm, Thur 1pm to 8pm. **Casa Ludovice,** Rua de São Pedro de Alcantara no. 45. **Casa Museu Dr. Anastácio Gonçalves,** Av. 5 de Outubro 8, Tue-Sat midday to 6:30pm, closed Sundays and Mondays. **Estufa Fria,** Parque Eduardo VII, 10am-5:30pm (in summer until 6pm). **Casa-Museu João da Silva,** Rua Tenente Raul Cascais 11. **Palácio dos Marquêses da Fronteira,** Largo de S. Domingos de Benfica 1, Mon and Wed 10am-3pm, Sat 3:30pm-5pm. **São Vicente de Fora,** 9am-1pm and 3pm-6pm. **Bullfighting Arena,** Campo Pequeno, in Summer fights are announced, usually on Sundays, often on Thursdays.

MUSEUMS: **Museu da Agua Manuel da Maia,** Rua do Alviela 12, Porto de Lisboa, Tue-Sat 10am-12:30pm and 2pm-5pm, closed Sundays and Mondays. **Museu Arqueológico do Carmo,** Largo do Carmo, 10am-1pm and 2pm-5pm, closed Sundays. **Museu Nac. de Arte Antiga,** Rua das Janelas Verdes 9, 10am-6pm, Tue 2pm-6pm, closed Mondays. **Museu Artes Decorativas,** Largo das Portas do Sol 2, Tue/Thu 10am-midday, Sun/Wed/Fri/Sat 10am-5pm, closed Mondays. **Museu de Arte Sacra,** Largo da Trindade Coelho, 10am-5pm, closed Mondays and holidays. **Museu Nac. do Azulejo,** Rua da Madre de Deus 4, Tue 2pm-6pm, Wed-Sun 10am-6pm, closed Mondays.

Museu do Chiado, Rua Serpa Pinto 6, 10am-6pm, Wed and Sat 10am-8pm, Mon and Tue 2pm-6pm. **Museu da Cidade,** Campo Grande 245, 10am-1pm and 2pm-6pm, closed Mondays. **Museu da Ciência,** Rua da Escola Politécnica 56, Mon-Fri 2pm-5pm. **Museu do Cinema,** Rua Barata Salgueiro 39, 9:30am-12:30pm and 2:30-5:30pm, closed Sat-Sun. **Museu Nac. de Etnología,** Av. Ilha da Madeira, 10am-12:30pm und 2pm-5pm, closed Mondays and holidays. **Museu Calouste Gulbenkian** and **Centro de Arte Moderna,** Av. de Berna 45, Wed, Fri, Sat, and Sun 10am-5pm. Thu and Sat 2pm-7:30pm, closed Mondays and holidays. **Museu Militar,** Largo dos Caminhos de Ferro, 10am-4pm, closed Mondays. **Museu Rafael Bordalo Pinheiro,** Campo Grande 382, 10am-1pm and 2pm-6pm, closed Mondays. **Museu da Marioneta,** Largo Rodrigues de Freitas 19A, 11am-5pm, closed Mondays and holidays. Guided tours on weekends. **Museu Nac. do Teatro,** Palácio de Monteiro Mór, Estr. do Lumiar 12, Tue 2pm-6pm, Wed-Sun 10am-6pm, closed Mondays. **Museu Nac. do Traje,** Largo Júlio Castilho, Parque do Monteiro Mor, 10am-1pm and 2pm-5pm, closed Mondays and holidays.

Shopping

Shopping streets: Rua Augusta, Rua Garrett, Rua da Mouraria.

Antiques: Rua Pedro V., Rua São José, Rua de São Bento. Dona Antiguidade, Rua Garcia de Orta 71 C, Lojas 6 e 20. Loja da Calçada, Calçada de São Vicente 51. **Ceramics and Tiles:** Viúva Lamego, Calçada do Sacramento 29. Ratton, Rua da Academia Ciências 2C. Olaria do Desterro, Rua Nova do Desterro 14. Santa Ana, Rua do Alecrim 95. Vista Alegre, Largo do Chiado 18. Oficina 59, Rua de São João da Mata 59. **Cloth:** Souleiado, Largo do Carmo 11. **Cork products:** Rua da Escola Politécnica 4. **Delicatessens:** Casa Simoes, Largo do Chiado 17, Wine shop. Martins and Costa, Rua A. Herculano 32. Manteigaria Silva, Rua D. Antão de Almada 1D. Manuel Tavares, Rua da Betesga 1A/B. **Gift shops:** Unika, Rua Garret 32. Costa & Branco, Rua de Assunção 75. A Havanza, Largo do Chiado 25. **Glass market:** Depósito da Marinha Grande, Rúa de São Bento 243-418. **Handicrafts:** Mercearia Liberdade, Av. da Liberdade 207. Arameiro, Pr. dos Restauradores 62-64. Centro de Artesanía, Rua Dr. Joaquim Manso 3B. **Haute Couture:** Ana Salazar, Av. de Roma 16E and Rua do Carmo 87. Augustus, Rua Augusta 55. Mario Matos Ribeiro, Tv. do Poço do Cidade 46. Gardenia, Rua Garret 54. Bazar da Rua do Conde, Rua do Conde 34. Lena Aires, Rua da Atalaia 96. **Jewelry:** Rua Aurea, Rua da Prata. **Music:** Valentim de Carvalho, Av. de Roma 49 and Rossio 59. A large selection of Portuguese long-playing records and CDS. Discoteca do Carmo, Rua do

Carmo 63. Good selection. Associação José Afonso, Rua Voz do Operário 623. Traditional Portuguese music, with an art gallery. Contraverso, Trav. da Queimada 33. All the newest sounds on the rock market. **Stationary**: Rua Atalaia 114. Livraria Barata, Av. de Roma 11A.

Markets

Grocery: Covered market on Av. 24 de Julho, open daily until noon. Mercado do Bairro Alto, Rua da Atalaia. **Fish market**: Cais do Sodré. **Flower market**: Praça Dom Pedro IV. **Philately and numismatics market**: Praça do Comercio, Sunday mornings. **Fleamarket**: Feira da Ladra, Campo de Sta. Clara, Saturday and Sunday 7am-6pm. **Handicrafts market**: July 1-August 29 in Estoril.

Festivals

Prozession do Senhor dos Pasos da Graça on March 6. *Sto. Antonio* on June 13 in Alfama. *Santos Populares*, i.e. the festival celebrating various patron saints in the city districts, June 12-29. *Feira da Luz*, first Sunday in September.

Public transport

Train stations: Rossio – Trains for Sintra. Sta. Apolónia, Av. Infante Dom Henrique, destinations to the north and east; Cais do Sodré – suburban trains in the direction of Cascais; Ferry from Est. Fluvial, Pr. do Comercio to Barreiro, from there trains heading south.

Boat excursions: Estação Fluvial do Terreiro do Paço, Praça do Comerçio. Trips include longer rides to the estuary of the Tejo, also nights. **Bus stations**: To points north and east: Av. Casal Ribeiro 18. To points south: Av. 5 de Outubro 75.

Airport information: Tel: 802060.

Inner city transportation: For busses, elevators, tramways use the same ticket. The same applies for the cable cars of Lavra, Bica, Glória as well as the elevator of Sta. Justa. Tickets come in ten-packs of five tickets, each of which can be used twice. One can also buy a 0ne- or three-day ticket. Four- and seven-day tickets can also be used in the subway.

City tours: Tramway line Nr. 28 is the cheapest way to visit the city and get a look at everyday Lisbon life. Watch out for pickpockets in the narrow trolley cars! Special trains with varying departure times leave from Pr. do Comerçio in summer to Linha das Colinas and Linha do Tejo.

Taxis: Radio-Taxis, Tel: 8155061. Tele-Taxis, Tel: 8152076.

Practical addresses

Hospital: Sta. Maria, Av. Egas Moniz, Tel: 7979459. São José, Rua José A. Serrano, Tel: 8860710. **Emergencies**: 617777. **Post office**: Praça dos Restauradores, open from 8am to 8pm. **Tickets**: For the theater: Av. da Liberdade 140, Tel: 3425360. For the theater and soccer matches: ABEP

Pavilion, Praça Restauradores, Tel: 3475824, Mon-Sat 9am-9:45pm, Sun 10am-7pm.

Rental cars and motorbikes

Rental cars: All rental companies have offices at the airport. **Rent-A-Car**, Tel: 8495523. **Avis**, Tel: 8494836. **Europcar**, Tel: 801163. **Hertz**, Tel: 801496. City offices: **Avis**, Av. Praia Vitória 12C, Tel: 3462676. **Europcar**, Av. António A. Aguiar 24, Tel: 9422306. **Hertz**, Av. 5 Outubro 10, Tel: 9422306. **Motorcycle rentals**: Gesrent, R.S.J. Nepomuceno 32A, Tel: 691499, 9-19.30 Uhr tägl.

Tourist information

Office of tourism: Palácio Foz, Pr. dos Restauradores, Tel: 3463624, daily 9am-8pm.

SUBURBS
QUELUZ, BELÉM AND ODIVELAS
Restaurants and Cafés

BELÉM: A Commenda, Restaurant in the Centro Cultural de Belém. **Pasteis de Belém**, Rua de Belém 84. Here you'll find the best *Pasteis de Nata*: Strudel dough cake filled with cream and sprinkled with cinnamon sugar.

QUELUZ: Cozinha Velha, Palacio de Queluz, Tel: 4350232. Luxury restaurant in the oldcastle kitchen; belongs to the Pousada chain.

Sightseeing and museums

BELÉM: Aquario Vasco da Gama, Rua Direita, 10am-5:30pm (in summer until 6pm). **Mosteiro dos Jerónimos**, 10am-1pm and 2:30pm-5:30pm, Sun 10am-1pm, closed Mondays and hollidays. **Museu Nac. de Arqueología**, Tue 2pm-6pm, Wed, Fri, Sun 10am-6pm, Thu, Sat 10am-7pm Uhr, closed Mondays. **Museu Nac. dos Coches**, Praça Afonso Alburquerque, Wed, Fri, Sun 10am-6pm, Thu, Sat 10am-7pm, Tue 2pm-6pm, closed Mondays. **Museu de Arte Popular**, Av. Brasilia, Belem, 10am-12:30pm and 2pm-5pm, closed Mondays and hollidays. **Museu de Etnologia**, Av. Ilha da Madeira, Restelo, 10am-12:30pm und 2pm-5pm, closed Mondays and Fridays. **Museu da Marinha**, Praça do Imperio, 10am-5pm, closed Mondays and Fridays. **Centro Cultural Belem**, daily 11am-8pm. **Palácio Nacional da Ajuda**, Largo da Ajuda, 10am-5pm, closed Mondays and hollidays. **Planetarium**, demonstrations Wed, Thu 11am, 3pm, and 4:15pm, Sat and Sun 4pm. **Torre de Belem**, 10am-6:30pm (in winter until 5pm).

ODIVELAS: Cistercian Cloister: open Mon-Fri 10am-midday and 2pm-4pm.

QUELUZ: Palácio Nacional: open 10am-1pm und 2pm-5pm, closed Tuesdays.

Tourist information

QUELUZ: Office of tourism: Palacio Nacional, Tel: 4363415. 10am-1pm and 2pm-5pm Uhr, closed Tuesdays.

ALTANTIC COAST
AROUND LISBON

0   5   10   15 km

EXCURSIONS AND BEACHES AROUND LISBON

**THE SUNSHINE COAST
THE ESTREMADURA COAST
ESTREMADURA
MAFRA AND SINTRA
SOUTH OF THE TEJO**

Not only is Lisbon one of Europe's most attractive cities, but its inhabitants are also fortunate enough to live in close proximity to some marvelous scenery, all within day-trip range. To the south, between the estuary channels of the Tejo and Sado Rivers, are long sand beaches; the Serra de Arrábida has pleasant hiking trails and restaurants; to the west, the coast of Costa de Lisboa leads into the elegant resort suburbs of Estoril and Cascais; and to the north lies the Serra de Sintra, a landscape of romantic cliffs, fishing villages, and vineyards.

THE SUNSHINE COAST

Costa do Sol, the Sunshine Coast, is what Lisboners call the stretch of coastline to the west, on the open sea. The once-mundane vacation resorts that lined this coast are today among the tonier suburbs of Greater Lisbon. Local trains take about 35 minutes to cover the distance between the station on Cais do Sodré and Cascais, and travel along a beautiful, albeit uninterruptedly built-up coast. Below the tracks and the four-lane arterial road known as the *Marginal* are a

Preceding pages: Azenhas do Mar clusters atop a cliff that overlooks the Atlantic Ocean.

large number of small beaches. Beyond **Caxias**, whose gigantic São Bruno fortress was an infamous high-security prison in the days of Salazar, come **Paço do Arcos**, **Oeiras**, with the palace of the Marquis of Pombal, and **Carcavelos**, with the São Julião da Barra fortress. The best beaches begin at this point, adjacent to such places as **Estoril**, where one finds opulent villas from the turn of the century and a casino with revues and variety shows of international class, and the former fishing village of **Cascais**. Farther to the west are golf courses, riding clubs, luxury hotels and a slew of restaurants catering to the needs of holidaymakers. In spite of heavy tourism, however, the old center of Cascais has maintained a good deal of its charm. Pleasant villas, old and new hotels, a good choice of restaurants, and a picturesque pedestrian zone contribute to the town's flair. The **City Museum**, in the palace of the Dukes of Castro Guimarães, stands in the park behind the Citadel, which was built in 1681. Its unique rooms contain works of art by local painters, Indo-Portuguese furniture, and an outstanding library.

Cascais has a fishing port and three beaches, of which the middle one, tucked away amidst cliffs, is by far the most beautiful. It is known as *Praia da Rainha*, or the Queen's Beach. Just be-

hind the lighthouse is the **Boca do Inferno**, which translates as the "Abyss of Hell," an opening in the sheer cliff face that the waves continue to gnaw away at with unchecked fury. Along here, the whole coast is steep and rocky. Halfway to the Cabo da Roca, framed by pine forests and sand dunes, is the large, attractive **Praia da Guincho**. Wind and wave surfers usually met here and at the"Abyss of Hell."

THE ESTREMADURA COAST

Cabo da Roca, a rocky cape (as the name indicates) that defies the wild Atlantic swell, is continental Europe's westernmost point. It's an ideal spot for admiring the endless cliffs, which yield, in places, to small bays. The coast from here to Cape Carvoeiro has managed to maintain much of its original, unique mixture of fishing villages alternating with green, hilly farmland tended by small farmers and vintners. The harsh and windy Atlantic climate has served to check the influx of mass tourism, but not of surfers, who find the massive waves here quite a challenge. The small beaches, which fishermen use to park their boats, are hardly built up, but more and more weekend houses have started appearing around the villages, and their denizens fill the area's myriad fish restaurants to overflowing on weekends, as well.

The beach **Praia das Maçãs**, accessible in summer using a tramway from **Colares**, is one of the most popular. The town's coat-of-arms shows three necklaces. According to legend, in the 11th century a Scandinavian princess bought a parcel of land from the Moorish king, and payed for it with her jewelry. In the former royal wine-cellars with their huge tiled wall, exquisite wines are pressed and aged in large wooden barrels. The wines here come out of a particularly old tradition: the local vineyards were the

Above: Estoril, a popular seaside resort (with a casino) on the Costa do Sol. Right: The art of lace-making in Peniche.

only ones in Europe that were spared the devastating phylloxera epidemic of 1865.

At the foot of the cliffs along the coast between Praia das Maçãs and Ericeira are a number of small beaches. One village of note is **Azenhas do Mar**; its houses lie one above the other like little boxes stacked up the cliff. Its tiny bay boasts a natural salt-water swimming pool.

São Julião is a former fishermen's community; its diminutive houses are spread out along the top of the cliff. It fills up with people on weekends and in summer. Locals belong to the Society of the Friends of Saint Julian; and the chapel, decorated with ancient tile pictures, is also dedicated to that holy man.

Ericeira is the only village with a harbor along this stretch of coast. In 1910, Manuel II, Portugal's last king, embarked here on his journey into exile in England after the proclamation of the Portuguese Republic. Sand beaches lie to both sides of the harbor. This fairly large fishing and resort village has preserved much of its original look, barring a few taller

modern buildings that have been planted along the main street. On the wharf overlooking the beaches, where the fishing boats lie about safe from the pounding surf, old men sit around chatting or watching, as from a balcony, the fishermen at work below. Also here is a pretty tiled chapel dedicated to Saint Sebastian.

Continuing northwards, you arrive at more small sand beaches; then the outlying beach district of Torres Vedras, **Praia Santa Cruz**, which consists almost exclusively of apartment houses; and finally, past the windswept beach of **Santa Rita**, an unsightly golf hotel standing alone at the top of a cliff. The best way to endure this is to stay in it; that way, you don't have to look at it. To get a real taste of the secluded-beach experience, get a room in one of the small pensions in **Porto Novo**.

This section of coast ends at the **Peniche** Peninsula, which was still a full-fledged island at the time of the Romans. In the 17th century, this small town sprawling on a sandy isthmus was built up into Portugal's most powerful coastal fortress. A massive fortified wall shields it on the inland side, and along the harbor is a gigantic bulwark, the **Baluarte de Redondo**, that served until 1974 as a maximum-security prison during the rule of Salazar. Nowadays it houses a local museum and a fishing museum. More forts can be found along the northern side of the peninsula and on the 7.5-mile-long (12 km) Berlenga Island.

These days Peniche is a major fishing center with a busy harbor and lots of excellent fish restaurants. The 2-mile (3 km) peninsula, which ends at the Cape Carvoeiro lighthouse, is a barren, rocky plateau that is becoming a popular spot for vacation homes. Walkers should negotiate it on foot: the trail leads along steep cliffs, past caverns washed out by the rambunctious waves, to the cape itself and the lookout called Varanda de Pilatos. On the way back to town you will come across the Remédios Chapel. To the north of Peniche one can see the expansive sand beaches that begin around Baleal, a small vacation resort – almost an island, in fact – that is connected to the mainland by a narrow, sand-blown isthmus.

Berlenga Island lies about 7.5 mile (12 km) offshore opposite Peniche. It, together with a few smaller islands, has been made into a nature conservation area. The only houses are the lighthouse and those of a small fishing village offering very modest accommodations. A narrow gangplank connects the island to the fortress of **São João Baptista**, which was erected in the 18th century. Otherwise there are a few restaurants, a camping site, and hiking trails. Boats shuttle from Peniche to the island in summer. In order to pitch a tent here, however, you need special permission from the tourist office in Peniche.

Right: The medieval town of Óbidos is still for the most part intact.

Further inland, the towns around the wooded Serra de Montejunto chain only get the Lisbon throngs on summer weekends. The rest of the year they are pleasant country towns and villages, such as Bombarral, with its tiled train station, or Cadaval and Rio Maior. A worthwhile sight is the early-Gothic church of **Atouguia da Baleia**. The ceiling structure originally consisted of whale ribs, which gave the town its name (*baleia*).

Óbidos

When the legendary king Dom Dinis married Isabella, who was later canonized, he gave her the town they spent their honeymoon in as a wedding present. This tradition was kept up until the secularization of Portugal: **Óbidos** was the dowry for all Portuguese queens. The medieval town has been well preserved over the centuries. It takes a solid hour to walk all around the old city wall. Eleganty set between its fortress and defensive tower, Óbidos suggests a movie set. Little white houses with yellow and blue trim are pressed together on the sloping terrain. Along its pretty streets are city gates, Baroque fountains, the *pelourinho*, Baroque or Baroquely redone churches, a 16th-century aqueduct, and little squares, or house walls adorned with window-boxes and flowerpots overflowing with blossom. The only straight street, **Rua Direita**, consists of a long string of souvenir shops, ceramics workshops, galleries, and restaurants. Still, a stroll through the side alleys will always bring to light another gentle detail in this carefully tended ensemble; the full impact of its charm becomes clear at night, when the street lights come on and the last tour bus has taken off to other climes.

The community church of **Santa Maria** is coated with 17th-century tiles. Around the altar hang several paintings by the Baroque artist Josefa de Ayala of Seville. She settled in Óbidos in the

middle of the 17th century and later became famous under the name Josefa de Óbidos. She is buried in the São Pedro Church. A collection of her paintings is also exhibited in the fine **museum** in the old Town Hall, along with other paintinngs, sculptures and archaeological finds.

In the 15th-century **Royal Palace** inside the fortress is one of the country's most attractive Pousadas. To get one of the nine rooms, one must book ahead; but there are also other similarly furnished accommodations to be found in Óbidos.

Beyond the city wall is a vast and fertile plain. In the Middle Ages, Óbidos' lake used to reach the town limits, but it has since silted up to about a third of its original size. Heading toward Caldas da Rainha on the main road, you'll come across the Baroque, octagonal pilgrimage church **Jesús da Pedra**.

Caldas da Rainha

Queen Leonor founded the thermal spa of **Caldas da Rainha**, hence the name "Queen's Spa." Apparently she was journeying through the region once when she spotted peasants tumbling about in the mud. She stopped and asked what the reason was for this peculiar behavior. On hearing that the mucky water had healing properties, she decided at once to benefit from it herself. Nowadays, cures for cardiovascular and pulmonary problems are confined to the hospital, which is located near the spa park, the Queen's Palace and the Manuelistic church.

Otherwise modern in aspect, the town has become a center for the fine arts, with numerous painters' and sculptors' studios. The museum in the park has an excellent collection of paintings and sculptures by local artist José Malhoa, and gives a great deal of information about the work of Portuguese artists over the past two centuries.

Caldas' pedestrian zone is an agreeable place for shopping. The colorful market on **Praça da República** has not surrendered any of its rustic character to modern life, and the nearby beach of **Foz do**

Arehlo promises some enjoyable hours of swimming and sunbathing.

ESTREMADURA

The territories which the Asturian kings reconquered from the Moors in the early Middle Ages were called *estremadura*, meaning "outlying area." As the *Reconquista* progressed, further tracts of land were given the same name. Spain's midwestern section and Portugal's far west retained it.

The Estremadura between the Tejo and the Atlantic coast has always been the turf of small farmers, who planted the fertile land with vegetables, vineyards and orchards. Many of the hills still sport windmills, a hallmark of the region. A number of what used to be tiny villages have developed into popular tourist destinations, and have been expanded by the holiday cottages of many Lisboners.

Above and right: Some of the old windmills of the Estremadura are still operational.

Among the prettiest landscapes in the Estremadura is the wine region of **Arruda dos Vinhos**.

Torres Vedras, which clusters around a medieval fortress, has already acquired a healthy measure of traffic congestion and stress – more typical characteristics of the towns within reach of Lisbon. At the center of town, housed in a former monastery, is the museum, which has a lovingly presented collection of artifacts relating to local history and culture. To the southwest lies an arch of hills more than 25 miles (40 km) long. In 1810, the Duke of Wellington had a dual fortified line of 152 forts and castles built along them, the Torres Vedras line, which even the French armies, so accustomed to battlefield victory, failed to break through.

MAFRA

The giant complex of the **Mafra Monastery** and the Royal Palace is visible from a great distance. Around the turn of the 17th century, gold and diamonds were discovered in Brazil, which made the Portuguese monarchy extremely rich overnight. The exploitation of these mines took place during the reign of João V, and the resulting wealth is reflected in the monastery of Mafra. José Saramago wrote an entire novel, *The Memorial*, about the project, describing the construction of this building, which was supposed to surpass any other in terms of size and splendor. The initial impetus was a vow taken by the young king, whose wife, Marianne of Austria, had not yet produced an heir to the throne. If she gave birth within a year, he swore to build a Franciscan monastery. Lo and behold, the queen bore a daughter, Barbara, who later married Fernando VI of Spain. The cornerstone of the cloister was laid in 1717.

At the time Portugal lacked any architects capable of executing a project of such vast dimensions (760 by 683 feet/232 by 209 m), and so the German architect Ludwig and his sons were contracted to draw up the plans. All building materials with the exception of the stones and the colored marble were shipped in from abroad; artists in Italy wrought sculptures of Carrara marble sculptures, some of which reached a height of up to 16 feet (5 m), for the basilica. Laborers were drafted from throughout the kingdom by force, and 7,000 soldiers were brought in to keep an eye on 45,000 workers. The official statistics note that 1,338 men died on the construction site.

After 13 years of work, the basilica was consecrated on the king's birthday in 1730. It's a solemn building of black, red, white, and blue marble. In 1744 the Franciscans moved into the monastery, which could accommodate up to 342 monks and 150 novices. Work on the exterior ended in 1750, the same year in which João V died. His son, José I, continued with the interior decoration.

In 1754, the Italian artist Alexander Giusti opened a school of sculpture in Mafra so that Carrara marble could be worked on the spot. It produced some extremely fine students, notably Machado de Castro and José de Almeida, whose style was known as "Pombalistic" after the omnipotent Marquês de Pombal. By 1806, work had progressed enough that the court – under João VI – could move in and take up residence. Two years later, Napoleon arrived on the scene with his revolutionary armies, and the royal family and its entourage fled to Brazil, taking some of the finest art treasures of Mafra with them. The monks, too, were forced to leave. The French, and later the British, set up their military headquarters in the buildings. After returning from Brazil, the court only used the palace sporadically as a summer residence or for brief hunting jaunts until the Portuguese monarchy ended in 1910. Thus Mafra, for all its glory, never really fulfilled its projected function as a royal residence.

The one-hour tour of the place covers a considerable distance and shows countless suites of rooms that all seem uninhabited and for that matter uninhabitable, even though a children's room and the the apartment of the king and queen are given as evidence to the contrary. The most impressive sight is the 556-foot (170 m) hallway in the rear of the second floor. The experts are not all in agreement with one another, but the official publications mention 880 rooms, 300 monastic cells, 4,500 windows and doors, 29 interior courtyards, and 154 stairways. One memorable room is the dining room, which was used during the hunting trips; all of its furniture, including the chairs, is made of antlers. On the second floor are the rooms of the monastery, with the apothecary and the sick bay, the kitchen, religious sculptures, liturgical garments, and more. The most beautiful room is the library, whose Rococo decoration is still unfinished. It is about 260 feet (80 m) long and contains 36,000 invaluable volumes.

Needless to say, the sheer size of the monastery and palace literally dwarfs the town of Mafra proper. Nevertheless, don't overlook the simple, early Gothic Church of Santo André at the other end of town. Behind the monastery is the royal hunting preserve, **Tapada Nacional**, a forest of around 8 square miles (20 sq. km) that has remained unchanged since 1747. It is now a nature conservation area. Visitors are only allowed in on Sundays and then only accompanied by an official guide.

SINTRA

The **Serra de Sintra** forms a barrier between the western outskirts of Lisbon and the rustic hinterlands of the Estremadura. Even 19th-century travelers, among them Lord Byron and Hans Christian Andersen, agreed that this part of the

Above: The Palácio da Pena in Sintra, a 19th-century fairy-tale castle. Right: A pretty tiled fountain in Sintra.

country was by far the most beautiful: a huge park landscape with luxuriant vegetation, seas of flowers, villas, cultivated gardens, and forests: a perfect oasis on hot summer days. The kings were aware of this as well. Afonso Henriques overran the Moorish stronghold high above the town of Sintra in 1147, and in the 15th century, King João II began building a royal palace on the ruins of the Arab castle below. Manuel I continued work on this summer residence, known as **Palácio Real**, at the beginning of the 16th century.

From the outside, the whole ensemble seems a little run-down. Particularly noticeable are the huge conical chimneys. But this makes the interior all the more fascinating. Medieval building methods were so sound that the place survived the 1755 earthquake, hence early and late Gothic styles can be found in their original form. The tour guide leads visitors up and down stairs, to grandiosely furnished rooms, through courtyards, bathing rooms, a chapel, the kitchen, the

room in which Afonso VI's brother locked him up for eight years, and the room emblazoned with the coats-of-arms of all Portuguese noble families. Every room has its own legend, each piece of furniture its story to tell. Every decorative element has been chosen with care, be it a coffered ceiling with magpies or with swans, beautiful Moorish tiles, or a *mudejar* wooden ceiling.

The palace dominates the little summer resort of Sintra; but the churches of **Santa Maria**, **São Martinho**, and **São Pedro**, which were originally Gothic and later revamped in more modern style, are also worth a visit, as is the regional museum. And you can take pleasant strolls through the town park **Parque da Liberdade**, around the Moorish castle and the palace, or in the English garden of the exotic, romantic **Palace of Monserrate**, where there are more than 3,000 plant species from all over the world. And throughout the Serra and its villages are pretty restaurants ideal for day-trippers.

Atop the mountain, at an altitude of

some 1,635 feet (500 m), and commanding a view of Lisbon and the sea, the entire mountain range, and to the north as far as Mafra, is the fairy-tale castle **Palácio da Pena**. This was built in the mid-19th century as a whim of Ferdinand of Coburg-Koháry, second husband of Queen Maria II da Gloria, on a spot where the earthquake, the revolutionary French armies, and secularization had combined to destroy a monastery. A Renaissance chapel and cloister of the original building were rebuilt and incorporated into the newer building. The palace, painted in bright yellows and reds, is an eclectic hodgepodge of medieval towers and Moorish arches, a playful demonstration of wealth and feasibility.

The **Capuchin Monastery of Santa Cruz** seems incomparably modest next to da Pena. This 150-year-old monastery was built into the rocks in the midst of a forest between Sintra and Colares. Its tiny, cool cells, which the monks insulated with cork, exude a cavernous feeling.

73

SOUTH OF THE TEJO

Since 1966, after completion of the Salazar Bridge – later renamed Bridge of April 25 to commemorate the end of the Salazar dictatorship – **Almada** has developed into a suburb of Lisbon. To get into the capital each day, its residents either have to endure the monstrous bridge's permanent traffic jams, or take the ferry from Cacilhas. Since 1959, the **Cristo Rei**, a gigantic figure of Christ, has been welcoming people to the left bank of the Tejo. This 360-foot (110 m) statue was created by the sculptor Francisco Franco. An elevator carries visitors up to the platform at the statue's base, from which you have a spectacular view of Lisbon and the entire Tejo bay.

Locals call the river's vast estuary *Mar de Palha*, sea of straw. On the left bank are a few towns and old fishing villages, where cork-making has been established since time immemorial. Lisbon's inexorable growth has, however, swallowed them up, and uncontrolled building sprees have to a great extent ruined what was once a beautiful landscape. All that remains are some pretty harbors with good fish restaurants, a few beaches of doubtful cleanliness, and some sights: the museum of **Seixal**, where traditional shipbuilding is demonstrated; the church of **Arrentela**, with interesting Baroque ornamentation; the church of **Moita**, with a painted wooden ceiling; the windmills and tidal mills of **Barreiro** and **Corroios**; the salt ponds of **Alcochete**; and the bullfight arena of **Montijo**.

Located on the Atlantic coast of Almada is the favorite beach of Lisboners, **Costa da Caparica**. Above it stands a restored Capuchin monastery that is used for a summer music festival. The town of Caparica itself bristles with hotels, highrises, restaurants and snack bars. In summer, the 18.5-mile (30 km) sand beach, the **Praia do Sol**, is awash with people seeking rest and recuperation from the capital's infernal temperatures. The first 6 miles (10 km), which is accessible by local trains from Lisbon, are naturally the most crowded. The forest around the **beach lagoon of Albufeira** has been declared a conservation area and is therefore largely free of buildings; a golf club has settled here instead.

The farther southeast you go, the rockier and steeper the coast. The peninsula ends at **Cabo Espichel**, a crag bearing a lonely lighthouse and a pilgrimage church with accommodations for the pilgrims.

The Serra da Arrábida

The sheltered southern side of the peninsula, **Costa Bela**, between the Tejo and Sado Rivers, is bordered to the south by the **Serra da Arrábida**, a mountain range that rises almost perpendicularly from the ocean. Because of its Mediterranean vegetation, it has been placed under protection, and is an excellent place for excursions and hikes.

The resort of **Sesimbra** lies at the foot of the Serra, framed by steep, rocky cliffs. The medieval fortress, still the site of the town cemetery, looks out over modern Sesimbra, the wide **Praia do Espadarte**, and the protected harbor, **Porto do Abrigo**. It is one of the most colorful fishing ports along the entire coast. In the old town center are a Renaissance church, the town museum, and another fortress.

You should only attempt the panoramic road running along the southern edge of the mountains if you're sure you don't suffer from vertigo. On a clear day the views of the Sado estuary and the Tróia Peninsula is truly breathtaking. But you should also avoid the road on weekends, as the traffic jams often reach from Sesimbra all the way to Setúbal.

Right: Colorful fishing boats brighten the view in the harbor of Sesimbra.

The Franciscan monastery standing at the top of the mountain is not open to the public. The road winds its way up to an altitude of 1,635 feet (500 m); from the top, you look down a sheer wall to the crystal-clear blue sea below. Tucked away at the foot of the cliffs are tiny sand beaches, veritable Edens for swimmers and snorkelers.

The northern slopes of the Serra are somewhat gentler. The grapes for Setúbal's famous sweet muscatel grow here. Old *quintas*, noble palaces, stand amid the vineyards, many of them now restaurants or hotels. Casais da Serra, Vila Nogueira de Azeitão, and **Villa Fresca da Azeitão** (famous for its tile paintings) are the starting points for hiking trails through the mountains, along slopes covered with strawberry trees, laurel, pine, oak, and juniper.

Your first sight of **Setúbal** from afar will be smoking chimneys and the great drydocks. However, the city center turns out to be lively and surprisingly pretty, with a pleasant pedestrian zone and stylish cafés. Activity here centers around the Praça Bocage, a square sporting a statue of this Romantic-era poet, who lived in Rúa São Domingos nearby.

The foundations of the old town bear witness to the ancient birth of this important salt-trading port: under the glass floor of the tourist office, you can make out the remains of a Roman mill. The 1755 earthquake destroyed much of Setúbal with the exception of the Manuelistic façade of the São Julião Church on Praça Bocage and the **Monastery of Bom Jesús**, the first-ever example of the Manuelist style. The latter was built in the 15th century during the brief period when João II made Setúbal his residence. Manuel I continued and completed the work. The church, standing on a generous square, seems simple and unadorned from the outside. The main portal leads directly into the long nave, where you discover that the interior of this three-aisled church, where the columns separating the two side aisles from the central nave are twisted like a ship's rope, is one

of the most significant examples of Manuelism. The chancelry and sacristy are decorated with tiles from the 16th and 17th centuries.

The **Museum** of Setúbal is in the adjacent rooms of the cloister. Its exhibits include paintings that used to hang in the church, regional archaeological finds, and Portuguese art from various periods.

Setúbal was always well protected. The castle of **São Filipe**, commissioned in 1590 by King Filipe I, watches over the harbor. In its chapel, tile paintings tell the story of Saint Philip. Within view is the fort of **Palmela**, another powerful defensive bulwark that harks back to the Moorish period, and secures the inland side of town. The Knights of Saint James integrated one of their monasteries into it in the 15th century. Both fortresses have been turned into hotels of the Pousada chain; have a coffee on the terrace of one, and an aperitif at the bar of the other.

Above: On the beach, peddlars hope to find relaxed and willing customers.

Palmela town has long, old streets, a handsome Baroque fountain, an elegant Renaissance Town Hall and a 16th-century *pelhourinho* (pillory). On the crest of the Serra do Louro, beside the fortress, a series of old windmills stands along a breezy high road.

Behind Setúbal are the marshes of the Sado estuary. The area has been declared a nature preserve and a bird sanctuary, along with the salt marshes of Mitrena and the pine forests around Gãmbia. Luckily for the nesting birds, most of the marsh is only accessible in the flat-bottomed boats of the estuary fishermen.

An enjoyable ferry ride leads from Setúbal to **Tróia**, whose striking high-rises can be spotted from far away. The long beach following a 17-miles (28 km) sand bar, with a golf club and other fancy establishments, has made this island another favorite for Lisbon's huddled and overheated masses. A bumpy road leads through a pine forest to the neglected remains of the Roman fish-pickling plant of **Cetóbriga**.

EXCURSIONS AROUND LISBON – NORTH OF THE TEJO
Accommodations

ARRUDA DOS VINHOS (063): *TURISMO RURAL:* **Quinta de São Sebastião**, tel. 9501340.

CALDAS DA RAINHA (062): *MODERATE:* **D. Carlos**, Rua de Camões 39A, tel. 832551, Fax: 831669. **Dona Leonor**, Hemiciclo João Paulo II. 6, tel. 842171, Fax: 831509. **Estremadura**, Largo Dr. José Barbosa 23, tel. 832313. *CAMPING:* **Orbitur**, Parque D. Leonor, tel. 832367. **Foz do Arelho**, Lagoa de Óbidos, tel. 979101. *TURISMO RURAL:* **Casa dos Plátanos**, Rua Bordalo Pinheiro 24, tel. 841810.

CASCAIS (01): *LUXURY:* **Quinta da Marinha**, Hotel & Village Resort, tel. 4869881/9, Fax: 4869032. **Guincho**, Praia do Guincho, tel. 2850491, Fax: 2850431. **Forte Muchaxo**, Praia do Guincho, tel. 2850221, Fax: 2850444. **Mar do Guincho**, Praia do Guincho, tel. 2850251. MODERATE: **Inglaterra**, Rua do Porto 1, tel. 4684461, Fax: 4682108. CAMPING: **Guincho**, Areias, tel. 2850450.

COLARES (01): *MODERATE:* **Miramonte**, tel. 9291230, Fax: 9291480. **Conde**, Quinta do Conde, tel. 9291652. *TURISMO RURAL:* **Quinta da Pedra Firme**, Av. Dr. Brandão Vasconcelos, Várzea de Colares, tel. 9290553, Fax: 9292533.

ERICEIRA (061): *MODERATE:* **Turismo**, tel. 864045, Fax: 63146. Huge and a bit run-down, but right on the water. **Vilazul**, tel. 864101, Fax: 62927. **Pedro Pescador**, Rua Dr. Eduardo Burnay 22, tel. 864302, Fax: 62321. New and elegant. *CAMPING:* **Mil Regos**, tel. 62706.

ESTORIL (01): *LUXURY:* **Palácio do Estoril**, Rua do Parque, tel. 4680400, Fax: 4684867. *MODERATE:* **Alvorada**, Rua de Lisboa 3, tel. 4680070, Fax: 4687250. *BUDGET:* **Lido**, Rua do Alentejano 12, tel. 4684123, Fax: 4683665.

LOURINHÃ (061): *LUXURY:* **Bela Vista**, Rua D. Sancho I. tel. 414164, Fax: 414138. **Areia Branca**, Praia da Areia Branca, tel. 412491, Fax: 413143. *MODERATE:* **Rossio**, Rua Bombeiros Voluntarios, tel. 423049. *BUDGET:* **Mar do Norte**, Ribamar, Praia Porto Dinheiro, tel. 423100, Fax: 411713. *CAMPING:* **Praia da Areia Branca**, tel. 412199. *TURISMO RURAL:* **Quinta do Bom Sucesso**, Moita dos Ferreiros, tel. 921220. **Quinta da Moita Longa**, Toxofal de Cima, tel. 422385. **Quinta de Santa Catarina**, Rua Visconde de Palma de Almeida, tel. 422313.

MAFRA (061): *MODERATE:* **Castelão**, Av. 25 de Abril, tel. 812050, Fax: 51698.

ÓBIDOS (062): *LUXURY:* **Pousada do Castelo**, tel. 959105, Fax: 959148. **Rainha Santa Isabel**, Rua Direita, tel. 959323, Fax: 959115. **Josefa d'Óbidos**, Rua D. João d'Ornelas, tel. 959228, Fax: 959533. **Convento**, Rua D. João d'Ornelas, tel. 959217, Fax: 959159. *MODERATE:* **Louro**, Casal da Canastra, tel. 950183. **Alcaidaria-Mor**, Amoreira, tel. 969947. *TURISMO RURAL:* **Casa do Poço**, Trav. da Rua Nova, tel. 959358. **Casa do Relógio**, Rua da Graça, tel. 959282. **Casa do Pinhão**, Bairro da Senhora da Luz, tel. 959078.

PENICHE (062): *MODERATE:* **Félita**, Largo Prof. Franc Freire, tel. 782190. *BUDGET:* **Mar e Sol**, Berlenga-Insel, tel. 750331. *CAMPING:* **Peniche Praia**, tel. 783460. **Balealcampismo**, Baleal, tel. 769333. *TURISMO RURAL:* **A Coutada**, Atouguia de Baleia, tel. 759733. **A Casa das Marés**, Baleal, tel. 769255. **Quinta das Tripas**, Atouguia de Baleia, tel. 759733.

RIO MAIOR (043): *LUXURY:* **Quinta da Ferraria**, Ribeira de São João, tel. 95001, Fax: 95696. **Rio Maior**, Rua F.Barbosa, tel. 92087. *TURISMO RURAL:* **Quinta da Cortiçada**, Outeiro da Cortiçada, tel. 479182, Fax: 479772. **Moinho da Senta**, Rua da Boavista 10, tel. 92551.

SINTRA (01): *LUXURY:* **Seteais**, Rua Barbosa de Bocage 8, tel. 9233200, Fax: 9234377. **Palast. Gruta do Rio**, Rio de Mouro, tel. 9164146, Fax: 4953876. *MODERATE:* **Sintra**, Trav. dos Avelares 12, São Pedro, tel. 9230738. **Bristol**, Rua Visconde de Monserrate 40-52, tel. 9233852. *BUDGET:* **Adelaide**, Av. Guilherme Gomes Fernandes 11, tel. 9230873. **Nova Sintra**, tel. 9230220. *CAMPING:* **Capuchos**, tel. 3152715. *TURISMO RURAL:* **Quinta da Capela**, Estrada de Montserrate, tel. 9290170. Belongs to a cinema owner, exclusive & stylish. **Quinta de São Tiago**, Estrada de Montserrate, tel. 9232923. **Patio do Saloio**, tel. 9241520. **Quinta das Sequoias**, Estr. de Montserrate, Tel/Fax: 9230342.

TORRES VEDRAS (061): *LUXURY:* **Golfmar**, Praia Porto Novo, tel. 984157, Fax: 984621. *BUDGET:* **Promar**, Praia Porto Novo, tel. 984195, Fax: 984220. **O Forte**, Praia Porto Novo, tel. 984472. **Berco Mar**, Praia Porto Novo, tel. 984262.

Restaurants / Cafés

AZENHAS THU MAR: do Zé, Fontanelas, tel. 9292209. **CALDAS DA RAINHA: Páteo da Rainha**, Rua Camões 39, tel. 35658. **Portugal**, Av. Alm. Cândido Reis 30, tel. 34280. **Adega do Borlão**, Rua Eng. Cancela Abreu, tel. 842690. **CASCAIS: A Taberna de Gil Vicente**, Rua dos Navegantes 22, tel. 4832032. **A Traineira**, Rua A. Herculano 25A, tel. 4862739. **Maré Alta**, Rua do Cobre, tel. 4843845. **Ponto Final**, Praça Costa Pinto 33, tel. 4831345. **Tosca Bar**, Rua Marquês Leal Pancada 28A. **COLARES: Tita**, Mucifal, tel. 9291582. **Bistro**, Largo da Igreja, tel. 9290016. **A Casa do Luís**, Azóia, Cabo da Roca, tel. 9292721.

ERICEIRA: **Miradouro da Baleia**, Praia do Sul, am Südstrand. **Mar d'Areia**, Rua Fonte do Cabo 75, tel. 62222. **Toca do Caboz**, Rua 5 de Outubro, tel. 62248. **Gaivota**, Rua Capitão J. Lopes 18, tel. 62161. **Cantinho Madeirense**, Praça dos Navegantes, Lote 17, tel. 63969. **Pedro O Pescador**, R. Dr. Eduardo Burnay 22, tel. 864032. **ESTORIL**: **A Bolina**, Praia do Pescoço do Cavalo, tel. 4687821. **A Choupana**, Estr. Marginal, São João do Estoril, tel. 4683099. **Jackpote**, Rua de Lisboa 1, tel. 4670754. **MAFRA**: **O Pateo**, Rua Serpa Pinto 19, tel. 811137. **Solar d'el Rei**, Rua da Quinta Nova. **O Escondidinho**, Trav. Quinta Nova. **Paris**, Praça da República 14. **ÓBIDOS**: **A Ilustre Casa de Ramiro**, Rua Porta do Vale, tel. 959194. **O Caldeirão**, Largo do Sr. da Pedra, tel. 959839. **D. João V.**, Largo do Sr. da Pedra, tel. 959134. **Alcaide**, Rua Direita, tel. 959220. **A Vila de Dona Josefa**, Rua D. J. de Ornelas, tel. 959228.

PENICHE: **Gaivota**, tel. 782202. **Onda Azul**, tel. 787224. **Abrigo do Pescador**, tel. 783436; **Loja do Mar**; **Mar à Vista**, tel. 784502, alle 5 am Hafen, Largo da Ribeira. **Amigos do Baleal**, Praia do Baleal, tel. 769173. **Nau dos Corvos**, Cabo Carvoeiro, tel. 782410. **SINTRA**: **Adega das Caves**, Rua da Pendoa 2A, tel. 9230848. **Flor da Várzea**, Várzea de Sintra, tel. 9232741. **O Chico**, Rua do Arco do Teixeira 4-6, tel. 9231526. **Cantinho de São Pedro**, Praça D. Fernando II., tel. 9230267. **Solar de São Pedro**, Praça D. Fernando II., tel. 9231860. **Tacho Real**, Rua da Ferraria 4, tel. 9235277. **Palacio de Seteais**, Estr. de Colares km 1,5, tel. 9233200.

Sights/Museums

CALDAS DA RAINHA: **Museu de José Malhoa**, 10am-12:30pm, 2pm-5pm, closed Mondays. **CASCAIS**: **City Museum**, **Palace of the Condes de Castro Guimarães**. **MAFRA**: **Monastery/Palace**: 10am-1pm and 2pm-5pm,closed Tuesdays. Glockenspiel: Sun 4pm, demonstration of the mechanism: Sun 2pm and 3pm.
ÓBIDOS: **Museu Municipal**: 10am-12:30pm and 2pm-6pm, closed Mondays. **PENICHE**: **Fort/Museum**: 10am-midday and 2pm-5pm, closed Mondays. **SINTRA**: **Palacio Nacional**: 10am-1pm and 2pm-5pm, closed Wednesdays. **Palacio da Pena**: 10am-1pm and 2pm-5pm, closed Mondays. **Castelo dos Mouros**: 10am-6pm (in winter until 5pm); **Convento dos Capuchos**: 10am-6pm (in winter until 5pm). **Park der Pena**: 10am-6pm (in winter until 4:30pm); **Park von Montserrate**: 9am-6pm. **Museu Regional**: Praça da República 23; **Museu Ferreira de Castro**: Rua Consigliéri Pedroso 34; **Casa Museu Anjos Teixeira**, Volta do Duche; **Casa Museu Leal da Câmara**, Cacém near Sintra; Tue-Fri 9:30am-midday

and 2pm-6pm, Sat, Sun, Fri 2pm-6pm, closed Mondays. **Roman excavations of Odrinhas**, 15 km north of Sintra, 10am-noon and 2pm-6pm, closed Tuesdays. **TORRES VEDRAS**: **Museu Municipal**, Praça 25 de Abril, Convento da Graça, 10am-1pm and 2pm-6pm, closed Mondays.

Tourist information/Useful addresses

ARRUDA DOS VINHOS: **Tourist Office**: Praça Miguel Bombarda, tel. 95436/97004. **CABO DA ROCA**: **Tourist Office**: Azóia, tel. 01-9280081. Winter 9am-7pm, summer 9am-8pm. **CALDAS DA RAINHA**: **Tourist Office**: Praça 25 de Abril, tel. 831003, Mon-Fri 9am-7pm, Sat-Sun 10am-1pm and 3pm-7pm. **CASCAIS**: **Tourist Office**: Rua Visconde da Luz, tel. 4868204. **COLARES**: **Tourist Office**: Alameda Coronel Linhares de Lima, tel. 9292638. Winter 9am-7pm, Summer 9am-8pm. **ERICEIRA**: **Tourist Office**: Rua Eduardo Burnay 33A, tel. 63122, daily 9am-8pm, Fri-Sat 9am-10pm. **ESTORIL**: **Tourist Office**: Arcadas do Parque, tel. 4681697. **LOURINHÃ**: **Tourist Office:** Praia da Areia Branca, tel. 422167. **MAFRA**: **Tourist Office**: Av. 25 de Abril, Mon-Fri 9:30am-6pm, Sat-Sun 9:30am-1pm and 2:30pm-6pm, in summer until 7:30pm. **Post**: Av. 25 de Abril. **Reiten**: Rua de S. Miguel, Alcainça, tel. 9862222. **ÓBIDOS**: **Tourist Office**: Rua Direita, tel. 959231, daily 9:30am-1pm and 2pm-6pm, in summer until 7pm. **PENICHE**: **Tourist Office**: A. Herculano, tel. 789571, in summer daily 9am-8pm, winter 10am-1pm and 2pm-5pm. ‾**Boat Excursions**: Berlenga Turpesca, tel. 789960/783013. Viamar, tel. 782153. **RIO MAIOR**: **Tourist Office**: Praça da República, tel. 92199.

SINTRA: **Tourist Office**: Praça da República 23, tel. 9231157/9241700. winter 9am-7pm, summer 9am-8pm. **Post**: Praça da República 26. **Taxis**: At the train station and at the palace (unmetered). **Horse carriages**: Centro Equestre, tel. 9233778. **Train station**: Largo D. Manuel I. (to Lisbon every quarter hour). **Buses**: Av. Dr. Miguel Bombarda 59. **TORRES VEDRAS**: **Tourist Office**: Rua 9 de Abril, tel. 314094, 10am-1pm and 2pm-6pm.

Festivals

CALDAS DA RAINHA: 2nd half of August, fruit festival. **ÓBIDOS**: January 17, pilgrimage São António. **PENICHE**: August 15, Na. Sa. de Bom Viagem. **SINTRA**: June 29, São Pedro. **TORRES VEDRAS**: Carnival.

SOUTH OF THE TEJO
Accommodations

ALCOCHETE (01): *TURISMO RURAL:* **Casa de Moyzém**, Largo Alm. Gago Coutinho 1, tel. 234066. **AZEITÃO** (01): *LUXURY:* **Club d'Azeitão**, Quinta do Bom Pastor, Vila Fresca, tel. 2182267, Fax: 2191629. *TURISMO RURAL:*

Quinta das Torres, tel. 2180001, Fax: 2190607. **Quinta do César**, Vila Fresca, tel. 2180387. **Quinta da Arrábida**, Casais da Serra, tel. 2183433. **Quinta de Santo Amaro**, Aldeia da Piedade, tel. 2180030, Fax: 2183190.
COSTA DA CAPARICA (01): *MODERATE:* **Real**, Rua Mestre Manuel 18, tel. 2901701, Fax: 2901701. **Capa Rica**, Rua dos Pescadores 5, tel. 2900242, Fax: 541427. *BUDGET:* **Copacabana**, Rua José Alves Marins 14, tel. 2900103. *CAMPING:* **Orbitur**, Monte da Caparica, tel. 2900661. **Praia da Saúde**, tel. 2902272. **Lagoa**, Southern shore in Albufeira, tel. 2684777. *TURISMO RURAL:* **Quinta de Vale Mourelos**, Sobreda, Vía Rápida km 2,3, tel. 2954871, Fax: 2942566. **MONTIJO** (01): *MODERATE:* **Havaneza**, Rua Man. de Almeida 7, Tel./Fax: 2303457. *TURISMO RURAL:* **Palacio de Rio Frio**, tel. 2303401. Private palace, wonderful tile paintings. **PALMELA** (01): *LUXURY:* **Pousada**, tel. 2351226, Fax: 2330440. *MODERATE:* **Varanda Azul**, Rua Hermenegildo Capelo 3, tel. 2331451/2/3, Fax: 2331454. *TURISMO RURAL:* **Quinta do Chaparro**, Orvidais, tel. 2350431. **O Moinho**, tel. 2351033. Windmill. **SESIMBRA** (01): *MODERATE:* **Varandas da Falésia**, Ponta d'Argéis, tel. 2230586, Fax: 2233769 (Apartements for 4 people). **Quinta do Rio**, Alto das Vinhas, tel. 2081043. *CAMPING:* **Forte do Cavalo**, tel. 2233694. *TURISMO RURAL:* **Casa de Nossa Senhora**, tel. 7971984 or 2230637.
SETÚBAL (065): *LUXURY:* **Pousada S. Filipe**, tel. 523844, Fax: 532538. **Setúbalense**, Rua Major A Pala 17, tel. 525790, Fax: 525789. *MODERATE:* **Bocage**, Rua S. Cristóvão, tel. 21598, Fax: 21809. *CAMPING:* **Outão**, Estr. da Figueirinha, tel. 538318. *TURISMO RURAL:* **Quinta do Patrício**, Estr. do Castelo S. Filipe, Tel./Fax: 33817.

Restaurants / Cafés

SESIMBRA: Aqualeme, Av. dos Náufragos 31, tel. 2235396. **Toca do Leão**, Rua Amélia Frade 12, tel. 2231649. **O Farol**, Largo da Marinha 4/5, tel. 2233356. **Beira-Mar**, Portinho Arrábida, tel. 2080544. **Ribamar**, Av. dos Náufragos 1. tel. 2234853. **SETÚBAL: A Roda**, Trav. Postigo do Cais 7, tel. 29264. **Cactus**, Rua Vasco da Gama 81, tel. 34687. **O Beco**, Rua da Misericórdia 24, tel. 524617. **Albarquel**, Praia Albarquel, tel. 35438. **O Casario**, Av. Luisa Todi 85, tel. 29268.

Sights / Museums

ALCOCHETE: Museu Municipal and **Museu de Arte Sacra**: Wed-Fri 2pm-6:30pm, Sat-Sun 3pm-7pm. **ALMADA: Cristo Rei**: daily 9am-6pm, in summer until 7pm. **Museu Municipal**: Mon-Fri 10am-6pm, Sat-Sun 3pm-23. **Casa da Cerca**, Centro de Arte Contemporanea 10am-6pm,

closed Mondays. **Museu Naval**, Olho de Boi, 10am-12:30pm and 2pm-5pm, Sat-Sun 2pm-5:30pm, closed Mondays. **Museu de Arqueología e Historia**, Olho de Boi, Tue-Fri 10am-12:30pm and 2pm-5pm. **AZEITÃO: Quinta da Bacalhoa**, Park, Mon-Sat 9am-6pm. **BOMBARRAL: Museu Municipal**: Tue-Fri 9am-12:30pm and 2pm-5:30pm, Sat-Sun 10.30-1pm and 2pm-5:30pm. **MONTIJO: Museu Municipal**: 10am-midday and 2pm-6pm, Sat-Sun 2pm-6pm, closed Mondays. **Museu Etnografico**: Mon-Fri 9am-1pm and 3pm-6pm. **SEIXAL: Ecomuseu**, Torre da Marinha: Tue-Fri 10am-midday and 2pm-5pm. **Museu Naval Histórico**, Arrentela, Tue-Fri 10am-midday and 2pm-5pm, Sat-Sun 10am-5pm, closed Mondays. **Moinho de Maré** (Gezeitenmühle), Corroios, 10am-midday and 2pm-5pm, Sat-Sun 2pm-5pm, closed Mondays. **SESIMBRA: Museu Municipal**: Mon-Fri 9am-12:30pm and 2pm-5pm.30. **SETÚBAL: Igreja de Jesus** and **Museu de Setúbal** in the Convento de Jesús : Mon-Fri 9am-12:30pm and 2pm-5:30pm. **Arch. and Ethnol. Museum**: Tue-Sat 9:30am-12:30pm and 2pm-5pm, Sun 9:30am-12:30pm, closed Mondays. **Oceanographic Museum**, Portinho da Arrabida: Mon-Fri 10am-4pm, Sat-Sun 2pm-6pm. **Casa de Bocage**: Mon-Fri 9am-midday and 13.30-5pm, Sat 3pm-7pm. **TRÓIA: Roman excavations**: 9am-1pm and 3pm-6pm, closed Wed and Thu.

Tourist information

ALMADA: Tourist Office: Av. D. Nuno Alvares Pereira 14N, tel. 2747854. **AZEITÃO: Tile art**: São Simão, Rua Almirante Reis 86, Vila Fresca de Azeitão. **BOMBARRAL: Tourist Office:** Palacio do Gorjão, Praça do Município, tel. 61145. **COSTA DA CAPARICA: Tourist Office**: Praça da Liberdade, tel. 2900071. **MOITA: Tourist Office**: Praça da República, tel. 2892818. **MONTIJO: Tourist Office**: Pr. da República, tel. 2894540. **PALMELA: Tourist Office**: Largo do Chafariz D. Maria I. tel. 2350089. **SEIXAL: Tourist Office**: Praça da República, tel. 2227054. **SESIMBRA: Tourist Office:** Largo da Marinha, tel. 2235743. **SETÚBAL: Tourist Office**: Trav. Frei Gaspar, tel. 524284, Tue-Fri 9am-7pm, Mon and Sat 9am-12:30pm and 2pm-7pm. **Car rental**: Alucar, Av. dos Combatentes 60, tel. 533285, Fax: 525405. Avis, Av. Luisa Todi 96, tel. 526946. Facilcar, Av. Luisa Todi 27, tel. 528038.

Festivals

ALCOCHETE: Easter: Seaman's Pilgrimage; Barrete Verde and Salines festival 2nd week in Aug. **PALMELA**: Wine festival, first Sunday in Sept. **SESIMBRA**: Na. Sa. do Cabo last Sunday in Sept, Cabo Espichel. **SETÚBAL**: Santiago: Week of July 25. Week of Sept 15, musical & cultural events.

THE ALENTEJO

THE UPPER ALENTEJO
THE LOWER ALENTEJO
THE ALENTEJO'S ATLANTIC COAST

The gently undulating hills and austere landscapes of the Alentejo are a fragile green in spring, golden yellow in summer, and arid brown in autumn. This sparsely-populated region is dotted with isolated cork oaks, modest olive groves, and the small adobe houses of peasants who eke out a living from wheat, olives, animal husbandry, and cork. Cork, the cambium of the oak tree, is peeled from the trunks every eight to ten years; after being peeled, the trunks are a bright ochre yellow, then turn red-brown before settling back to their usual grayish brown. Portugal is the world's leading cork producer, but it is processed in factories around the big cities, so little of the income flows back into the Alentejo.

Alentejo, meaning "beyond the Tejo," comprises a quarter of Portugal's surface area and has a population of half a million; it's also known as Latifundium. The huge estates here are mostly in the hands of a few wealthy land-owners, descendants of the old landed gentry. They took over ownership from the military orders, who in turn had received it as a reward for services rendered during the campaigns of the *Reconquista* and as a means

of ensuring the future defense of the country. The bulk of the population, therefore, basically owns nothing, and for the past two or three centuries have put themselves to service as day laborers for harvesting, cork-peeling or pruning trees. They generally live in small whitewashed houses with blue trim and huge chimneys over the smoky but warm kitchens which serve as a family's main living quarters. Typical of the Alentejo are small towns with houses clustered around a fortress that protected them in days of yore.

The revolution of 1974 provided the Alentejans with an opportunity for change. The land was divided up or assigned to cooperatives. The people got to work cultivating tracts that had previously lain fallow. The results were promising; but the euphoria was short-lived: the first democratic cabinets rescinded the expropriations, and the people of the Alentejo were returned to their original unpropertied state. Few of the cooperatives survived, and only a few farmers continue to make a living from working their own land. Emigration from the region is proceeding at a steady pace, even though the government and the European Union have been funding developmental programs to support business initiatives, regional agricultural products, rural tourism, and local crafts.

Preceding pages: Martelo's famous painted plates attract people to Redondo from far and wide. Left: The old town of Évora Monte.

83

Yet *Hope in the Alentejo*, a novel by Saramago, gave rise to a renewed sense of local pride in the region. Local newspapers and radio and television stations began to spring up, giving serious coverage to events and problems in the Alentejo. Folkloric groups started reviving traditional dances and songs with traditional costumes and original local instruments. Young people began to swell the ranks of the old-fashioned men's choruses, now receiving a good deal of competition from similar groups for women. Regional products have become another source of pride: these include Alentejan wines from Reguengos, Redondo or Vidigueira, the cheese of Serpa, and solid peasant dishes such as *migas*, a kind of giant bread dumpling accompanied by a selection of offal.

For travelers, the Alentejo is an excellent destination thanks to its fine beaches, its hunting and riding, its tastefully furnished country homes in the midst of pristine nature, and some of the most attractive Pousadas in all of Portugal. The best time of year to visit is in the spring, when the fields are fresh and green and not yet harvested, and the houses have been freshly whitewashed in expectation of the long and dusty summer. The small rivers all carry water, and the storage lakes are still full. Almond trees are in full bloom around the farmyards, or *montes*, and the orange and lemon orchards are heavy with fruit. Little white villages on hilltops, accented, as often as not, by a mighty fortress, seem to greet approaching travelers from afar.

These defensive systems originated for the most part with the Arabs, and most of those were built on Roman foundations. When the Christians retook the land they usually built churches in the fortresses as a demonstrative gesture of their return to power. The villages are dreamy little places that sometimes have, besides their fort, two or three interesting churches, a pillory, a decorative fountain, a local mu-

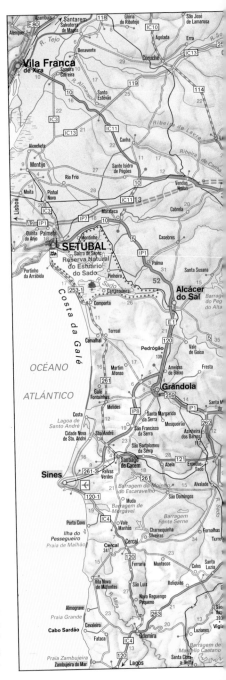

ALENTEJO

0   5   10   15 km

seum, a few picturesque squares, and a slew of comfortable cafés.

THE UPPER ALENTEJO

Between the Tejo and the old Roman road that leads from Badajoz via Elvas, and Évora to the coast, the villages are few and far between. But every one of them has its special highlight: in Brotas it's a tower from a 14th-century palace; Fronteira has a tiled chapel with a painted coffered ceiling; in Monforte, you find a Roman bridge, a fascinating ossuary chapel in the community church, and reputable stud farms throughout the surrounding area. In the middle of **Pavía** stands a dolmen, a stone tomb thousands of years old that has been turned into a chapel.

Avis lies atop a granite cliff. Its imposing fortress, once belonging to the Knights Templar, dates from the 13th

Above: The Baroque fountain at the entrance to Arraiolos with the blue trimming so typical of the Alentejo.

century. After the order was dissolved, the castle was given to the Avis Order, which was founded in the town. João I, the illegitimate son of Pedro I, was the 20th Grand Master. After he ascended the throne, he named his dynasty after the seat of the order. The steep streets of the village lead up to the Baroque gateway of the castle district, where one can see remains of the fortress, the convent, and the *pelhourinho* with the coat-of-arms of the order, an eagle with spread wings.

Arraiolos is proud of its blue-trimmed houses, which give the village around the fortress's oval wall an impression of uniformity. The monastery of Quinta dos Lóios at the northern edge of town, which is decorated with wonderful old tiles, is currently being turned into a Pousada. Arraiolos' claim to fame, however, are its brightly-colored wool rugs that have been used in many of Portugal's palaces since the 17th century. Particularly beautiful specimens can be seen in the Town Hall, and the cooperative shop opposite sells them in all price categories. Another

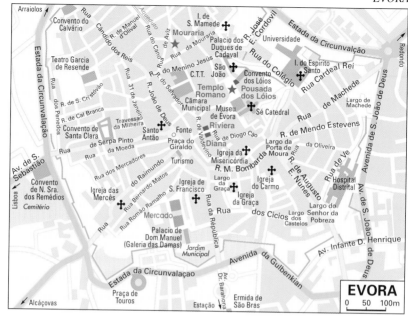

sight is the Baroque fountain near the entrance to the town, which once supplied the whole place with water.

All that remains of the vast castle area of **Montemor-o-Novo**, which once encompassed four church parishes, is a pile of ruins. You can still visit the remains of the churches, the ducal palace, and the Saudaçao Convent from the 16th century. After the Middle Ages, the village – where St. John of God was born – expanded beyond the castle walls; today, this inviting area still has countless Baroque churches, pretty streets and squares to beguile passers-by. The former Dominican Monastery houses a comprehensive **archaeological museum.**

Évora

Évora, the old Roman town *Liberalitas Julia*, the bishopric of the Visigoths, a major trading center of the Moors, and, finally, seat of the court in the 16th century, is the capital of the province of the same name and of the Alentejo. It also serves as a traffic hub between northern and southern Portugal, Spain and Lisbon, and with its 50,000 inhabitants is the most important town between the Tejo and the Algarve. The historic old town, still tucked within its 14th-century city wall, has been entirely placed under the protection of the UNESCO; measuring 3,924 feet (1,200 m) in diameter, it encompasses the old town, the former Roman district and the early medieval town. Four important architectural monuments stand cheek by jowl at the highest point: the remains of a 3rd-century temple, discovered in a slaughterhouse in the 19th century; the Manuelistic Lóios Monastery, which has been turned into an elegant *pousada*; the Jesuit university, dating from the 16th century, which became a state university in 1945; and, finally, the Cathedral.

From the outside the **Sé** (Cathedral) has kept the features of an early Gothic fortified church from the 12th and 13th centuries. The entrance portal is decorated with very expressive figures representing the twelve apostles. It is Portugal's largest cathedral, and its interior conveys an impression of great space and calm. The main chapel, with a Baroque altar, was completely redone in the 18th century by the German architect Johann Friedrich Ludwig. The Renaissance choir and the 16th-century organ are especially beautiful. From the Gothic cloister, you have an excellent view of the rose window in the transept. Spiral staircases in the corners lead up to the roof, which is also accessible via the labyrinthine **Cathedral Museum**. Among the collection of liturgical articles and garb, images and shrines displayed here is a particularly beautiful portable altar, a statue of the Madonna that opens up to reveal minute and detailed ivory carvings.

In the upper part of the Old Town, the *Acropolis*, as the Évorans call it, is the old bishop's palace, where the **Museu de Évora** displays various items from the days of Rome and some notable works from the Gothic and Renaissance periods. One of the finest exhibits is an enamel triptych from Limoges, France. Next to the Lóios Monastery stands the private palace of the Dukes of Cadaval; its pentagonal tower has given it the nickname the "**Palace with the Five Corners.**" It comprises the Gothic Church of St. John, a delightful building decked out in blue tiles. The palace has a private museum, and a tour includes inspection of the tombs of the Melo dynasty.

To the west of the inner circle of the Old Town is **Praça do Giraldo**, with the Church of Santo Antão and a 16th-century marble fountain that is the epicenter of town nowadays. The old houses here have lovely, dignified façades, but the Town Hall had to give way to the Bank of Portugal. The original wave of secularization did its best to rid the town of many of its monasteries, and the royal palace,

built in the 16th century, stood in the way of a market and a barracks. Only one wing of this opulent edifice remains, the so-called **Ladies' Gallery**, which is located in a park at the southern edge of town, and used for special exhibitions.

Before the walls of the early medieval Old Town, between Rua Serpa Pinto and Rua Raimundo, are the streets and alleyways of the former Jewish quarter. To the north of the Old Town, on both sides of Rua de Avis, is the **Mouraria**, where the Moors once lived, with the narrow alleys and dead-end streets typical of Arab city planning. Here, too, ends the 16th-century aqueduct, with its *agua da prata*, or "silver water." The southern edge of the old town also has a Moorish touch. When you emerge from the cramped streets to the Porta de Moura, you don't actually pass through a city gate, but you do feel you've gone through a medieval city wall. The square here is graced with an old fountain, but the view nowadays is obstructed by the heavy flow of traffic.

The royal **Church of São Francisco** holds a particularly grisly sight for its visitors: one of the side chapels has been entirely built of human bones, a morbid decorative touch typical of the 15th-century *Zeitgeist*. The inscription over the door explains that the bones assembled here await our own.

There are numerous other churches to see, many built in the 16th century, redecorated with tiles in the 17th and 18th centuries, but they are not always open: the Carmo Convent, the Misericordia, and the churches of Graça and Santa Clara. Outside of town is the **Chapel of São Bras**, built in the 15th century, whose exterior buttresses end in little towers, a characteristic feature of early Gothic churches in the Alentejo.

Back to the Stone Age

Rechts: The Praça do Giraldo, with its marble fountain, is the center of Évora.

Searching out the most interesting highlights in the ample testimony to the

early settlement of the region can lead to fairly long excursions around Évora. The town's tourist office is well supplied with information as to where to find menhirs, cromlechs, and dolmens, known here as *antas*. Such sights are also signposted along the main roads; reaching them usually involves following a dirt road.

An itinerary might begin, for example, with a visit to the **Cromlech dos Almendres**, west of Évora, a mysterious oval ensemble comprised of more than 90 stones arranged around a menhir, which may have served as a kind of calendar about 6,000 years ago. Another curiosity is the chapel in the **Dolmen of São Brissos**. The 20-foot (6 m) *anta* of Zambujeiro is particularly well preserved.

At the end of the tour is **Santiago do Escoural**, which boasts a cave with stalagmites and 20,000-year-old drawings carved into the rock; only a small section of the cave is open to the public. Another stately dolmen stands near Igrejinha on the way to Arraiolos.

Estremoz

A mighty reverential tower rises like a beacon above the castle district of **Estremoz**. It was completed in the 13th century during the reign of Dom Dinis, and is known as the **Tower of the Three Kings**, because three kings participated in its construction. Dom Dinis lived in the fortress with his wife Isabel, who was later canonized, but it was destroyed in the 17th century when the arsenal blew up. The Pousada in the **Royal Palace**, which was rebuilt in Gothic style by João Vin the 18th century, was named for Queen Isabel, who was known for her charity. The room in which she died was turned into a chapel in the 17th century and decorated with painted tiles depicting scenes from her life.

A modern marble memorial to Isabel has been placed on the square in front of the royal palace. Three other buildings here warrant attention. The first is the city museum, with displays of folk art and Roman relics. The second is the Manuelistic **Igreja de Maria do Castelo**, which contains an impressive collection of works by Portuguese Old Masters. The last is the so-called audience palace of Dom Dinis, a medieval grain market that was given a Manuelistic facelift in the 16th century and now houses a museum of modern design. Through the **Arco da Frandina**, one of the city gates, you come to a *pelhourinho* crowned by an armilary sphere – a medieval astronomer's instrument – and continue on to the lower town, which is surrounded by a ring wall from the 17th century.

This section of Estremoz also has some significant architectural monuments to show for itself. The lower town centers around the broad square of the **Rossio**, which transforms into a colorful marketplace on Saturdays. Here, too, is the Town Hall, once the palace of the Viceroy of India, and the former monastery of the Knights of Malta, later a hospital, with its two-story Renaissance cloister and beautifully decorated Misericordia church with a crèche by Machado de Castro. Beside the church is the **Museum of Folk Art** with a collection of *bonecos*, painted clay figures typical of Estremoz. North of the Rossio, on Largo do General Graça, stands the 17th-century **Tocha Palace**, adorned with painted tiles. Next to it is a former Franciscan monastery that, after secularization, turned into a barracks, but managed to retain its Gothic church with sarcophagi, altar, and cloister. Finally, there's the **Praça Fonte da Gadanha**; its central fountain, crowned with a statue of Saturn, is so large that locals generously term it the *lago*.

The spacious quarters of an old grain mill on the edge of town have been converted into a museum of agricultural equipment, the **Museu da Alfaia Agricola**. A great deal of effort was put into gathering used equipment and other

Right: When a pig is slaughtered it's a neighborhood affair (near São Brissos).

farming paraphenalia from the region and presenting them here.

Serra de Ossa

The **Serra de Ossa** rears up from to the south on the plateau surrounding Estremoz. On one of its peaks, near the edge of the range, is the little village of **Évora Monte** and a fortified tower in Manuelistic style that has been newly, and not altogether tastefully, replastered. From here, there's a view over half of the Alentejo. To the west, you can make out a forest of cranes and hill-sized piles of rock; these mark a marble quarry on a vein 4 by 25 miles (6 by 40 km) in size, which has brought the region between Vila Viçosa and Sousel much of its wealth. The remaining supply is estimated at 40 million tons.

Vila Viçosa is a Renaissance town whose dominant feature is the 16th-century **Paço Ducal**, the palace of the Dukes of Bragança. A 20th-century memorial to João IV by Francisco Franco stands on the huge deserted square **Terreiro do Paço** that sprawls before it. The palace, with its broad marble façade, was used by the Portuguese kings as a summer residence up until the end of the monarchy. The guide recounts with obvious relish the story of the first duchess who lived in the palace: in 1512, her husband caught her *in flagrante* with her 14-year-old page, and killed her. Some of the rooms and the well-stocked library have been arranged as the **Museum of the Dynastic House of the Braganças**.

Opposite the palace is the church of the erstwhile Augustine convent (17th-18th centuries) with the sarcophagi of the Bragança dukes; the duchesses were buried in the Chagas Convent, which is next to the palace. Finally, to the north of the palace, is the **Porta dos Nós**, the so-called "Knot Gate." It's a typically Manuelistic affair built of stone and shaped like a huge knotted rope.

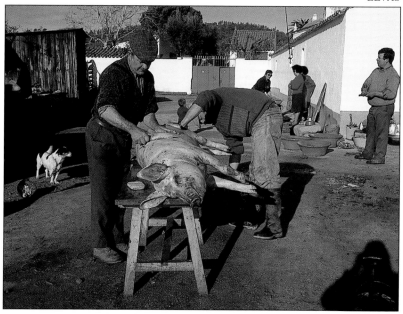

Still guarding the city is the perfectly preserved old fortress surrounded by a double fortified wall. It was built in the 13th century and extended in the 17th. The moat and the drawbridges are still intact; inside, the rooms have in part been taken over by the **Archaeological Museum** and a **Hunting Museum**. The space between the castle and the outer defensive ring has little streets with quaint houses and the **Igreja da Conceição**, a Renaissance church revamped during the 18th century. The first king of the Braganças, João IV, entrusted his crown to the patron saint of this church, a Gothic Madonna, in 1646. Since that time no Portuguese king has worn a crown.

The modern outer districts of Vila Viçosa show all the signs of flourishing economic activity. Marble is king nowadays. Everything in this region, right down to the curbstones, is made of that noble stone, and the air is filled with its dust mixed with that of red clay. Nearby **Borba**, with its medieval old town, is also full of marble. The chalky earth here is excellent for growing grapes, and hence the local wines are in a class of their own.

Redondo is also known for its wines, and besides it has a 14th-century fortress. But its most famous attraction is a little old man named Martelo, whose studio churns out artistically painted plates. He works steadily, creating new and inspired patterns that go beyond the standard folk "naive style," and customers flock in from far and wide.

Border Fortresses

Due to its location on the country's border, **Elvas** has always been extremely well defended. Its grand medieval castle, mighty walls, extended bastions, and two flanking forts, **Forte da Graça** (18th-century) in the north and **Forte de Santa Luzia** (17th-century) in the south, kept the famous "Elvas lines" intact during the War of Restoration against Spain in 1659. Even today, building activity in this town, which is surrounded by peace-

91

ful olive groves, has been confined to the space within the old walls from 1643.

Elvas was the seat of the bishopric before Évora assumed this role. On **Republic Square**, which is paved like a giant Roman mosaic, stands the erstwhile cathedral **Nossa Senhora da Assunçao**. A string of other churches in town date from the 13th to the 18th centuries, including the Baroque chapel that was built over the defenses of the western city gate. The most beautiful is the church of the Consoling Madonna, **Igreja de Nossa Senhora da Consolação**, which originated in 1543 as a small, octagonal chapel and has just been restored, with gilded marble columns and ornamental 17th-century tiles lining the dome. The **Museu Regional** in the former Jesuit monastery displays a hodgepodge of objects ranging from Roman mosaics to art from the African colonies.

Above: A street in Monsaraz with a pelourinho. Right: Laundry is still done in the traditional way in many villages.

At the northern end of town, still within the fortifications, is the **Castelo**, with a defiant barbican and a small **military museum**. The castle itself was built by the Moors in the 13th century and enlarged in the 15th. The streets around it, the oldest section of Elvas, are awash with colorful flowers. Entering the town on the west is the majestic **Amoreiras Aqueduct**, 5 miles (8 km) long, up to 100 feet (31 m) high, and borne on 843 arches. Construction of this marvel began in 1498 on the foundations of a Roman aqueduct, according to plans by Arruda, but the job was not completed until 1622.

The pilgrimage church **Jesus da Piedade**, which stands on the edge of town near a splendid fountain and a pleasant restaurant, was built in the 18th century and bears witness to the profound faith and superstition of the Portuguese. Miracles are ascribed to the church's figure of Christ, and a small museum preserves the collection of more than 5,600 *ex votos* that have been sent in over the centuries by the healed and saved. Those of more

recent date are usually just photographs, whereas the older ones depict and describe the miraculous event in a rather naive way. Body parts made of wax – the ones that were healed, of course – are also part of the collection.

The castle of **Campo Maior**, commissioned by Dom Dinis in the 14th century, was later expanded to serve as a border fort. For a while it was used as as an arsenal until, in 1732, it blew up, killing most of the people living in the area. In 1766, a grisly memorial chapel was built of their bones. It can be visited next to the community church. Today, however, the air is laden not with the smell of cordite, but rather the penetrating aroma of coffee from the roasters, who until recently ran a profitable smuggling operation with Spain.

Every five years, there's a major festival on Campo Maior in the first week of September (1997 is the next). All 90 streets in town are given special decorative treatment on the occasion. Trying to create the most beautiful street is a matter of local pride, and each block committee keeps its decorating plans strictly secret until the eve of the festival.

Another impressive sentinel fort is **Monsaraz**, almost 50 miles (80 km) to the south. The two long streets of the town, lined with white houses, lie within the fortifications along the crest of the mountain. On weekends the streets, the well-equipped hotels and bed-and-breakfasts, and the restaurants fill up with tourists. Even today, the castle's courtyard does double duty as a bullfighting arena on special occasions.

The community church with its advanced Gothic *pelhourinho*; the Misericordia church; and the two chapels Santa Catarina and São João Batista are veritable gems. Within view, beyond the Guadiana River, is **Mourão**, which also boasts a fortress.

In the 19th century, a large part of the Monsaraz population left the safe but impoverished haven of their fortified mountain for the fertile plain below, where they founded **Reguengos de Monsaraz**.

93

This was a smart move, for the region now produces one of the best Alentejan wines. **Corval**, not too far away, is known nationwide for its 36 ceramics studios. Furthermore, in the surrounding area anyone looking for traces of the Stone Age will find a wealth of megalithic tombs and menhirs, including the 18-foot (5.6 m) phallic **Menhir of Outeiro**, and the cromlechs of Farisoa and **Xerez**. The latter stands very photogenically with the fortress of Monsaraz in the background.

THE LOWER ALENTEJO
Beja

The main town of the Lower Alentejo is **Beja**, known to the Romans as *Pax Julia*, a pretty, provincial town with a 13th-century crenellated castle tower in its midst, good restaurants and pleasant

Above: The orange-red trunks of peeled cork oaks are a dominant feature of the Alentejan landscape.

shops. Two monasteries are particularly worth a visit: The former **Convent for Franciscan Nuns**, which now functions as a Pousada, still has its Gothic chapel, cloister, chapter room, and refectory. The **Convent of Nossa Senhora da Conceição** was once inhabited by the order of Poor Clares, but all that remains of it is the church and the cloister. This is where the legendary nun Mariana Alcoforado (1640-1723) lived, who had been confined to the nunnery by her family since her childhood. Peering out of the barred window of her cell, she fell madly in love with a passing French nobleman, the Marquis de Chamilly. The two did ultimately get together, but their relationship ended abruptly when the Marquis returned to his native France. The unanswered love letters of Mariana Alcoforado comprise Portugal's most important literary work of the 17th century; although it's open to question whether the real author of the letters was not a Frenchman named de Guilleragus, who had been inspired by the nun's story.

Having stood empty since the end of the 19th century, the convent was, in 1927, turned into a **regional museum** named after the duchess of Beja, Queen Leonor, whose parents founded the convent in 1459. The museum's treasure's are substantial, notably the Roman mosaics, a superb collection of *azulejos*, fine folk art, furniture, and paintings by, among others, the Spaniard Ribera. The architecture, influenced by the Manuelistic style, and the well-preserved 16th-century tiles in the cloister and the chapter room make the entire convent a pleasure for the eye.

The museum has a subsidiary in the **Capela de Santo Amaro** that displays Visigoth finds. This early Romanesque church, the oldest in the city, is impressive for the scale of its architecture. Not far away is the **Castelo** of King Dinis I, built on Roman foundations. Its 131-foot (40 m) tower is the tallest in Portugal. The castle houses the **Museu Militar do Baixo Alentejo**.

Taking a leisurely stroll through the streets of Beja, you'll pass such gems as a Manuelistic window in the Rua dos Mercadores; Republic Square, with its winding *pelourinho*; the Gothic church of Santa Maria near the convent, its flying buttresses ending in turrets (an architectural flourish typical of the region); and numerous restaurants serving hearty local fare.

In the Land of Cork Oaks

One nice excursion from Beja leads north into a hilly landscape of cork oak forests around the reservoirs of Odivelas and Alvito; the road then proceeds to Cuba, Vila Alva, Vidigueira, and Viana. **Cuba** is considered the Alentejo's center of a capella choral singing. Every village around here has at least one chorus, either men's, women's, or mixed; if you're lucky, you may stumble on a café or a pub where one of them happens to be re-hearsing. The texts are easy to understand even if you are unfamiliar with the language: these simple country people usually sing melancholy songs about their hard lives, the beauty of their homeland, and hopes for better times, all with great seriousness and depth of feeling.

The villages around here are white and flat, with grain silos the size of fortresses, and small churches from the 16th and 17th centuries. A visit to the castle of Alvito, which has been a *pousada* for several years now, reveals the mighty structure of what was once not a border fort, but rather a retreat for King João II in the case of war. The three-aisled Renaissance church. **Igreja Matriz**, is decorated entirely with 17th-century tiles. The **São Sebastião Chapel** is a further example of a Gothic fortified church. By contrast, the **Santa Luiza Chapel**, with some fine 17th-century frescoes, has an unusual dome that suggests something Moorish.

Vidigueira already had vineyards in the days of the Romans. There were remains of that early settlement near **São Cucufate**. In the Middle Ages, the Knights of St. James built a monastery on the Roman foundations; you can visit its ruins today.

Another fortress of imposing dimensions, complete with integrated church, can be seen in **Viana do Alentejo**. In the pilgrimage church of **Nossa Senhora dos Aires** on the edge of town, one finds – as in Elvas – a large collection of *ex votos* sent by pilgrims who were miraculously cured.

Moorish Forts

In the eastern part of the Lower Alentejo lie a sprinkling of communities that time seems to have totally forgotten. The little town of **Moura**, "the Moorish," is laid out around a medieval fort. Besides its thermal spa with a pretty park, it has lively shopping streets and a small *mouraria*, or Moorish quarter, with numbered streets. The **Church of São João** has an ornate Manuelistic portal. The cloister and Renaissance church of the oldest Carmelite convent in Portugal, **Nossa Senhora do Carmo** (founded around 1250), are open to the public, and also serve as a museum of sacred art. To the north of town, the government is building the huge Alqueva storage lake that will supply much-needed water to the southern part of the Alentejo and parts of the Algarve. A number of the side valleys will also be flooded when the project is completed.

Up on the 938-foot (287 m) hill known as Alto de São Gens is a pilgrimage church to the Virgin of Guadalupe, and a *pousada*. The view from here stretches over olive groves, cork oaks, and **Serpa**. This little white town is surrounded by a Moorish wall, has a crumbling castle from the 13th century housing an archaeological museum; a Gothic church, Santa Maria, all decked out in tiles; an aqueduct along the top of the old Moorish town wall; a number of Baroque churches; and quaint, narrow cobblestone streets.

Mértola is the town that has best preserved its medieval character. Known to the Romans as *Myrtilis*, the town was a Moorish fortress from the 13th to the 15th centuries, and then the residence of the Knights of St. James. It is picturesquely located on a rocky promontory at the confluence of the Oeiras and the Guadiana. Its houses nestle tightly around the craggy stronghold, guarded by the castle and a fortified church, **Igreja Matriz**, once a mosque that was converted into a Christian house of worship in the 16th century. It was built on a square ground plan, and still has its *mihrab*, a prayer niche orientated towards Mecca, scalloped arches, a horseshoe arch over the sacristy, and a beautiful Renaissance portal. The Moorish fort

Above: The Arab fortress and the salt marshes gave Alcacér do Sal its name.

Castelo dos Mouros didn't succumb to the Christians until 1233, and was rebuilt at the end of that century. Its two museums display exhibits relating to the area's Roman and Moorish past.

About 15.5 miles (25 km) north of Mértola, the Guadiana, which you can reach from Amendoeira along a dirt road, has carved out a canyon-like bed for itself in the rocks. The **Pulo do Lobo**, or "wolf's leap," is a 65-foot (20 m) waterfall; excursions to this spot, however, would be even nicer if the river weren't so polluted as to take away some of one's pleasure in the sight.

THE ALENTEJO'S ATLANTIC COAST

The landscape of the Alentejo becomes more diversified as you approach the coast. The cork oak forests begin to alternate with pine woods or small fields with isolated farmhouses. Here and there, picturesque windmills adorn the hilltops; no longer operational, they serve today as landmarks or vacation homes. Small industries, ports, fishing and tourism are the main source of economic activity in the towns. The beaches of the Alentejo are generally wild and undeveloped. In the southern part, between Cabo Sardão and the Ponta da Atalaia, where the region adjoins the western Algarve, the beaches are small and usually tucked away between the steep, rocky walls of the coastal cliffs. To the north and south of Sines, long sand beaches line high bluffs or majestic dunes. Access is seldom easy, so there is much undisturbed room for nature exploration. Large hotels and vacation communities are almost completely absent from the landscape.

Alcácer do Sal was named after its Moorish fort (*kasr*) and the salt ponds that glisten white between the rice paddies in the flats around the Sado estuary. So many cultures have passed through here over the centuries that hardly a trace

is left of the free Roman city of *Salacia*. The Arabs also valued the salt and built up the town's defenses. After German crusaders freed it from the Moors in the 13th century, it became a headquarters of the Knights of St. James. This little town with its large castle breathes fresh sea air, and lives off busy trading and fishing in the Sado estuary. One of its most interesting sights is the **Chapel of the 11,000 Virgins** in the former Monastery of São Antão. The tile images in the Church of São Tiago retell Alcacér do Sal's past. As for archaeological finds from the area, they are exhibited in the little Church of Espirito Santo.

Today, the Sado has been declared a nature conservation area, which effectively protected it from the threatening expansion of Greater Lisbon. **Carrasqueira** has even succeeded in keeping the pile houses of its fishing port, and here and there you can even spot a reed hut. Idyllic tranquility rules on the beaches of Comporta, Carvalhal, Galé Fontaínhas, Melides, and Santo André,

tucked away amidst lagoons, dunes and pine forests.

A little ways inland is **Grândola**, lively and business-minded, a market and school town for the surrounding rural region. The name was immortalized in a famous song by José Afonso: "*Grândola, vila morena,* a friend on every corner, equality in every face." When these forbidden lines were broadcast on April 25, 1974, it marked the start of the famous "Carnation Revolution." People thronged the streets, and the little Alentejan town became a symbol of freedom after a half century of dictatorship.

Santiago de Cacém, which was important even in Roman times, nestles between a fortified mountain and a long crest with a string of windmills, one of which can be visited. Next to what was once an Arab fort and now mere walls – with a cemetery inside – is the Church of St. James, rebuilt after the 1755 earthquake. It contains numerous votive offerings to its patron saint and to the order of St. James. On the main square in the

97

newer part of town, which lies at the foot of the fort, is the former district prison, now a fine **museum**. Here, among other things, you can examine the most interesting finds excavated from the old Celtic and later Roman Miróbriga. The excavation site itself (including the ruins of a Roman temple and a Roman road) is over a hill behind the windmills. The Santiago train station is also worth a visit for its folk tile decor dating from the 1930s.

Sines is southern Portugal's only major industrial center. In its gigantic, newly-developed, oil harbor, pipelines, wind generators, and a refinery fulfill the power needs for this part of the country. Industrial activity has overwhelmed the old fishing village and vacation resort; the only part of town that has maintained a modicum of its old charm is around the old fort, where Vasco de Gama was born in 1469. However, some of the beaches here are fantastic, notably those stretch-

Above: Housewives pride themselves on the flowers around their front doors.

ing northward to the lagoon and the sandbank of São André, and the isolated ones along the bays in the south near the fishing village **Porto Covo**, which gradually open up into a long tract of dunes. The island of **Pessegueiro** lies just offshore here. Fishing boats will take you over to it if you wish to explore the Roman ruins or the remains of a 17th-century fort built to defend against pirates.

The entire coast between Sines and the Algarve has been made a nature preserve to protect the birds that nest here and the plants that hold the dunes together from the effects of unregulated building. Some of the beaches here are particularly beautiful, notably Malhão, Alvados, **Vila Nova de Milfontes** – a pretty community at the mouth of the Mira River – and Praia Grande near Almograve. The little village of **Cavaleiro** has a colorful bar on the main square, the striking lighthouse of **Cabo Sardão**, and sandy bays along a dramatic cliffside well-known to smugglers. **Zambujeira do Mar** is a pleasant resort with fine fish restaurants.

THE ALENTEJO
Accommodations

ALCÁCER DO SAL (065): *MODERATE:* **Herdade da Barrosinha**, E.N. 5, Barrosinha, tel. 62363.

ALJUSTREL (084): *TURISMO RURAL:* **Monte Aguetinha do Campo**, Messejana, tel. 65251, Fax: 65252.

ALVITO (084): *LUXURY:* **Castelo do Alvito**, tel. 48343, Fax: 48383. Pousada in an old castle. *CAMPING:* **Markádia**, Barragem de Odivelas, tel. 76141. *TURISMO RURAL:* **Quinta dos Prazeres**, Largo das Alcaçarias, tel. 48170.

ARRAIOLOS (066): *TURISMO RURAL:* **Horta da Parreira**, tel. 48114. **Monte das Oliveiras**, tel. 42507, Fax: 42508. **Herdade das Lages**, São Gregório, tel. 46221. **Solar Cor de Rosa**, Rua Melo Mexia 29, tel. 41431. **Quinta da Espada**, Estr. Évora-Arraiolos, tel. 734549.

AVIS (042): *CAMPING:* **Albufeira do Maranhão**, on the Raia storage lake, tel. 42452.

TURISMO RURAL: **Solar Santa Teresinha**, Rua Machado dos Santos 24-26, tel. 42588.

BEJA (084): *LUXURY:* **Pousada São Francisco**, Largo D. Nuno Alvares Pereira, tel. 328441. *MODERATE:* **Coelho**, Praça de la Republica 15, tel. 32403, Fax: 328939. **Santa Barbara**, Rua de Mértola 56, tel. 322028. **Cristina**, Rua de Mértola 71, tel. 322035, Fax: 329874. *BUDGET:* **Thomas**, Rua A. Herculano 7-11, tel. 324613, Fax: 320796. *TURISMO RURAL:* **Monte da Diabrória**, São Brissos, E.N. 121, tel. 98177, Fax: 98069. Estate with wonderful day rooms, swimming pool.

BORBA (068): *BUDGET:* **Chuabo**, Rua da Cruz 2B, tel. 94376. *TURISMO RURAL:* **Casa de Borba**, Rua da Cruz 5, tel. 94528.

CAVALEIRO (083): *TURISMO RURAL:* **Moita Nova**, tel. 64357, Fax: 64167. Riding and riding lessons on Arabians. Quiet, near the cliffs, nice, large apartments with fire places.

CASTRO VERDE (086): *MODERATE:* **Aparthotel do Castro**, Rua da Seara Nova, tel. 22713.

CORUCHE (043): *TURISMO RURAL:* **Quinta Moura**, Rua S. Torcato, tel. 60168.

ELVAS (068): *LUXURY:* **D. Sancho II**, Praça República 20, tel. 622684, Fax: 624717. **Eixadal Parque**, Varche, tel. 623036, Fax: 623729. **Varchotel**, Varche, tel. 621621, Fax: 621596. *MODERATE:* **D. Luis**, Av. de Badajoz, tel. 622756, Fax: 620733. *BUDGET:* **Luso-Espanhola**, Rua Rui de Melo, tel. 623092. *CAMPING:* Piedade, tel. 623772. *TURISMO RURAL:* **Monte da Amoreira**, São Brás, tel. 622817, Fax: 624683.

ESTREMOZ (068): *LUXURY:* **Pousada Rainha Santa Isabel**, Largo D. Dinis, tel. 22618, Fax: 23982. *MODERATE:* **Carvalho**, Largo da

República 27, tel. 22712. *BUDGET:* **Alentejano**, Rossio Marquês de Pombal 14/15, tel. 22834. *TURISMO RURAL:* **Monte dos Pensamentos**, Estr. da E. de Ameixial, Santa Maria, tel. 22375 oder 01-3967906. **Monte Gil**, Casas Novas, tel. 332996.

ÉVORA (066): *LUXURY:* **Pousada dos Loios**, Largo Conde Vila Flor, tel. 24051/2, Fax: 27248. **Dom Fernando**, Av. Dr. Barahona 2, tel. 741717, Fax: 741716. **Monte das Flores**, Estr. das Alco Çovas, tel. 25490, Fax: 27564. **Poquer**, Quinta Vale Vazios, tel. 734696, Fax: 33710. *MODERATE:* **Eborense**, Solar Monfalim, Largo da Misericórdia 1, tel. 22031, Fax: 742367. Alter Palast. **Riviera**, Rua 5 de Outubro 49, tel. 23304, Fax: 20467. **Diana**, Rua de Diogo Cão 2, tel. 22008, Fax: 743101. In the pedestrian zone. **Santa Clara**, Trav. da Milheira 19, tel. 24141, Fax: 26544. *BUDGET:* **Giraldo**, Rua dos Mercadores 27, tel. 25833. **Os Manuéis**, Rua do Raimundo 35, first floor, tel. 22861. *CAMPING:* **Orbitur**, tel. 25190. *TURISMO RURAL:* **Casa de S. Tiago**, Largo A. Herculano 2, tel. 22686, Fax: 02-6000357. **Quinta da Espada**, 4 km toward Arraiolos, tel. 93130. **Quinta de S. Luis**, Estr. da Igrejinha, tel. 26983. **Monte da Serralheira**, tel. 743957/25017. 3 km south of **Monte do Azinhal**, São Matias, tel. 31181.

ÉVORAMONTE (068): *TURISMO RURAL:* **Casa da Vila**, Rua de Santa Maria, tel. 95137. **Monte da Fazenda**, tel. 95172.

GRÂNDOLA (069): *MODERATE:* **Vila Morena**, Av. Jorge Nunes, tel. 42095/6. Central and modern. *BUDGET:* **Paraíso do Alentejo**, Rua D. Nuno A. Pereira, tel. 56405. **Fim do Mundo**, Av. Jorge Nunes 6, tel. 42061. *TURISMO RURAL:* **Monte Cabeço do Ouro**, Courelas dos Daoeiros, tel. 51292. **Moinho Velho**, Melides, tel. 97323, Fax: 97320.

MÉRTOLA (086): *BUDGET:* **San Remo**. Av. Aureliano Mira Fernandes. *TURISMO RURAL:* **Casa das Janelas Verdes**, Rua Dr. Manuel Francisco Gomes 38-40, tel. 62145. In the Old Town.

MONSARAZ (066): *LUXURY:* **Monsaraz**, Largo de S. Bartolomeu, tel. 55112, Fax: 55101. *MODERATE:* **Horta da Monsaraz**, tel. 55206/45, Fax: 55241. *TURISMO RURAL:* **Casa do Embaixador**, Largo da Igreja, tel. 55432. **Casa de D. Nuno**, Rua José F. Caeiro 6, tel. 55146. **Casa de S. Tiago**, tel. 55159. **Casa do Quintal**, tel. 55149. **Casa do Condestável**, tel. 55181.

MONTEMOR-O-NOVO (066): *MODERATE:* **Monte Alentejano**, Av. Gago Coutinho 8, tel. 82141. *TURISMO RURAL:* **Herdade da Comenda de Igreja**, São Geraldo, tel. 84104.

MOURA (085): *MODERATE:* **Hotel de Moura**, Pr. G. Coutinho 1, tel. 22494. *BUDGET:* **Alentejana**, Lg. J. M. dos Santos 40, tel. 22529.

ODEMIRA (083): *MODERATE:* **Ondazul**, Zambujeira do Mar, tel. 61450. **Duna Praia**, Almograve, tel. 64115. *BUDGET:* **Paulo Campos**, São Salvador, Almograve, tel. 64118. **Rita**, Zambujeira do Mar, tel. 61330. **Solpraia**, Almograve, tel. 64115. *CAMPING:* **Zambujeira**, Zambujeira do Mar, tel. 61172. *TURISMO RURAL:* **Monte da Alcaria do Demente**, S. Teotónio, tel. 95628.

REDONDO (066): *LUXURY:* **Convento de São Paulo**, Aldeia da Serra, tel. 999100, Fax: 999104. *TURISMO RURAL:* **Quinta da Talha**, Estrada do Freixo, tel. 999468.

SANTIAGO DO CACÉM (069): *LUXURY:* **Pousada de Santiago**, Rua de Lisboa, tel./Fax: 22459. *MODERATE:* **Gabriel**, Rua Egas Moniz 24, tel. 22245, Fax: 826102. *CAMPING:* **Parque de Campismo**, Lagoa de St. André, tel. 79151.

SERPA (084): *LUXURY:* **Pousada São Gens**, Alto de São Gens, tel. 53724, Fax: 53337. *MODERATE:* **Serpinia**, Rua Serpa Pinto, tel. 53055, Fax: 53961. *CAMPING:* **Municipal**, tel. 53290. *TURISMO RURAL:* **Herdade do Topo**, Monte do Topo, tel. 59136. **Casa de São Bras**, São Bras, tel. 90272.

SINES (069): *LUXURY:* **Veleiro**, Rua Sacadura Cabral 19A, tel. 634751, Fax: 634803. *MODERATE:* **Carvalho**, Rua Gago Coutinho 13, tel. 632019. *CAMPING:* **S**. **Torpes**, tel. 632105. **Porto Covo**, tel. 95136.

VILA NOVA DE MILFONTES (083): *LUXURY:* **App**. **Quinta das Varandas**, tel. 96155. *MODERATE:* **Eira da Pedra**, Eira da Pedra, tel. 99662. Fax: 99664. **Duna Parque**, Eira da Pedra, tel. 96451, Fax: 96459. Hotel village. *BUDGET:* **Castelo de Milfontes**, L. da Barbacã, tel. 96108.

VILA VIÇOSA (068): *MODERATE:* **Calipolense**, tel. 98392. *TURISMO RURAL:* **Casa de Peixinhos**, tel. 98472.

Restaurants / Cafés

ALANDROAL: **A Maria**, Rua João de Deus 12, tel. 431143.

ALCÁCER DO SAL: **Estrela do Sado**, Av. dos Aviadores, tel. 622917. **A Bica**, Torre, tel. 97168. **O Poço**, Largo Luís de Camões, tel. 622310. **Jardim do Sado**, Parque Municipal, tel. 623143.

ALVITO: O Américo, Largo do Relógio 7.

BEJA: **Os Infantes**, Rua dos Infantes 14, tel. 22789. **O Aficionado**, Rua Acoutados, 38, tel. 23964. **Luis da Rocha** Rua Capitão J. F. de Sousa, tel. 23179. **Dom Dinis**, Rua Dom Dinis 11, tel. 22976. **Novo Mundo**, Rua da Mértola 41, tel. 25018. **Alentejano**, Largo dos Duques de Beja, tel. 23849. **Gatus**, Rua João Conforte 16-18, tel. 25418. *BARS:* **Laterna Azul**, Rua da Moeda 11. **A Floresta**, Largo da Conceição 2, tel. 329578.

CORUCHE: **Café Grande**, Rua de Santarém.

ESTREMOZ: **Aguias d'Ouro**, Rossio, tel. 22196. **Zona Verde**, Largo Dragões de Olivença 86, tel. 24701. **Kimbo**, Rua 31 de Janeiro 20, tel. 23664. **Figo**, Rua da Restauração 36, tel. 24529. **O Faisão de Estremoz**, Rua J. Felix Ribeiro 27, tel. 23926. **Ze Varunca**, Av. Tomaz Alcaide, tel. 23567. **Arlequim**, Rua Dr. Gomes Resende Jr. 15 R/C, tel. 237328. **São Rosas**, Largo do Castelo.

ÉVORA (066): **O Aqueducto**, Rua Esplanada. **O Antão**, Rua João de Deus 5-7, tel. 26459. **Jardim do Paço**, Palacio das Cinco Quinas, Esplanada, tel. 744300. Terrace with a view of the temple. **Burgo Velho**, Rua Diogo Cão 37. **A Muralha**, Rua Diogo Cão 21. **Aquário**, Rua de Valdevinos 7, tel. 29403. **Lampeão**, Rua dos Mercadores 72, tel. 26495. **A Grelha**, Rua de Machede 46, tel. 744861. **A Cozinha de Santo Humberto**, Rua da Moeda 39, tel. 24251. **Fialho**, Trav. das Mascarenhas 16, tel. 23079. **Luar de Janeiro**, Trav. do Janeiro 13, tel. 24895. **O Grémio**, Alcárcova de Cima 10, tel. 742931. **Cozinha São Francisco**, Rua Romão Ramalho 56. **Liz'as Pizza Place**, Patio do Salema, Ecke Rua de Diogo Cão. *BARS:* **Quarta Feira**, Rua do Inverno 16-18. Weinstube. **Amas do Cardeal**, Rua Amas do Cardeal 4A, tel. 21133. **Molhóbico**, Rua de Aviz 91, tel. 744343. **Os Meninos de Graça**, Trav. do Landim 1. **Slide**, Rua Serpa Pinto 135. Xeque Mate, Rua de Valdevinos 21B.

MOURA: **Guadiana**, Rua da Latoa 1, tel. 22157. **Mourense o Carlos**, Rua da República 37, tel. 22598. **O Arcada**, Pr. 25 de Abril 24, tel. 93164. **O Emigrante**, Rua Serpa Pinto 23, tel. 22145. **O Mario**, Rua da Oliveira 14, tel. 23188.

SANTIAGO DO CACÉM: **O Retiro**, Rua Machado dos Santos, tel. 22659. **Flor Alentejana**, Largo 5 de Outubro 2, tel. 23368. **Cozinha do Jardim**, Pr. do Municipio 11A, tel. 23322. **Quinta do Antonio**, Estr. das Cumeadas, tel. 826248. **O Refugio do Mirante**, Estr. das Cumeadas, tel. 22732. **Retiro dos Caçadores**, Cumeadas.

SERPA: **Alentejano**, Praça da República, tel. 53335. **Lebrinha**, Rua do Calvario 6-8, tel. 90311. **Cuiça-Filho**, Rua Portas de Beja 18, tel. 90566.

SINES: **O Castelo**, Rua João de Deus 22. **A Palmeira**, Rua Marquês de Pombal 41, tel. 634170. **A Caravela**, Rua Marquês de Pombal 32, tel. 632298. **Varanda do Oceano**, Rua da Rampa 1, tel. 632303. **Porto do Céu**, Rua Poeta António Aleixo 10, tel. 632317. **A Ilha**, Ilha do Pessegueiro, Porto Covo, tel. 95113. Auf der Insel. **Vista do Mar**, Vale Vistoso, Porto Covo, tel. 95126.

Sights / Museums

ALCÁCER DO SAL: **Museu Municipal**, Largo Pedro Nunes, 9am-12:30pm and 2pm-5:30pm.

BEJA: **Museu Rainha Leonor** and **Santo Amaro**: 9:45am-1pm, 2pm-5:15pm, closed Mon

and holidays. **Fortress**: 9am-1pm and 2pm-5pm.
BORBA: Museu dos Cristos: daily 9am-8pm.
ELVAS: Museu Tomas Pires, Burg, closed
Thursdays. **Igreja Na. Sa. da Consolação**, closed
Mondays. **Igreja Assunção**, closed Tuesdays.
Igreja S. Domingos, closed Wed. **Igreja dos
Tercios**, closed Fridays: 9:30am-12:30pm and
2:30pm -7pm, in winter only until5:30pm. **Jesus da
Piedade**, pilgrimage church, daily 9am – 6pm.
ESTREMOZ: Museu Alfaia Agricola, daily
9am-midday and 2pm-6pm, closed Saturday and
Thursday mornings. **Museu de Arte Rural**:
9:30am-12:30pm and 3pm-6pm, closed Mondays.
Museu Municipal and **Museu de Disenho**: 9am-
11:45am and 2pm-5:45pm, closed Mondays.
ÉVORA: Cathedrale (Sé), **Museu de Arte
Sacra** (Cathedral museum), **Museu de Évora,
Igreja das Mercês**: 10am-12:30pm and 2pm-5pm,
closed Mondays and holidays. **Igreja São João** and
Museum of the Mélo: private guides. **Capilla dos
Ossos** (ossuary chapel) in the **Igreja Real de São
Francisco**: daily 8:30am-1pm and 2:30pm-6pm,
Sun: 10am-11:30am and 2:30pm-6pm.
MÉRTOLA: Islamic Museum and **Roman
Museum**, in the Town Hall: workdays 9am-
12:30pm and 2:30pm-5:30pm, on weekends at 11am
and 3pm tours arranged by the tourist office
**MONTEMOR-O-NOVO: Archaeological
Museum**, Dominican monastery: 10:30am-
12:30pm and 2:30pm-6pm, closed Mon
SANTIAGO DO CACÉM: Museu Municipal,
Pr. do Município, 10am-12:30pm and 2:30pm-6pm,
Sat and Sun 3pm-6pm, closed Mon. Excavations of
Miróbriga, Estr. das Cumeadas, 9am-midday and
2pm-5pm, closed Mon.
SANTIAGO DO ESCOURAL: Caves: 9am-
midday and 1:30pm-5pm, closed Monand holidays.
SERPA: Museu Arqueológico, in the fortress:
daily 9am-12:30pm and 2pm-5:30pm. **Museu Et-
nológico**, Largo do Corro: daily 9am-12:30pm and
2pm-5:30pm.
SINES: Museu Arqueológico, Rua Francisco
Lopes, 9:30am-midday and 2pm-5pm, closed Mon-
days. **Museum of Natural History** in the fortress
tower: 9am-1pm and 2pm-6pm, closed Tues.
VIDIGUEIRA: São Cucufate, Vila de Frades
(Roman ruins, cloister): 10am-5pm, closed Mon.
VILA VIÇOSA: Paço Ducal: 9:30am – 1pm and
2:30pm-6pm (in winter: 2pm-5pm), closed Mondays, last entrance 45 minutes before closing.

Tourist information

ALCÁCER DO SAL: Tourist Office: Rua Rui
Salema, tel. 622603. **Market**: First Saturday in the
month.
ARRAIOLOS: FRACOOP, Rug Cooperative,
Praça Lima e Brito 4. **BEJA: Tourist Office**: Rua

Capitão João Francisco de Sousa 25, tel. 23693, in
winter: Mon-Sat 10am-6pm, in summer daily 9am-
9pm. **Market**: Saturdays in the castle district.
CAMPO MAIOR: Tourist Office: Rua Mayor
Talaya, tel. 68104. **Riding**: Herdade de Oliva.
ELVAS: Tourist Office: Praça da Republica,
daily 9am-7pm, in winter 9am-6pm, tel. 622236.
Post: Rua Cadeia. **Hospital**: tel. 622177.
ESTREMOZ: Tourist Office: Rossio Marquês
de Pombal, tel. 22783.
ÉVORA: Tourist Office: Praça do Giraldo 73, tel.
22671, 9am-7pm, on weekends 9am-12:30pm and
2pm-5:30pm. **Post**: Rua de Olivença, 9am-6pm.
Parking spaces: outside the city walls, esp. near
the southern entrance. **Rent-a-bike**: Ctra. On the
way to Estremoz, tel. 761453. **Handicrafts**: Av.
dos Salesianos 21, tel. 20076. **Excursions**: Tu-
rAventur, bicycle tours, Rua João de Deus 21, first
floor left, Tel/Fax: 743134. Safaris and balloon
tours: Turi Balão, Rua Miguel Bombarda 44. **Hospital**: Largo Senhor da Pobreza, tel. 25001.
GRÂNDOLA: Tourist Office: Rua Dr. José Pereira Barradas, tel. 42052. **Market**: 2nd Monday in
the month. **Bus station**: Rua Afonso Henriques.
MÉRTOLA: Tourist Office: Mon-Fri 9am-
12:30pm and 2pm-5:30pm. **MONSARAZ: Tourist Office**: Largo D. Nuno A. Pereiro, tel. 55136,
daily 10am-1pm and 2pm-6pm. **MONTEMOR-
O-NOVO: Tourist Office**: Largo Calouste Gulbenkian, tel. 82071. **MORA: Tourist Office**: Casa
da Cultura, Rua S. Pedro, tel. 43378.
MOURA: Tourist Office: Largo de Santa Clara,
tel. 24902, Mon-Fri 9am-midday and 2pm-5:30pm.
Market: first Saturday of the month.
REDONDO: Potters, Adriano Rui Martelo, Rua
Cândido dos Reis 35. **Wine cooperative**, Rua
Conde de Monsaraz 5.
**REGUENGOS DE MONSARAZ: Tourist Of-
fice**: Rua 1 de Maio, tel. 52229, Ext. 21. Weekdays
9am-12:30pm and 2pm-6pm, Sat and Sun from
10am on. **Market**: first Friday of the month.
ODEMIRA: Tourist Office: Trav. do Botequia,
tel. 22247.
SANTIAGO DO CACÉM: Tourist Office:
Praça do Mercado, tel. 826696. **Bus station**: Rua
Cidade de Setúbal.
SERPA: Tourist Office: Largo D. Jorge Melo 2/3,
tel. 53727, daily 9am-12:30pm and 2pm-5:30pm, in
summer 4pm-7:30pm.
SINES: Tourist Office: Jardim das Descobertas,
tel. 634472. 10am-1pm and 2pm-6pm, closed weekends in winter. **Bus station**: Largo Afonso Albuquerque. **Hospital**: Rua Cândido dos Reis, tel.
632172.
VILA VIÇOSA: Tourist Office: Praça da República, tel. 98305.

THE ALGARVE

FARO
SERRA DO CALDEIRÃO
ALGARVE SOTAVENTO
ALGARVE BARLAVENTO
SERRA DO MONCHIQUE

Algarve, from *al gharbe,* the Arabic name for the western edge of the Caliphate of Córdoba, is a magic word for thousands of European retirees, synonymous with a pleasant winter retreat, and for even greater crowds denoting a few weeks of guaranteed sun, long beaches, and clean water between Easter and autumn.

The Algarve coast extends for some 93 miles (150 km) in the south of Portugal. Most of it is protected from the Atlantic storm systems by three mountain ranges: the Serra de Espinhaço de Cão, the Serra de Monchique, and the Serra do Caldeirão. This topographical situation means that this southwesternmost region of Europe, although on the Atlantic Ocean, is dominated by a Mediterranean climate. In January the orange trees are laden with fruit and the almond trees are in full bloom; gardens are filled with a profusion of colorful flowers year-round; and even in the rainy season bad weather seldom holds for longer than three days at a time.

International investors have conveniently exploited pallid North Europeans'

Preceding pages: These small coves with sand beaches embraced by limestone cliffs are typical of the western Algarve. Left: Getting ready for a night out fishing.

thirst for the sun in the past few decades, by blanketing the most beautiful parts of the coast with acres of vacation homes, massive hotel colonies, slews of bungalows, and elegant club complexes. It would be unfair to use the verb "ruined" here; this could only apply to certain spots that are particularly densely built up, such as Albufeira or Praia da Rocha. It would be more appropriate to say that the character of certain areas has been completely changed. What was once a sparsely populated region south of the coastal mountains, where people eked out a living fishing or farming on a fairly small scale, is now a thoroughly urbanized zone catering to the needs of an international society with a lot of spare time on its hands. The architecture, where it doesn't follow standard international models, tends toward the Mediterranean style found in Ibiza or the Costa del Sol: that is, a kind of pseudo-Moorish style which is supposed to conjure up for Northern Europeans all the exotic charm of the Arabian Nights mingled with all the standard, modern comforts of home.

There are 70 beaches to choose from between Odeceixe on the west coast and the estuary of the Guadiana on the Spanish border; 45 of these have been granted a blue flag for special amenities and cleanliness. The villages have long adapted their infrastructures to the armies of tourists: nowhere else in Portugal can you find such a concentration of restaurants. Many of them display menus in German and English, and serve international dishes as well as local fare. Pubs, bars, inns and discos provide for an active nightlife, and water parks and riding clubs ensure daytime entertainment for people of all ages. For golf players, the Algarve coast is a veritable El Dorado: 17 courses compete for clientele, and their prices guarantee exclusivity.

About 330,000 people live year-round in the Algarve. For the British, Germans, and Dutch who have settled here for good, it has become more than just another geographical region; rather, it is the epitome of Mediterranean lifestyle, a dolce vita in all senses of the word. These expatriates have developed their own subculture, which even overshadows the locals' in some places. They run shops and restaurants, keep their own clubs, organize special events, and have their own newspapers and doctors.

The throng doubles in size during the high season, congesting streets and roads beyond endurance. The only time to enjoy long, solitary strolls along the beach, excursions up to idyllic mountain villages, or reading the newspaper on a sunlit café terrace, is in the off season; the best time is during the wonderful early spring.

The Algarve coast can be divided up into three distinct parts: Sotavento, meaning "over the wind," with generally flat, sand beaches stretching between Faro and the Spanish border; the adjoining region of Barlavento, "under the wind," which consists of steep limestone cliffs that the sea has hammered into sometimes bizarre formations that only allow space for small beaches between Quarteira and Portimão; and finally the harsher, windier southwestern corner that runs from Lagos to Cabo Vicente and then northward to Aljezur.

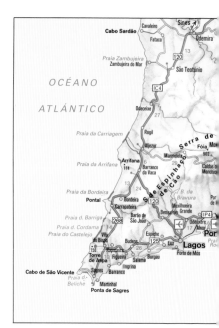

FARO

Faro, the largest town of the Algarve, has the region's only international airport. Founded as a Phoenecian trading post and equally significant under the Romans, Visigoths, and Moors, it finally became a bishopric in the 16th century. In 1596, an English raid left the town in ashes. Then, in 1755, the earthquake repeated their performance. After reconstruction, in 1756, it was made capital of the Algarve. Today, the town is marked by unshackled growth, although the tiny Old Town is sheltered from the brunt of the hectic activity by the original defensive wall. The **Cathedral** is a miscellany of architectural styles from the Romanesque to the Baroque; its organ dates from this latter period. Opposite stands the Bishop's Palace, a proud 18th-century building.

The old Convent of **Na. Senhora da Assunção**, founded in 1518, now houses the Archaeological Museum, with items excavated from Roman Milreu, ceramic

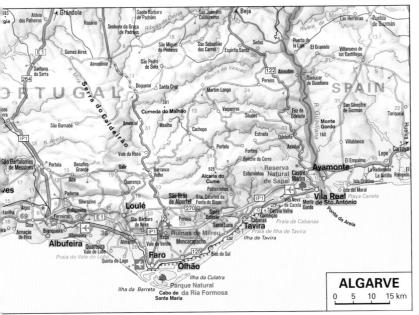

exhibits, and art. The two-story Renaissance cloister within the convent is in itself worth a visit. Baroque churches are by no means lacking in Faro: São Francisco, Misericordia, São Pedro, São Luis, São Sebastião, and the Carmo Church with a small charnel chapel standing on the adjacent cemetery. The **Regional Museum** shows some local folk art and handicrafts, and the life of the fishermen on the Algarve coast is explored in the **Museu Maritimo**, which also displays model ships. On the northern end of **La Doca**, the yacht harbor, is **Baixa**, the pedestrian zone, with a profusion of small shops and snack bars.

A great piece of architecture stands alongside the road northwest of Faro, just before Almansil. The **Igreja São Lourenço** was built in the 15th century, but thoroughly revamped in the 18th. Blue and white tiles line the entire inside, right up to the dome, painting the picture of the patron saint's martyrdom.

To the southeast of Faro sprawls the nature park **Ria Formosa**, which is more than 34 miles (55 km) long and has a surface area of approximately 17,000 hectares. The dune and saline vegetation, marine fauna and fish of the lagoon landscape are all protected, and form the habitat of millions of migrating birds. Because of the park, this strip of coastline and the parallel sand bank have been protected from the building boom of the past decades. The vacation communities are located away from the shore, and the beaches of the sand bank are seldom overcrowded. While the **Praia de Faro**, the city beach, is still accessible using normal roads, **Ilha de Faro**, **Farol**, and **Culata** can only be reached by boat from Faro or Olhãos.

SERRA DO CALDEIRÃO

To the north of Faro, along the foothills of the mountains, isolated villas stand in the midst of orchards, almond and orange groves. Their residents not only have a splendid view, but also enjoy peace and quiet and a modicum of cooler

air in summer. The small villages of the Serra, such as **São Brás de Alportel**, are traditional summer retreats, oases in an arid landscape of maquis, almond and carob trees.

Loulé lies above the coastal plain. Rife with tradition, this village boasts a series of Gothic and Renaissance churches and cloisters. The **Igreja São Clemente** was built in the 13th century on the site of a mosque, whose minaret was used as its tower. The town's art gallery was recently established in the **Convent of Espirito Santo**. The local **Museum** is located in a section of the old Moorish wall. Near the **fortress**, which also dates back to the Moorish days of the 12th century, is a small church, **Nossa Senhora da Conceição**, dating to the 16th century and decorated with old tiles. Loulé attracts locals and foreigners alike on Saturdays in particular, thanks to the weekly

Above: The fish market of Olhão. Right: Tavira is considered the most beautiful town in the eastern Algarve.

market around the covered market hall, built in neo-*mudejar* style.

An 18th-century nobleman's palace, which has stood abandoned for years, is one of the main sights in **Estói**; you can visit its playful park and ascend the tiled double stairway leading over a grotto or stroll around and enjoy the refreshing shade of its spreading old trees. Nearby are the Roman ruins of **Milreu**, with remains of a 3rd-century villa and baths, their basins decorated with fish mosaics. Only a few of the finds are still here; most of them have been transported to the museum in Faro (see above), while some of the mosaics are displayed in the Estói villa.

ALGARVE SOTAVENTO

This sandy stretch of the Algarve extends from Faro to the Guadiana River, which forms the border with Spain. The villages here are influenced less by tourism than by their past as trading posts and fishing ports, in particular tuna fishing.

Olhão calls itself "cubist town." The white houses of the local fishermen, with their flat roofs, look more like Berber than Portuguese architecture. From the tower of the parish church, you have a lovely view of the whole place. Olhão also has the most picturesque fishing harbor of all the villages of the region. You can conclude a leisurely walk through its lovely streets with lunch or dinner at one of its fine fish restaurants.

Many agree, however, that the most beautiful town along the coast is **Tavira**. Again, one has to climb a little to get an overview, namely up to the fortress, from where one can see the distinctive roof-scape of the old town, the Roman bridge, the spires of around 20 churches, and the shining white façades of the houses on the opposite bank of the river. About a mile (2 km) out of town, by the mouth of the Gilão, the best restaurants are concentrated by the pier for boats running to and from the sand bank and beaches.

Other places worth visiting are Luz, Santo Estêvão, Conceição, and the fish-

ing village of Santa Luzia. The best beaches are on the islands and sand bars off Tavira and Cabanas, which can be accessed by boat if you don't feel lik wading out to them at low tide or driving to one of the handful of narrow bridges. The island **Ilha de Tavira** has more than 6 miles (10 km) of sand beach, lined with a thin stand of trees that provide some much-needed shade.

The nature preserve of Ria Formosa extends all the way to **Cacela Velha**. In spite of its breathtaking location in an old fortress towering over a sand beach, this village still consists merely of a dozen or so houses, thanks to very strict building regulations. It's virtually impossible to park in the tiny town, but the pretty path leading down to the sea, lined with almond trees, and the sand bars when you get there, are well worth the hike.

The easternmost point on the Algarve coast is **Vila Real de Santo Antonio**. It was commissioned by the Marquês de Pombal after the earthquake of 1755 destroyed the old Santo António, and was

constructed within five months on a strict grid pattern. As a border town, it generally has a healthy measure of Spaniards on shopping jaunts or enjoying the neaerby beaches of Monte Gordo. For travelers in the Algarve, Vila Real is the last stop on the coastal railway. A ferry crosses the Rio Guadiana, just in case you would like to go on a day trip to **Ayamonte** in Spain.

Upstream lies **Castro Marim**, whose mighty castle was the first seat of the Knights of Christ, an order founded in 1319. In 1356 they moved to the fortified monastery of Tomar. The Inquisition's court later used Castro Marim as a prison. Another fortress, **Castelo São Sebastião**, built in the 17th century, stands on another hill. Both forts offer a panoramic view out over the vast saline landscape of the Sapal nature reserve and all the way

Above and right: Albufeira, with its extensive vacation communities and large hotels standing on the cliffs, is still one of the most popular sea-side resorts in Portugal.

to Spain, which has come a little closer to Portugal ever since the construction of the elegant bridge over the River Guadiana in 1992. About a mile (2 km) to the south of Castro Marim, at the foot of a long vineyard, a dirt path leads off the main road. It's a perfect spot to park your car and take a tour on foot to the dams of the salt ponds where flocks of flamingos make their home. A word of warning, however: photographers stalking these majestic wading birds for illustrative purposes should take care not to leave the paths on the dams.

Only the lower section of the Guadiana is navigable nowadays, although the Romans used it all the way up to Mérida, the capital of Lusitania, in Spain's Extremadura. Only small boats can make it to **Alcoutim**, a modest little village at the foot of a fortress ruin, once a major river harbor. Historians still recall this backwater; the Peace of Alcoutim was signed in 1371 by the kings of Portugal and Castile on a boat on "neutral grounds," namely in the middle of the river.

ALGARVE BARLAVENTO

West of Faro, one famous beach gives way to another, one golf course follows another, and a host of hotels all compete with one another to demonstrate the greatest number of swimming pools, tennis courts, and exotic bars. Towns with such promising names as Quinta do Lago or Vale do Lobo turn out to be the sites of exclusive club complexes. In Quarteira, Vilamoura, and Branqueira, travelers have a wide choice of hotels and apartments in all price categories. **Vilamoura** was established as the largest private vacation facility in all of Europe. It includes no fewer than two 18-hole golf courses and one with 27 holes. The yacht marina, with 1,000 berths and a wide selection of water sports, is considered the most fashionable spot along the coast. A casino, a riding club, and a shopping center round off the available amenities.

The most famous beaches of the Algarve are here, and the chic clientele of the local luxury hotels mills about in Vale do Lobo, Falésia, Olhos de Agua and Maria Luisa.

A photogenic stretch of rocky coastline begins just before **Albufeira**, which was once the number-one destination for foreign tourists in the Algarve, and remains so to a certain extent. Back in the 1960s, direct access to the beach was brutally blocked by a barrier of hotels; today, the town is linked to the beaches by tunnels. Nevertheless, the gold-colored sandstone cliffs and the beach used by fishermen, separated from the rest by another rocky promontory, still leave a lasting impression of beauty. The town itself, built like an atrium along the bluffs, has a special atmosphere all its own.

West of Albufeira, you can take marvelous hikes along the cliffs; below you, you can spot little sand beaches tucked between the rocks. Clambering down to them is often a breakneck enterprise; particularly exclusive hotels have built elevators down to their – private – beaches.

The beach of **Armção de Pêra** is somewhat broader than the others. It has

enough space to accommodate both beach enthusiasts and fishermen, who are often here working on their boats or repairing their nets. From the beach, you can reach small caves that the waves have carved into the soft cliffs, but keep an eye on the tides. Fishermen take passengers out to some of the more hidden caves. Most of the towns between Albufeira and Portimão, such as Pêra, Porches, the erstwhile fishing village of Carvoeiro, Estômbar, with its late-Manuelistic church, or **Lagoa**, famous for its wine, are now surrounded by a ring of vacation homes; still, they have all preserved their pretty old town centers.

The little pilgrimage church **Nossa Senhora da Rocha** stands on a promontory high over the sea. Both sides overlook a picture-perfect combination of sun, sand and rock. White sails seem to hover over the water, and through the fa-

Above: Relaxing atmosphere for the vacationers in Lagos. Right: The bizarre rocks and grottos of Ponta da Piedade.

mous rock window you can now and then spot the colorful sails of windsurfers.

Portimão, shopping center and unofficial capital of the whole region, is a lively place where foreigners rub elbows with locals sauntering about the streets or exploring the shops. The pedestrian zone echoes with all the languages of the Western Hemisphere. In the evening the bars and restaurants gradually fill up, while the younger crowd heads for the discos at the edge of town. From the waterfront promenade wafts the unmistakable odor of charcoal-broiled sardines, a specialty that every visitor should make an effort to sample. Portimão's fishing port is in **Ferragudo**, which lies on the opposite bank of the Arade River, and is a good deal quieter and more romantic than the main city.

Praia da Rocha, the beach area of Portimão, is the largest vacation resort in the Algarve, and possesses a very impressive high-rise skyline. One giant hotel or apartment block rises after another. At the end of the coastal road, at

the mouth of the Arade, stands a fort which commands a view of the entire bay of Praia da Rocha.

The adjoining segment of coast, from here to **Alvor**, is more exclusive. Tastefully done holiday communities and golf clubs have transformed the maquis into a veritable park. The beaches of Vau, Tres, Irmãos and the tiny bights at the bottom of the steep cliffs along the shore up to Meia Praia just before Lagos, are by and large reserved for residents of the vacation complexes. Of course, no one is allowed to build on the beaches themselves, but as the carefully fenced-in and guarded private plots usually extend all the way to the edge of the cliff, getting to one of these beaches without a boat is fairly difficult.

In 1578, **Lagos** was the port from which the young and enthusiastic king Sebastião set forth to Morocco with an army of 17,000 knights to wage war against the Saadi Sultan. He drowned in the River Loukos in the disastrous battle of Ksar-el Kebir. As no knight was allowed to survive his king, the fact of his death remained a secret, and everyone "expected" him to return some day. A controversial modern statue on Praça Gil Eanes portrays Sebastião as a creature from outer space who could land any day.

Behind the high walls of the fortified town is one of the Algarve's most charming towns, with pretty streets reserved for pedestrians, many cafés and other establishments whose tables overflow onto the sidewalks, old churches, and a wide harbor promenade. On Republic Square stands the Gothic edifice that once housed the **slave market** where the first black Africans were sold in the 15th century; it's now used for exhibitions.

Lagos has a number of 15th- and 16th-century churches, but all of them were either renovated or completely rebuilt after the earthquake of 1755. The most significant ones are São Sebastião, Carmo, and Misericórdia. Next to the **Igreja Santo António** (1769) is the **Museu Regional** with an interesting and eclectic collection ranging from archaeo-

113

logical finds and religious and folk art to Angolan spearheads and stuffed birds from the coastal region. Beyond the fort **Pau de Bandera**, which dates from the 17th century, is a lookout called **Ponta da Piedade**, a picturesque and much-photographed spot along this craggy coast; you can descend to it down a long flight of steps between the rocks. Approaching by boat gives you the best impression of this landscape. Farther on are the beaches of Porto de Mós and Luz, strongholds of sea-side tourism; before that, fascinating nature trails lead along the cliffs, such as those between Praia da Rocha and Alvor, or between Ponta da Piedade and Luz, Burgau and Salema.

SERRA DE MONCHIQUE

Should the heat along the coast become too oppressive in summer, then

Above: Harvesting oranges in the Serra de Monchique. Right: A bracing wind for the surfers near Sagres.

the mountains are the place to head for. The **Monchique** range, whose highest peak is the **Fóia** at an altitude of 2,950 feet (902 m), is of volcanic origin, and forms a kind of climatic barrier for the whole Algarve coast. On a clear day the view from the treeless summit extends all the way to the sea and into the lower Alentejo. The Monchique, Marmelete, and Alferce are sprinkled with little cafés and restaurants with nice terraces. Trails lead up to observation points, and one of them to the **Caldas de Monchique** spa. While the mountains' southern slopes are a sea of flowers and orchards, the northern and western slopes, which are subject to harsher climatic conditions, have been planted with pine trees and eucalyptus. A new road leads through both kinds of vegetation on its way from Caldas over Marmelete to Aljezur.

Another recommended excursion through the hinterlands is the route from Silves to Loulé. **Silves** is overshadowed by the Moorish fort **Castelo dos Mouros**, built of red sandstone. The three-aisled Gothic **Cathedral**, made from the same stone, was erected on the foundations of a 13th-century mosque; inside it are the tombs of several Crusaders. Silves was under Muslim rule from 711 to 1242, and during the Caliphate of Córdoba it functioned as the capital of the western province *Al Gharb* of the Moorish realm known as *Al Andalus*. Located behind a protective string of hills, and with a sufficient water supply, the area was ideal for growing vegetables and fruit; and the city of *Xelb*, as Silves was called in those days, was swimming in wealth. After the Christian armies had taken over, however, it lost all its significance. The area was settled even before the arrival of the Moors, as the local **Archaeological Museum** can demonstrate: it displays items dating from the Stone Age to the 17th century. By the eastern exit of town stands the **Cruz de Portugal**, a crucifix of white limestone carved in Manuelistic style in the 16th century. The Crucifixion is shown on one side, and the Descent from the Cross on the other.

Driving east from Silves in springtime is one of the loveliest experiences the Algarve has to offer. The agriculture here recalls the Arab tradition of landscape gardening: an Expressionistic palette of lush green, splashed with orange and radiant yellow, in the orange and lemon groves, where the trees are so laden with fruit that the branches can barely support the weight, alternates with the delicate hues of the almond trees, decked out in white and pink flowers against a perfectly blue sky. Sprinkled through the area are farmhouses surrounded by flowers and the occasional vacation villa or pretty, and largely untouristed, village.

Some particularly attractive towns are **São Bartolomeu de Messines,** with a 16th-century church; Salir; and **Alte**, where the carstic spring, **Fonte das Bicas**, and cafés draw sightseers. A sonnet which the poet Cândido Guerreiro

wrote to this idyllic spot is reproduced on tiles. The area's lovely countryside is ideal for walks.

Cabo São Vicente

The closer you come to Cabo São Vicente, the younger the crowd. Snorkelers, windsurfers, sailors, and those who enjoy the challenge of fishing from the cliffs are well served in this area. The landscape here is bizarre and barren; a strong wind blows year-round from the Atlantic; and even on calm days a steady ocean swell pounds steadily at the bluffs. The only beaches are little shell-shaped affairs tucked away at the bottom of the cliffs and difficult to reach. Holiday homes and hotels are few and far between; towns, such as the fishing village of Salema, small and rare. This stretch is perfect for those anyone who likes solitary hikes along the cliffs; sometimes you can even find a beach all to yourself. The nicest ones are at Figueira, Ingrina, Barranco and Martinhal.

115

The little village of **Sagres** is nestled in a depression of this high plateau. From here, it fulfilled its centuries-old task of defending the southwesternmost corner of Europe. The cliffs of this chalk peninsula rise vertically a good 165 feet (50 m) from the sea, as if designed for sentinels, the lighthouse, or the doughty fort. And it's precisely in these Godforsaken seas that the local fishermen earn their daily bread. Indeed, the cold currents here are rich in plankton, the staple food of the common sardine and other fish. Local anglers stand atop the cliffs, seemingly defying death, and cast their lines into the foamy maw below, to the constant roar of the waves that slam into the rocks and wash away the ground beneath their feet.

The fortress stands on a rocky promontory south of town. Modern buildings are currently being added on to complete a **Seafaring Museum**. Henry the Naviga-

Above: A hard way to earn a living – fishing from a wave-beaten cliff along the western Algarve coast.

tor (1394-1460) opened a school for mariners on this spot, which at the time was the last landfall of the known world. His aim was to train officers for voyages of discovery. Dating from this period is the great compass drawn in stones on the floor of the fortress, enigmatically divided into 42 parts.

The harbor of Sagres lies to the east of the cape in a cove. The beaches of Mareta and Baleira adjoin it. **Beliche** beach, whose powerful waves should only be negotiated by experienced swimmers and surfers, stretches between the rocky plateau of Sagres and the Cape of São Vicente. In the former castle of Beliche, hardly more than a large wall, is a restaurant. On the 203-foot-high (62 m) **Cabo São Vicente** is a lighthouse that can be seen from a distance. Henry the Navigator is said to have lived in the little village of **Vila do Bispo**. Legend has it that he used to pray in the little roadside Gothic chapel of the Virgin of Guadalupe, some 2.5 miles (4 km) east of town.

The first beaches of the Algarve's west coast begin near Vila do Bispo, a shoreline whose battered cliffs, plateaus, and wind-blown dunes clearly denote an Atlantic landscape. You won't find the usual tourist panoply of apartment houses, fashionable bars and restaurants, and souvenir shops along the beaches of Castelejo, Cordama and Barriga. For hikers, or anyone in search of a solitary place to pitch a tent, the road between Cabo São Vicente and Aljezur is a treasure trove, although one should note that access roads from Bordeira or Aljezur are veritable cross-country rides. But surfers will be rewarded for the bumpy and dusty drive: the beaches of **Castelejo**, **Carrapateira**, or **Bordeira**, about 12.5 miles (20 km) further north, provide good winds and excellent swell.

The Algarve ends after **Aljezur**, a nice farming town at the foot of a mountain bearing an old fortress, far from the maddening tourist crowd.

THE ALGARVE
Accommodations

ALBUFEIRA (089): *LUXURY:* **Cerro**, Cerro da Piedade, tel. 586191, fax: 586194. *MODERATE:* **Mar á Vista**, Cerro da Piedade, tel. 586354. **Torre Velha**, Sesmarias, tel. 591367. *BUDGET:* **Albufeirense**, Rua da Liberdade 18, tel. 512079. *CAMPING:* **Albufeira**, tel. 589505.

ALMANSIL (089): *LUXURY:* **Quinta do Lago**, tel. 396666, fax: 396393. *MODERATE:* **Santa Teresa**, Rua do Comercio 13, tel. 395525. *TURISMO RURAL:* **Quinta dos Amigos**, Escanxinas, tel. 395269, fax: 393283. **Quinta das Rochas**, Fonte Coberta, tel. 393165, fax: 399198.

ALTE (089): *MODERATE:* **Alte-Hotel**, Montinho, tel. 68523/4, fax: 68646. *TURISMO RURAL:* **Casa de Alte**, L. da Igreja, tel. 68426.

ALVOR (082): *LUXURY:* **Prainha Club**, tel. 458951/458561, fax: 458950. Apartment in a nice location, heated indoor pool in winter, private beach. *CAMPING:* **Dourada**, tel. 459178.

ESTÓI: (089): *LUXURY:* **Monte do Casal**, Cerro do Lobo, tel. 91503, fax: 91341.

FARO (089): *LUXURY:* **Moleiro**, Quinta da Bemposta, A. tel. 91495, fax: 91347. **Casa de Lumena**, Praça A. Herculano 27, tel. 801990, fax: 804019. **Aeromar**, Praia de Faro, tel. 817549, fax: 817512, on the island. *MODERATE:* **Oceano**, Tv. Ivens 21, tel. 823349, fax: 805590, centrally located. **O Farao**, Largo da Madalena 4, tel. 823356, fax: 804997. *BUDGET:* **Algarve**, Rua Francisco Gomes 4, tel. 823346. *CAMPING:* **Praia de Faro**, tel. 817876. *TURISMO RURAL:* **Quinta de Benatrite**, Santa Barbara de Nexe, tel. 90450.

LAGOS (082): *LUXURY:* **Casa de S. Gonçalo**, Rua Cândido dos Reis 73, tel. 762171, fax: 763927. **Rosas**, Albardeira, Meia Praia, tel. 768968, fax: 768970. *MODERATE:* **Cidade Velha**, Rua Joaquim Tello 7, tel. 762041. **Meia Praia**, Meia Praia, tel. 762001. **Marinha do Rio**, Av. dos Descobrimentos, tel. 769859. *BUDGET:* **Mar Azul**, Rua 25 de Abril 13, tel. 769143, fax: 769960. *CAMPING:* **Imulagos**, Porto de Mós, tel. 760031. *TURISMO RURAL:* **Casa do Pinhão**, Praia do Pinhão, tel. 62371.

LOULÉ (089): *MODERATE:* **Loulé Jardim**, Praça Manuel de Arriaga, tel. 413094/5, fax: 63177. *BUDGET:* **Cidem**, Trav. do Mercado 1, tel. 415553. *TURISMO RURAL:* **Quinta da Várzea**, Várzeas de Querença, tel. 414443.

MONCHIQUE (082): *LUXURY:* **Lageado**, Caldas de Monchique, tel. 92616. **Abrigo da Montanha**, Corte Pereira, Estr. da Fóia, tel. 92131, fax: 93660. *MODERATE:* **Bica Boa**, Estr. de Lisboa, tel. 92271, fax: 92360.

OLHÃO: *MODERATE:* **Bela Alexandra**, Bias do Sul, Moncarapacho, tel. 793371. Hotel village

Aldeia de Marim, tel/fax: 701327. *BUDGET:* **Bela Vista**, Rua Teófilo Braga 65-7, tel. 702538. *CAMPING:* **Orbitur**, Ilha de Armona, tel. 74173.

PORTIMÃO (082): *LUXURY:* Hotel village **Jardim do Vau**, Praia do Vau, tel. 401086. *MODERATE:* **Rio**, Largo do Dique 20, tel. 23041, fax: 411895. **O Patio**, Rua Dr. João V. Mealha 3, tel. 24288, fax: 24288. *CAMPING:* **Ferragudo**, tel. 461121. *TURISMO RURAL:* **Casa Três Palmeiras**, João d'Arens, tel. 401275, fax: 401029.

PRAIA DA ROCHA: *LUXURY:* **Bela Vista**, tel. 24055, fax: 415369. **Oriental**, tel. 413000, fax: 413413. **Vila Lido**, Av. Tomás Cabreira, tel. 24127, fax: 24246. *MODERATE:* **Pinguim**, Rua António Feu, tel. 24308, right on the beach. *BUDGET:* **Oceano**, Av. Tomás Cabreira, tel. 24309.

SAGRES (082): *LUXURY:* **D. Henrique**, Sitio da Mareta, tel. 64133. *MODERATE:* **Aparthotel Orquídea**, Baleeira, tel. 64340. **Baleeira**, tel. 64212, fax: 64425. **Gambozimhos**, Praia Martinhal, tel. 64318, nice location, solitary, inexpensive. *CAMPING:* **Sagres**, tel. 64351, at the top of the cliff. **Quinta dos Carriços**, Figueira, tel. 65201. Praia da Ingrina, tel. 66242, on the west coast.

SILVES: *LUXURY:* **Solar da Moura**, tel. 442682, fax: 443108. *BUDGET:* **Sousa**, Rua Samora Barros 17, tel. 442502. *TURISMO RURAL:* **Vila Sodré**, Cruz de Portugal, tel. 443441. **Quinta da Figueirinha**, tel. 442671.

TAVIRA (081): *LUXURY:* **Quinta de Pedrogil**, Rua Jacques Pessoa 15, tel. 22145. *MODERATE:* **Marés**, Rua José Pires Padinha 139, tel. 325815, fax: 325819. **Eurotel Tavira**, Quinta das Oliveiras, tel. 324324, fax: 325571. **Golden Club**, Cabanas, tel. 20517/20602, fax: 20513, Hotel village. **Pedras del Rei**, Santa Luzia, tel. 325352, fax: 324020,. *BUDGET:* **Castelo**, Rua da Liberdade 4, tel. 23942. *CAMPING:* **Ilha de Tavira**, tel. 23505. *TURISMO RURAL:* **Quinta do Caracol**, S. Tiago, tel. 22475, fax: 23175.

VILA REAL DE SANTO ANTONIO (081): *LUXURY:* **Guadiana**, Av. da República 94, tel. 511482, fax: 511478. **Oasis**, Manta Rota, tel. 951644, fax: 951660. *MODERATE:* **Apolo**, Parque de Bombeiros Volunt., tel. 512448, fax: 512450.

Restaurants / Cafés

ALBUFEIRA: **Borda d'Agua**, Praia da Oura, tel. 586541. **Vila Joya**, Praia Galé, tel. 591995. **Os Compadres**, Montechoro, tel. 514948. **O Montinho**, Montechoro, tel. 513959. **A Ruína**, Praia, tel. 512094. **ALMANSIL:** **Casa da Torre-Ermitage**, Estr. Vale do Lobo, tel. 394329. **Adega Cova**, Vale d'Eguas, tel. 395281 **FARO:** **Cidade Velha**, Largo da Sé 19, tel. 27145. **Roque**, Praia de Faro, tel. 817868. **Taverna da Sé**, Largo da Sé. **Sousa**, Largo do Pé da Cruz, tel. 826725. **LAGOA:**

117

Casa Velha, Rua Mouzinho de Albuquerque 60, tel. 342600. O Castelo, Carvoeiro, Rua do Casino, tel. 357218. La Romance, Quinta de Bemposta, tel. 341677, 1,5 km toward Estombar. O Manjar do Rei, Estr. do Farol 65, Carvoeiro, tel. 356527. LAGOS: Gilberto, Rua das Portas de Portugal 85, tel. 762336. Adega da Marina, Av. dos Descobrimentos 35. Lagosteira, Rua 1 de Maio 20, tel. 62486. Os Arcos, Rua 25 de Abril 30-36, tel. 63210. No Patio, Rua Lançarote de Freitas 46, tel. 763777 (Danish). LOULÉ: O Museu de Lagar, Largo da Matriz 8, tel. 63121. O Pescador, Rua José Fer. Guerreiro 54, tel. 62821. Horta Nova, Rua Major Manuel Olival, tel. 62429. Casa dos Arcos, Rua Sá de Miranda 23, tel. 416713. MONCHIQUE: Abrigo da Montanha, on the road to the Fóia, tel.92131. Paraíso da Montanha, Estr. da Fóia, tel. 92150. Central, Monchique, tel. 92203. Panorama Algarvio, Miradouro, tel. 92217. O Planalto, Fóia, tel. 92878.
OLHÃO: A Lagosta, Rua Mestre Joaquim Casaca, tel. 714179. Aquário, Rua Dr. João Lúcio, tel. 703539. Henrique, in the fishermen's quarter, tel. 713856. Marisqueira da Ponte, Rua 18 de Junho 70, tel. 703291. PORTIMÃO: Tio José, Rua da Barca. Casa Balau, Largo da Barca 10, tel. 23351. Casa de Jantar, Rua de Santa Isabel 14, tel. 22072. A Lanterna, Ferragudo, on the bridge, tel. 23948. O Gato, Estr. de Alvor, tel. 27674. Forte & Feio, Largo da Barca, tel. 25904. Dona Barca, Largo da Barca. Taberna da Mare, Largo da Barca, tel. 414614. Casa Bica, Lota do Cais, Av. 1, tel. 25944. PRAIA DA ROCHA: Serra e Mare, Rua Antonio Feu, tel. 26781. Fortaleza de Santa Catarina, tel. 22066.
QUARTEIRA: Quarteirense, Largo das Cortes Reais, tel. 380480. Adega do Peixe, Av. Infante de Sagres, tel. 312686. Rosa Branca, Av. Infante de Sagres, tel. 314430. O Pescador, tel. 314755. SAGRES: Fortaleza de Beliche, Estr. Cabo São Vicente, tel. 64124. Telheiro do Infante, Playa de Mareta, tel. 64179. Gambozinos, Praia Martinhal, tel. 64318. Moinho, Eiras, tel. 66159. SILVES: Casa Velha de Silves, Rua 25 de Abril 11, tel. 445491. A Mesquita, Rua 5 de Outubro 15, tel. 442721. Ponte Romana, Horta Cruz, tel. 443275. U Monchiqueiro, on the market, tel. 442142. Inglés, near the Cathedral. TAVIRA: Patio, Rua Antonio Cabreira 30, 1, tel. 23008. Quatro Aguas, at the pier, tel. 325329.
VILA REAL DE SANTO ANTONIO: Dom Jota, Ponta de Santo António, tel. 43151. A Caçarola, Av. da República, tel. 42641. Caves do Guadiana, Av. da República 89, tel. 44498. A Nau, Rua D. Pedro V. 69, tel. 511256. Joaquim Gomes, Rua 5 de Outubro 5, tel. 43285.

Sights / Museums
ALMANSIL: São Lourenço: 9:30am-1pm and 2:15pm-6pm, closed Sun. CASTRO MARIM: Fortress Museum and Information center of the Sapal nature park: Mon-Fri 9am-5pm.30. ESTÓI: Palace park: Tue-Sat 9am-12:30pm and 2pm-5:30pm. Roman excavations, Milreu: 10am-midday and 2pm-6pm, closed Mon. FARO: Archeol. Museum: 9am-12:30pm and 2pm-5:30pm, closed weekends. Ethnographic Museum: Mon-Fri 10am-6pm. Museu Marítimo: Mon-Fri 9:30am-12:30pm and 2pm-5:30pm, Sat 9:30am-1pm, closed Sun. S. António-Kapelle: 9am-1pm and 2pm-7pm. LAGOS: Museu Regional: 9:30am-12:30pm and 2pm-5pm, closed Mon. LOULÉ: Historic Museum in town wall and City Art Gallery: Mon-Fri 9am-noon and 2pm-5:30pm, closed weekends. PORTIMÃO: Museu Diogo Gonçalves: Mon-Sat 9:30am-12:30pm and 2pm-7pm, Sat and Sun 9am-1pm and 2pm-6pm. Igreja Matriz: 7am-noon and 3:30pm-7pm. SÃO BRÁS DE ALPORTEL: Museu del Traje: 10am-midday and 2pm-6pm, Sat-Sun 2pm-6pm. SILVES: Cathedral: 8:30am-6:30pm. Archeol. Museum: 10am-5pm, closed Mondays. TAVIRA: Fort: 8am-5:30pm, Sat and Sun 9am-5:30pm. VILA REAL DE SANTO ANTONIO: Nac. Galerie Manuel Cabanas, Praça Marquês de Pombal, 11:30am-12:30pm and 2pm-7pm, in summer: 2pm-8pm and 9pm-11pm, closed Mon.

Shopping
ALBUFEIRA: Casa Infante D. Henrique, Rua Cândido dos Reis 30: ceramics, porcelain. FARO: Aresta Viva, Rua Antero de Quental 22, tiles. PORTIMÃO: Vista Alegre, Rua de Sa. Isabel 21: porcelain. O Aquário II, Rua V. da Gama: copper, ceramics. Casco Garrafeira, Rua J. de Deus 24: wine, spirits. Tio José, Rua da Barca: wine.

Sports
EXCURSIONS: with Jeeps, canoes, mountain bikes, paragliders, boats, on horseback or on foot: Portitours, Emoção e Aventura, Rua Dr. Teófilo Braga, Ed. Pluma, Loja 2, Portimão, tel. 082-417978, fax: 412385. BICYCLE TOURS: Terras de Mu, Loulé, tel. 413138. FISHING: Sea Sports Centre, Av. dos Pescadores 4, Praia da Luz, tel. 082-789538. Cepemar, Portimão, tel. 082-25866. Surfpesca, Lagos, tel. 082-603147. Espadarte do Sul, Lagos, Docapesca, Armazém N 4, tel. 761820. Iate Estrêl do Rio, Porto da Baleeira, Sagres, tel. 082-415156. GOLF: Penina, Alvor; Alto Golf, Alvor; Vilamoura I, II and III; Vale do Milho, Carvoeiro; Vale do Lobo; Quinta do Lago; Palmares, Meia Praia, Lagos; Parque da Floresta, Vale de Poço, Vila do Bispo; Pine Cliffs, Albufeira; Vila Sol, Vilamoura; Euroactividades, Fer-

ragudo; **Penina**, Portimão; **Gramacho**, Carvoeiro; **Vale de Pinta**, Carvoeiro; **Pinheiros Altos**, Almansil. *RIDING*: Some vacation places such as the Hotel Alfamar, Falésia, or the Quinta do Lago, Pine Trees, in Almansil have stables. The largest center with organized horseback riding tours: **Quinta dos Amigos**, Escanxinas, tel. 395269, fax: 393283. **West-Algarve Riding Centre**, Quinta dos Almarjões, Burgau, tel. 765252. **Centro Hípico**, Vilamoura, tel. 380722. **Centro Hípico de Silves**, Cruz de Portugal, tel. 444120. **Centro Hípico**, Sítio do Rio, Carrapateira, Aljezur, tel. 082-97119. **Centro Hípico**, Vale de Ferro, Mexilhoeira Grande, Portimão, tel. 082-96444. **Quinta das Cinco Ferraduras**, Sítio da Pedragosa, Loulé, tel. 415709. *SEGELN*: **Sea Sports Centre**, Av. dos Pescadores 4, Praia da Luz, tel. 082-789538. **Marina de Vilamoura**, tel. 089-313933. Club de Vela, Lagos, tel. 082-62256. **Clube de Vela**, Tavira, tel. 081-23654. **Bom Sucesso**, Olhão, tel. 089-707744. *FLYING AND PARAGLIDING:* **Centro de Ultraleves do Algarve**, Aerodromo de Lagos, tel. 082-762906. **Aeroclube de Lagos**, tel. 082-760482. Round flights: **Aero Algarve**, Aeródromo de Portimão, Penina. *SQUASH:* **Tennis center and squash club Carvoeiro**, tel. 082-357847. **Quinta da Balaia**, Albufeira, tel. 089-586583. In the **Hotel village Aldea Turística**, Burgau. *DIVING*: **Sea Sports Centre**, Av. dos Pescadores 4, Praia da Luz, tel. 082-789538 (with diving bells, too). **Centro de Mergulho da Ingrina**, Praia da Ingrina, Vila do Bispo. **Centro de Mergulho Ilhas do Martinhal**, Sagres, tel. 082-64426. **Diver's Cove**, Quinta do Paraíso, Praia do Carvoeiro, tel. 082-356594. *TENNIS:* The largest hotel complexes generally have tennis courts for non-guests as well, e.g., Hotel Alfamar, Falésia and the **Carvoeiro Tennis Club**, tel. 082-357847. **The Roger Taylor Tennis-Centre** is in the Hotel Vale do Lobos. *WATER PARKS:* **Slide and Splash**, Vale de Deus, Estômbar. **The Big One**, Alcantarilha, E.N. 125 at km 4. *WATERSKIING*: **Marina de Vilamoura. Ocean Club Water Sports School**, Praia da Luz, tel. 082-789472. *WIND SURFING*: **Sea Sports Centre**, Av. dos Pescadores 4, Praia da Luz, tel. 082-789538. **Centro Náutico**, Alvor, tel. 458900. **Marina** de Vilamoura. Ferragudo, Windsurfing Centre, Pr. Grande, tel. 082-461115. **Centro de Windsurf e Desportos Náuticos**, Ar. de Pêra. **Centro Náutico**, Torralta, Alvor, tel. 082-459211.

Tourist information

ALBUFEIRA: Tourist Office: Rua 5 de Outubro, tel. 512144. **Car rental**: Auto-Jardim, Av. da Liberdade, Ed. Brisa, tel. 589715, fax: 587780. Auto Algarve, Montechoro, tel. 53987. Europcar, Rua Dr. Diogo Leote, tel. 52411. **Post office**: Largo Duarte Pacheco. **Motorbike rental: Vespa-a Rent, Tel**: 515485. **ALCOUTIM: Tourist Office**: Praça da República. tel. 46179. **ALJEZUR: Tourist Office**: Largo do Mercado, tel. 98229: Mon, Fri 9:30am-12:30pm and 2pm-7pm, Tue-Thu 9:30am-7pm, Sat-Sun 9:30am-12:30pm and 2pm-5:30pm. **ALMANSIL: Reiten**: Quinta dos Amigos, Escanxinas, tel. 395269. **ARMAÇÃO DE PÊRA: Tourist Office**: Av. Marginal, tel. 312145. **CARVOEIRO: Tourist Office**: Praia (Strand), Tel: 357728. **CASTRO MARIM: Tourist Office**: Praça 1 de Maio 2, tel. 531232. **FARO: Tourist Office**: Rua da Misericórdia 8-12, tel. 803604: Mon-Fri 9:30am-7pm, Sat-Sun 9:30am-5:30pm.. **Car rental**: Rentauto, Airport, tel. 818718, fax: 818189. Lusorent, Av. 5 de Outubro 19, Loja 1, tel. 812265. Hertz, Rua 1 de Maio, tel. 24877. Budget, Edificio Hotel Eva, tel. 803493. **Post**: Largo do Carmo.**LAGOS: Tourist Office**: Largo Marquês de Pombal, tel. 763031/4, 9:30am-5:30pm, im Sommer bis 7pm. **Car rental**: Luz Car, Largo Portas de Portugal 10, tel. 61016. B Car, Rua 1 de Maio 64, tel. 768930. **Post office**: Av. dos Descobrimentos.

LOULÉ: Tourist Office: Av. da República, tel. 63900, Mon-Fri 9:30am-12,30 and 2pm-5:30pm, Sat 9:30am-midday, Sun zu. **Market**: Saturday mornings. **MONTE GORDO: Tourist Office**: Av. Marginal, tel. 44495.

OLHÃO: Tourist Office: Largo da Lagoa, tel. 713936. **Info-Center** Parque Natural da Ria Formosa, Quinta de Marim, Quelfes, tel. 089-704134/5, fax: 704165.

PORTIMÃO: Tourist Office: Largo 1 de Dezembro, tel. 23695: 9:30am-7pm. **Car rental**: Locauto, Rua D. Carlos I., Tel 25038. Mova Rent a Car, Casa dos Arcos, Av. Comunidade Lusíada, tel. 83555. **Boat excursions**: Cepemar, Rua D. Carlos I, Ed. H4, Loja 10, tel. 25341, fax: 83590. **Market**: first Monday of the month. **Post office**: Rua Serpa Pinto. **Hospital**: tel. 415115. **PRAIA DA ROCHA: Tourist Office**: Rua Tomás Cabreira, tel. 22290. **Bicycle rentals**: Aventura Riders, tel. 416998.

QUARTEIRA: Tourist Office: Av. Infante Sagres, tel. 312217. **Car rental**: Rentauto, Rua Dr. José Soares, tel. 314071, fax: 315626. Budget, Av. Tomás Cabreira, tel. 25484. **SAGRES: Excursions**: Turinfo, tel. 64520. **SILVES: Tourist Office**: Rua 25 de Abril, tel. 442255.

TAVIRA: Tourist Office: Travessa da Fonte. **Motorbike rental**: Praça da República 10, tel. 325647. **VILAMOURA: Casino**: tel. 302999. **VILA REAL DE SANTO ANTONIO: Tourist Office**: Praça Marquês de Pombal, tel. 43272. **Casino**: Monte Gordo, tel. 512224.

ON THE BANKS OF THE TEJO

SANTARÉM
CROSSING THE RIBATEJO
FÁTIMA
TOMAR
CASTELO BRANCO
SOUTHEAST OF THE TEJO

The Tejo, at 624 miles (1,007 km) the longest river on the Iberian Peninsula, divides Portugal from east to west. North of its 170-mile (275 km) Portuguese segment is the mountainous region of the Beira and the Serra de Estrêla, to the south lies the Alentejo plateau. On its way from Spain the Tejo carves its way deeply into the rugged mountains along the border; in the narrow river valleys there's only room for small villages. The landscape opens up a little to the west of Abrantes to become a broad fertile alluvial plain where rice, grain, tomatoes, melons, corn, and wine are cultivated. On riverside terraces, protected from floods, larger towns have grown up at bridges and road intersections; these derive their revenue from agriculture and produce. Along the Ribatejo, the lower Tejo, proud castles and rich pasturelands characterize the landscape. Forts built by the military orders, who were granted this land in the 12th century after the *Reconquista*, tower over many of the villages and towns along this old defensive line against the Moors.

Racehorses and fighting bulls are reared on the *quintas* of the large land-

Preceding pages: A splendid view of Castelo de Vide. Left: Legion pilgrims light candles to the Madonna in Fátima.

owners. Both types of animal are employed in bullfights, which are particularly popular in this region. Of a total of 45 bull-rings, 30 are in the Ribatejo and the rest in the big cities or in coastal resorts where they provide entertainment mainly for the tourists.

SANTARÉM

Santarém is the most important town in the Ribatejo. Many Mediterranean towns boast of being built on seven hills and having roots in mythology, and Santarém is no exception. Its legends combine material from the Old Testament and the Odyssey with Roman and Lusitanian sagas. Odysseus is said to have reached Lisbon on his long voyage, where the sea nymph Calypso bore him a son. The child, named Abidid, was, at the order of his grandmother, placed in a basket and dropped in the Tejo. But countercurrents pushed the basket inland to the place where Santarém stands today; a she-wolf adopted the little boy and raised him. Years later some hunters found Abidis, and when his mother saw him she recognized him instantly. He was named king and promptly founded the town of Scallabidis (Abidis' nourishment) on his childhood stomping grounds. The name of the Roman town was *Julianum Sca-*

labitanum, and the people of Santarém are still called *escalabitanos* to this day.

Another legend is at the root of the current name of the town. The virgin Iria, or Irene, had vowed to enter a nunnery, but she was raped by her tutor. When her father found out that the girl was pregnant, he had her beheaded and thrown into the river. The corpse drifted to Santarém, which immediately adopted the name of the unlucky saint, Santa Irene.

This little town of many legends lies high above the Tejo, and its "seven hills" actually consist of one steep hillside divided up by deep ravines. A single narrow road leads from the bridge up to Santarém, but any attempt to drive through the town will end up in hopeless congestion. The best thing to do is park your car at the edge of the old town, near the **Covered Market**. The latter was built in 1927 and is decorated with bright blue painted tiles with scenes of life in the Ribatejo. A Jesuit church, **Igreja do Seminário**, stands on **Praça Sá da Bandeira**. It was built after the earthquake of 1755 on the site of one of João IV's palaces. The opulent façade has Baroque features, and inside are a splendid marble and alabaster altar, *talhas douradas* and *azujelo* paintings.

The old town of Santarém bubbles over with vitality. Besides small shops, it also has a number of very interesting churches, including, among others the **Marvila Church**, with 17th-century *azulejos* and a majestic 16th-century Manuelistic portal; the Renaissance **São Nicolas**; the **Misericórdia Church**; and the late Gothic **Graça Church** with a rose window whose dividers are made of stone. Pedro Alvares de Cabral, the seafarer who discovered Brazil, is buried in the chancel. Outside Santarém, to the northeast of the old town, is the early Gothic **Church of Santa Clara**, which boasts a wooden coffered ceiling. The interior of the **Santissimo Miracle** is in its original Renaissance style. The name

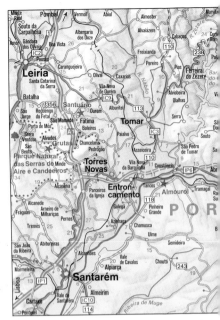

"Miracle of the Most Holy" is associated with yet another local legend, commemorated in an annual folk festival: a woman of Santarém who suffered a great deal from her husband's infidelity asked a witch for help. She was told to take a blessed host home with her from church in order to cast a spell on her unfaithful spouse. An unearthly light raised his suspicions, however, and he called in a priest. His wife confessed her heresy, and ever since then the host has been at its original location. The story doesn't say, however, whether her husband changed his wayward ways after this episode.

Santarém's archaeological museum is housed in the **Church of São João de Alporão**. This late Romanesque structure dating from the 12th century has ribbed vaulting over the chancel and a Gothic cenotaph. Opposite the church is the so-called "gourd tower," **Torre das Cabaças**, a surviving part of the old town wall where people used to hang empty gourds in order to amplify the sound of the church bells. A broad panorama

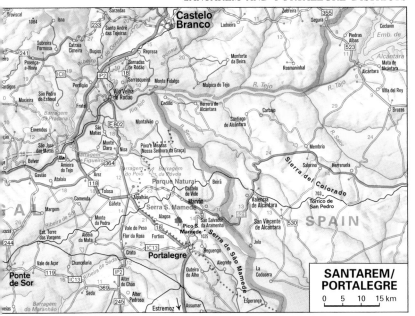

opens up from the Miradouro Portas do Sol at the end of Rua Serpa Pinto. The seemingly endless plain of the Tejo stretches all the way to the horizon, with its great tracts of cultivated fields. A little road tucked away in the southern part of town takes you down into this plain and to Caneiras, 5 miles (8 km) away.

CROSSING THE RIBATEJO

In the tiny village of **Caneiras**, the houses of the Tejo fishermen stand by the river on stone stilts to protect them from perennial floods. Living conditions are tough: the air is damp and swarming with mosquitos, and fishing from the Tejo no longer suffices to feed a family.

Cartaxo, a little ways downstream, is a small village where life centers on agriculture and wine. The local **wine museum** is located in large old storage halls; its exhibits, giving all the information you could desire on wine-making, are attractively and educationally presented. A tour of the place ends in a small bar with a sampling of the local wine, which is light and agreeable.

Palhota, not too far from Cartaxo, is another village with pile houses lying directly on the river, which you reach via an old Roman road. On the way there, stop off at the "Wine Cathedral," as the wine-cellar of the Quinta da Fonte Bela likes to be known, and at the **Solar dos Chavões**, a Renaissance country palace that now serves as the setting for an unusually good restaurant.

On the left bank of the Tejo opposite Santarém is **Alpiarça**. On the edge of town stands the **Museu dos Patudos**, lodged in the turn-of-the-century palace of the republican politician José Relvas (1858-1929). This impressive collection includes choice furniture, Arraiolos rugs, sculptures by Machado de Castro and Teixeira, and a gallery of paintings by Zubarán, Murillo, Rubens, Delacroix, Caravaggio, Memling, and Malhóa.

Further to the north is **Golegã**, a small farming community, whose church, always open to the public, boasts one of the

125

most beautiful Manuelistic portals in all of Portugal. "I am the memorial to him who built me," is inscribed on it, and it's thought today that this "him" is none other than the great Boytaca, architect of Manuel I himself. Opposite, right beside the Gothic *pelourinho*, is a museum devoted to the artist **Martin Correia**, in a building that was once a jail. The exhibition consists of more than 600 sculptures by the aged master and his students, indubitably among the most noteworthy examples of modern art in Portugal. Another museum is housed in the home of Carlos Relvas, the father of the politician from Alpiarça, and the nation's first professional photographer in the 19th century. Besides the stately furniture, visitors are presented with a host of interesting photographs and even, in Relvas's studio, the master's first photo plates.

Above: The poetic landscape on the banks of the Tejo near Cartaxo. Right: The village church of Golegã with one of the most beautiful Manuelistic portals in the country.

Further north is **Torres Novas**, a little town with a fort topped with eleven towers and enclosing a well-tended, shady park. An arm of the Almonda River serves as the moat, set off with more green spaces and a *noria*, a still-functioning Arabic water wheel. The pedestrian zone and the main square lie at the foot of the castle, as does the **Museu Carlos Reis**, devoted to the paintings of a native son (1863-1940). Also exhibited here are finds from the Roman ruins of Cardílio. The excavation site lies southeast of town, and consists of the remains of a Roman *vila* and baths that were built between the 1st and 4th centuries.

To the west is the town of **Lapa**, where, it's said, the living move around beneath the dead. This image becomes clearer when you investigate the system of man-made caves that extends beneath the church and the cemetery: innumerable galleries were carved out of the soft tufa, but no one knows why and by whom. They are said to reach all the way to the fortress of Torres Novas, but the old lady who keeps the keys to the entrance only shows visitors a few hundred meters of cave. She also enthusiastically recounts tales of the days before the caves were placed under state protection, when the village youth used them for parties and weddings.

The confluence of the quiet Zêzere and the quicker-flowing Tejo was called *Pugna Tegi* by the Romans; the name was gradually corrupted into Punhete. Since this name also means something akin to "accursed," local residents decided, in the 19th century, to change the name to Constância.

From the town's bridges, you have the best view of the attractive and well-tended town of **Constância**. Along the bank is a park with the ruins of the house where the great poet Camões lived for two years in exile because of a scandalous love affair in 1546. Just a few years later, the young king Dom Sebastião fled to Constância to escape the plague. From the river, sloping streets lead up to the church where the artist Malhoa painted an allegorical picture representing the confluence of the two rivers.

To the south, on an island in the Tejo, is **Almourol**, a castle of the Templars with twelve crenellated towers. Its reconstruction is of fairly recent date, however. As in the old days, a ferryman waits on the shore to take people over. The best view of the river with the castle in the middle is from the other bank. The road on the left bank, however, is in better shape than the one on the other side, and less trafficked to boot.

On the right bank of the Tejo lies **Abrantes**. Sole testimony to its turbulent past are the ruins of a fortress dating back to 1303. The Romans named the spot *Ourantes* after the gold (*oro*) that they used to pan out of the Tejo here. During the *Reconquista* the castle was on the front line of the Tejo and played quite an important military role. The armies of Alvares Pereira and João II met here before

heading to the battle of Aljubarrota. King João II and King Manuel I lived in the castle for some time. It later served as a barracks before being destroyed by Napoleon's troops in 1807.

The old town, with its flower-bedecked houses, extends around the castle district. Within the fortified walls stands the early Gothic **Church of Santa Maria do Castélo**, which in turn houses the **Museu Dom Lopo de Almeida**. It contains delightful *azulejos* (16th-century), Gothic sculptures, and gravestones. Other important sights in town include the **Misericórdia Church** with a Renaissance portal and paintings from the 16th century; the **Convento de São Domingo** (1492) with a two-story cloister; and the **Church of São João Baptista** with beautiful wood carvings and a coffered ceiling in Renaissance style.

With the advent of the railroad, Abrantes' riverine harbor diminished considerably in importance, but the pretty fishermen's district still exists. Today, however, it's industry and the processing of

agricultural products that provide the locals with their daily bread.

FÁTIMA

Once upon a time there was a Knight Templar, Gonçalo Hermingues, also known as "the Moor swallower," who kidnapped and then married Fátima, the beautiful daughter of the Moorish prince. She converted to Christianity and had herself christened Oureana. She died young, however, and the knight entered the monastery of Alcobaça. The towns of Fátima and Ourem were named after his beloved.

Day after day, **Fátima** welcomes thousands of pilgrims who arrive by bus, by car, on foot, or even on occasion on their knees. The significance of this pilgrimage shrine, whose fame goes well beyond Portugal's borders, cannot be under-

Above: Devotional dealership in Fátima.
Above right: Doing penance. Right: Olive
containers come in all shapes and sizes.

stated. Fátima is one of the most-visited shrines of Christendom, ranking with Lourdes and Santiago de Compostela, apart from places like Rome or certain sites in the Holy Land itself. On May 13, 1917, three shepherd children from Aljustrel, 7, 9, and 10 years of age, reported having seen a woman who "shone brighter than the sun" in an oak tree in Cova Iría near Fátima. The mysterious appeirition returned on the 13th day of each of the next five months, and in October 70,000 people witnessed a peculiar rotation of the sun. Two of the three children died early; the third died a few years ago in a monastery at an advanced age. All three are buried in the transept of the basilica of Fátima.

Work on the **Pilgrimage Church** was begun in 1928, and completed in 1953. Its ground plan was supposed to be in the shape of the Virgin Mary. The architect was the Dutchman Gerardus van Kriechen, and João de Souda did the windows. The giant square before the church and around the chapel, where the remains

of the oak tree are kept, is especially crowded on weekends and on the 12th of each month, when nighttime processions are held. Faith and superstition mingle in the masses of sick people and pilgrims from around the world. The **Wax Museum** of Fátima illustrates the tale of the shrine.

Ourem has grown up in the shadow of Fátima's crowds of visitors. Its old town lies a little further off, by the hill bearing the powerful medieval castle. The latter was originally erected by the Moors, and converted into a residential palace in the 15th century by Afonso V, a grandson of João I, as the inscription on his tomb in the Misericordia church indicates.

Southwest of Fátima lies the nature preservation area of **Serra de Aire**. The largest stalactite caves in Portugal formed in the limestone here, the **Grutas dos Moinhos Velhos**, with fascinating and bizarre formations and an underground lake. Not too far away are the caves of Alvados, Santo António, and São Mamede.

TOMAR

Tomar dates back to a Roman city founded on the left bank of the Nabão River. In the 12th century, Afonso Henriques granted the region to the Knights Templar. Grand Master Gualdim Pais had the order's main seat built on the hill above the town, and it remained there until the dissolution of the Templars in 1312. In 1356, castle and monastery were turned over to the Knights of Christ under their Grand Master, Henry the Navigator; after him, Manuel I, João III, and Filipe I all undertook various expansion projects on the complex. The town itself was seriously damaged by the French invasion of 1810, and secularization in 1834 did nothing to heal its wounds. However, a contemporary nobleman named Costa Cabral bought the monastery's southern and western wings and restored them for religious use.

The Templar castle **Convento de Cristo** is one of the most significant historical buildings in Portugal. Passing

through one of two gates, you come to the **Rotunda of the Templar Church** (begun in 1162), a 16-sided crenellated construction with a bell tower that replicates the rotunda in the Church of the Holy Sepulcher in Jerusalem. The octagonal Byzantine interior (*charola*), where the main altar is located, is luxuriously decorated with 16th-century gilded wood carvings and statues. Also ornamented in Manuelistic style, is the **Church of the Knights of Christ**, which was added on to the west side of the rotunda in the 1500s with the *charola* integrated as a chancel. This complex is accessed through the southern portal, which is decorated with statues. The Manuelistic architect Arrude managed to create an elegant link between the altar room of the rotunda and the church's nave.

Even though parts of the monastery are in ruins, the complex is impressive by

virtue of its imposing dimensions. The oldest of the cloisters is the one northeast of the Templar Church, the **Claustro do Cemitério** (Burial Cloister), decorated in *azulejos* in Mudéjar style. Its floor consists of gravestones of the deceased knights of the order. During the reign of Manuel I, the more august members of the order were granted especially opulent tombs set into the walls, such as those of Baltazar da Faria, a 16th-century Grandmaster, or Diogo da Gama, brother of the great explorer Vasco da Gama. The Philippine sacristy and the chapel of Portocarreros were extended during the reign of Filipe I. In the two-story **Claustro de Lavagem** (Cloister of the Laundry), the cistern illustrates how the monastery was originally supplied with water; the former wash-basins are now used for flowers. The smallest cloister, **Claustro de Santa Bárbara**, at the rear of the choir nave, has kept its original early Renaissance look. It provides a fine spot to examine the choir façade of the Church of the Knights of Christ, which boasts the

Oben: The Claustro do Cemitério is the oldest cloister in the Monastery of Tomar.
Right: In the Old Town of Tomar.

most famous Manuelistic window of all Portuguese architecture. It is framed in rich decorative elements, such as ship's ropes, garlands, tassels, and little towers, all surmounted by an elegant rose window. The two-story terraced cloister of João III, **Claustro dos Felipes** (1557-1562), with a 17th-century fountain, has been kept in Renaissance style, and leads to the dormitory tract. The "crows'" cloister, **Claustro dos Corvos**, leads to the monks' cells and to the refectory; the sick bay of the complex used to be located at the **Necessárias Cloister**, laymen and visitors used the **Hospedería Cloister**, and the **Micha Cloister** was where food was distributed to the poor.

Tomar itself has a delightful old town and a very lively modern section on the other bank of the Nabão. The **Church of São João Baptista** (1490), a flamboyant Gothic construction with an elegant Manuelistic portal and 16th-century paintings, stands on the main square along with a memorial statue of Gualdim Pais. The former synagogue from the 15th cen-

tury, located in a picturesque street in the Old Town, now houses the **Museu Abraham Zacuto**, a memorial to the Portuguese Jewish community.

Outside Tomar, near **Carregueiros**, is the **Aqueduct dos Pegões**, built between 1593 and 1613 during the reign of Filipe I to supply the monastery with water. An elegant construction, borne on 180 arches, it crosses the valley at a great height, carrying water over a distance of 3 miles (5 km) right into the well in the monastery garden.

CASTELO BRANCO

Beyond Abrantes, the estates of the Templars used to extend well into the Spanish Extremadura. This wide-open, harsh landscape, with its isolated olive groves, is sparsely populated. At this point, the Tejo's bed is so deep that the road can no longer follow its course. To the east, far from the other towns of the region and about 12.5 miles (20 km) north of the river, lies **Castelo Branco**,

the "White Castle," capital of Beira Baixa province. The name derives from a Templar fort that once stood here, of which only two towers remain. At the foot of these lies the old town, a charming tangle of small plazas and Manuelistic doors. The Cathedral is a Renaissance building also bearing the hallmarks of Manuelism. In Castelo Branco, Jews who had been forced to convert remained an influential force right up into the 18th century. From their ranks came doctors and intellectuals, notably the poet Ruis de Castelo Branco (16th century). His grave is in the restored Romanesque **Church of Santa Maria do Castelo**.

The main attraction of the town is the museum located in the **Palace of the Bishop of Guarda** and the Baroque park lying beyond it, the **Jardim Episcopal**. More than 300 granite statues grace the walls, balustrades, and fountains of this

Above: The kings of Portugal stand guard in the Jardim Episcopal in Castelo Branco. Right: Basket-weaving, a traditional craft.

beautiful 18th-century complex, depicting everything from allegories and signs of the Zodiac through the virtues to religious figures. All the kings of Portugal stand lined along the stairway leading to the entrance, and the gardener, with obvious relish, points out the three Spanish Felipes whose diminutive size makes them shrink beside the Portuguese kings.

SOUTHEAST OF THE TEJO

The Alentejo, a lonely region of maquis and cork oaks, begins on the south bank of the Tejo beyond Abrantes. The first town you come to is **Ponte de Sor**, named after the bridge over the Sor River built for the Roman road between Mérida and Lisbon. Beyond town is the large reservoir of Montargil, used for irrigation purposes. Water sports are also possible on the lake, and a "Hyper-camping" boasts no fewer than 3,500 lots.

Between Ponte de Sor and Portalegre lies an attractive landscape of undulating hills that is hardly settled, much less visited by tourists. Little villages with historically significant names, veiled in dreamy tranquility, lie clustered around mighty old fortresses.

The road from Ponte de Sor to Alter do Chão follows the old Roman road, crossing another Roman bridge behind Seda. The main square of **Alter do Chão** is framed by the Gothic residential castle of Pedro I and the Baroque (18th century) Alamo Palace with its beautiful park, the Jardim de Buxo. The palace is used nowadays as a cultural center. A host of other Baroque palaces, fountains, and churches testify to the fact that this market town in the valley stole the thunder of its neighbor, Alter Pedroso up in the hills, once the period of great wars ended. **Alter Pedroso** is a quaint old village lying at the foot of a ruined fortress, and offering a splendid view into the valley. North of Alter do Chão is **Coudelaria de Alter**, a stud farm founded in 1748 by João V. It began with 40 Andalusian mares and later bred its own Lusitanian race. One of these noble horses modelled for the equestrian statue of José I in Lisbon. You can visit the farm daily, and on April 24 there's the annual horse market.

The name **Crato** has always been present in Portuguese history. After being conquered by Afonso Henriques, the town was turned over to the Knights of St. John, who established their own priory here. All that remains of the palace of the prior, who had one of the most influential positions in the whole country, is a pretty, elegant Renaissance balcony. Otherwise, the town has a number of noble estates, a crenellated tower and a defensive wall. The **Monastery of Flor da Rosa** was built in 1356 as the headquarters of the Order; it has recently been turned into a luxurious Pousada.

For walkers, there are plenty of long, pleasant hikes in the area which lead to some of the region's 40-odd dolmens and megaliths. Nearby **Serra de São Mamede**, with the touristic triangle of

Portalegre, Castelo de Vide, and Marvão, also has its share of prehistoric sites and hiking trails. The range itself is a 30,000-hectare national park, whose highest point is the Pico São Mamede (3,352 feet/1,025 m). The last clouds ferried by the west wind usually rain themselves out here, so the streams and the reservoir of Apertura flow with fresh water.

Portalegre

Portalegre, known to the Romans as *Portus Alecer*, was converted into a fortress by Dom Dinis owing to its proximity to the border. Its Golden Age began in the 16th century after it was turned over to the Avis Order; testimony to this today are its many palaces. In the following century it developed into one of the nation's most important centers for textiles. The rug and tapestry manufacture founded by the Marquis de Pombal still exists to this day.

In the 18th century the seat of the diocese was moved from Castelo Branco

to Portalegre. The **Cathedral** (Sé), a proud Renaissance structure, crowns the hill facing the fort. The manneristic altars inside are among its most interesting features. Opposite the church, in the former monastery, the **Museu Municipal** has an impressive collection of religious art that was salvaged from churches and monasteries after secularization. Among the finest examples is a 15th-century *Pietà*, furniture, and a series of peculiar private collections such as one of more than 800 figurines of St. Anthony. The house of the writer José Regio, who died in 1969, is also a museum. Regio's novel *A Casa Velha* draws a fairly clear picture of society and its workings in Portalegre.

Other important monuments in town are the **Palácio Amarelo**, with 17th-century wrought-iron grates over its windows, the **Convento de Santa Clara**, with its very attractive cloister, and the

former **Monastery of São Bernardo** (1518), which now houses a police school. The chapel, where one finds the oversized 16th-century tomb of the founding bishop, Jorge de Melo, is open to the public. It is one of the last works of Nicolas de Chanterène.

The **old town** of Portalegre stretches along narrow streets between two hills. Just below the fortress is the erstwhile *mouraria*, the Moorish quarter, a labyrinth of cramped alleys and houses with pretty inner courtyards. Modern Portalegre lies a little further below, with **Avenida da Liberdade**, at its center, serving at once as a main thoroughfare and a park. In its middle is a banana tree more than 150 years old; its crown is some 325 feet (100 m) in diamter.

Castelo de Vide and Marvão

A short drive to the north along the foot of the Serra de São Mamede takes you to **Castelo de Vide**. The best view of the town, extending over its two hills,

Above: Mixing business and pleasure – crafts and local gossip. Right: The fountain in the Juderia of Castelo de Vide.

is from the Penha pilgrimage church. The town was simply called Vide until Dom Dinis had a castle built there to mark the signing of his marriage contract to Isabel of Aragón. It was incorporated into the Order of the Knights of Christ. Within the defensive walls, you can still see the old Gothic settlement with its two churches. The houses are all inhabited and give a good feeling of what life must have been like in the Middle Ages in this kind of castle quarter. The other communities around the São Tiago and São João churches arose in medieval times *extramuros*, or outside the city walls. When, in 1492, Jewish families fled Spain and settled in the border areas, the *juderia* sprang up, a district of narrow streets, full of Gothic portals, centered around the main square with the Fonte da Vila, the quarter's fountain. Halfway up to the fortress is the restored **Synagogue**. In the 15th century, this two-story building had space for a Torah school and religious services. In the 16th century, after the Jews were expelled from Portugal,

three curious grain silos were hewn into the floor of the lower storey.

Today's town center came into being in the 16th century as an extension of two large plazas separated by the Town Hall and the Baroque **Church of Santa Maria da Devesa**. The **Fortress of São Roque** was built in the 18th century, and the entire place was surrounded by a defensive wall. Today, Castelo de Vide is one of the best-preserved medieval towns in all of Portugal, and has a thermal spa to boot. Nearby are the neolithic necropolises of Santo Amarinho and Boa Morte, and the **Megalith Park of Coureleiros**, where a signposted trail leads visitors past the most important sights.

Marvão stands on an 2,830-foot (865 m) summit; Dom Dinis had this fortress built in the 13th century to defend against possible incursions by the Spanish. This little village tucked into the old defensive walls has a wonderful view of the region, romantic streets, flower-bedecked houses, a Pousada, and several restaurants welcoming weary hikers.

135

THE RIBATEJO
Accommodations

ABRANTES (041): *LUXURY:* **Turismo**, Largo de Santo António, tel. 21261, fax: 25218. **Abrantur**, Pego, E.N. nach Castelo Branco, tel. 93464. *MODERATE:* **Lírios**, Praça Barão da Batalha 31, tel. 22142. *BUDGET:* **Abrantes**, Rua D. Miguel de Almeida 17, tel.22119. **Aliança**, Rua Cidade Caldas da Raínha 50, tel. 22348. *CAMPING:* **Castelo de Bode**, tel. 992244. *TURISMO RURAL:* **Quinta dos Vales**, Tramagal, tel. 97363. **Monte Velho**, Concavada, tel. 92472.

CASTELO BRANCO (072): *LUXURY:* **Rainha Amelia**, Rua de Santiago 15, tel. 326315, fax: 326390. **Colina do Castelo**, Rua da Piscina, tel. 329856, fax: 329759. *MODERATE:* **Arraiana**, Av. 1 de Maio 18, tel. 21634, fax: 338814. **Caravela**, Rua do Saibreiro 24, tel. 23939. *BUDGET:* **Telhanense**, Rua das Damas 618, Tel 331545. **Ideal**, Av. Gen. Delgado 23, tel. 25604. *CAMPING:* **Municipal**, E.N. 18, tel. 21615.

CASTELO DE VIDE (045): *MODERATE:* **Garcia d'Orta**, Estr. de São Vicente. tel. 90621, Fax 90643. **Casa do Parque**, Av. de Aramenha 37, tel. 91250. **Isabelinha**, Largo do Paço Novo, tel. 91896. *TURISMO RURAL:* **Quinta da Bela Vista**, Póvoa e Meadas, tel. 98125, fax: 98132. **Casa da Meada**, Póvoa e Meadas, tel. 98116.

CONSTÂNCIA (049): *LUXURY:* **O Palacio**, tel. 99224. *MODERATE:* **João Chagas**, Rua João Chagas, tel. 99403, fax: 99378. *TURISMO RURAL:* **Quinta de Santa Bárbara**, tel. 99214. Former cloister. **Casa O Palacio**, tel. 99224.

CRATO: *TURISMO RURAL:* **Palacete Flor da Rosa**, Rua da Cruz 19, tel. 97451.

GOLEGÃ (049): *TURISMO RURAL:* **Casa da Azinhaga**, Rua da Misericórdia 26, Azinhaga, tel. 95146. **Casa de Santo António**, Rua Nova de Santo António, Azinhaga, tel. 95162.

FÁTIMA (049): *LUXURY:* **Tres Pastorinhos**, Rua João Paulo II, Tel/fax: 532429. *MODERATE:* **Dom Gonçalo**, Rua Jacinta Marto 100, tel. 52262. **Estrêla de Fátima**, Rua C. Formigão, tel. 51150.

MARVÃO (045): *LUXURY:* **Pousada de Santa María**, Rua 24 de Janeiro 7, tel. 93201, fax: 93202. *MODERATE:* **Sever**, Portagem, tel. 93318. **Casa Dom Dinís**, Rua Dr. Matos Magalhães, tel. 93236. *TURISMO RURAL:* **Quinta Curral da Nora**, Prado – Escusa, tel. 93558.

PONTE DO SOR (042): *MODERATE:* **Barragem**, Montargil, E.N. 2, tel. 94175, fax: 94225. *BUDGET:* **A Ponte**, R. B. Monteiro 3, tel. 22166.

PORTALEGRE (045): *LUXURY:* **D. João III**, Av. da Liberdade, tel. 330192, fax: 330444. **Quinta da Saúde**, Estr. Nac. 246-2, tel.22324. *MODERATE:* **Mansão Alto Alentejo**, tel. 22290. S.

Pedro, Rua da Mouraria 14, tel. 21129. *BUDGET:* **Nova**, tel. 21605. *CAMPING:* **Quinta da Saúde**, tel. 22848. *TURISMO RURAL:* **Quinta da Fonte Fría**, Fonte Fría-Serra, tel. 27575. **Quinta das Varandas**, Serra de São Mamede, tel. 28883.

TORRES NOVAS (049): *MODERATE:* **Cavaleiros**, Praça 5 de Outubro, tel. 812420, fax: 812052. **Solar São José**, Av. Dr. João Martins de Azevedo, tel. 22362. *BUDGET:* **Rui**, Tv. do Poço, tel. 24715. *TURISMO RURAL:* **Horta do Avô**, Vila do Paço, Zoudos, tel. 91116.

SANTARÉM (043): *LUXURY:* **Abidis**, Rua Guilherme de Azevedo 4, tel. 22017. *MODERATE:* **Alfageme**, Av. Bernardo Santareno 38, tel. 370870, fax: 370850. **Jardim**, Rua Florbela Espanca 1, tel. 20305, fax: 20305. **O Beirante**, Rua A. Herculano 5, tel. 22547. *BUDGET:* **Muralha**, Rua P. Canavarro 12, tel. 22399. *TURISMO RURAL:* **Casa da Pedra**, Rua das Pedras Negras 16, tel. 769754. **Quinta da Sobreira**, Vale de Figueira, tel. 420221. Swimming pool. **Quinta de Vale de Lobos**, Azóia de Baixo, tel. 429264. fax: 429313. **Casa dos Cedros**, Azóia de Cima, tel. 800986. Bicycles.

TOMAR (049): *LUXURY:* **Los Templários**, Largo Cândido dos Reis 1, tel. 321730, fax: 322191. **Santa Iria**, Parque do Mouchão, tel. 313326, fax: 321082. **Pousada de São Pedro**, Castelo de Bode, tel. 381159, fax: 322191. *MODERATE:* **Cavaleiros de Cristo**, Rua A. Herculano 7, tel. 321203, fax: 321192. **Sinagoga**, Rua Gil de Avô 31, tel. 316783, fax: 322196. *BUDGET:* **Luz**, Rua Serpa Pinto 144, tel. 312317. **Bomjardim**, Praceta Santo André, tel. 313195. *CAMPING:* **Poço Redondo**, tel. 376421, tel: 312265. **Municipal**, tel. 322607, fax: 321026. *TURISMO RURAL:* **Casa da Avõ Genoveva**, Rua 25 de Abril 16, tel. 92219. **Quinta da Anunciada Velha**, Cem Soldos, tel. 312648, fax: 321362. **Quinta do Valle**, Santa Cita, tel. 381941, fax: 381165. **Quinta do Triviscal**, Alverangel, tel. 371318. **Quinta de São Pedro**, São Pedro de Tomar, tel. 382333.

Restaurants / Cafés

ABRANTES: **Nora**, Concavada, E.N. 118, tel. 92272, **O Pelicano**, Rua Na. Senhora da Conceição 1, tel. 22317. **A Prensa**, Martinchel, tel. 99152. **Lacustre**, Martinchel, tel. 99151. **Casa do Pastor**, Cabeça Mós-Sardoal, tel. 95255. **Cantinho do Caçador**, Cana Verde-Alfarrarede, tel. 23587.

ALMEIRIM: **Páteo D'Al-Meirim**, Rua das Cancelas 10, tel. 52836. **Retiro do Campino**, Largo da Praça de Touros 1, tel. 52528.

CARTAXO: **Solar dos Chavões**, tel. 770006,

fax:770807 (only weekends). **Marisqueria Rosa de Ouro**, Rua Luís de Camões 42, tel. 779063. **CASTELO BRANCO**: **Praça Velha**, Lg. Luís de Camões, tel. 328640. **Zé dos Cachopos**, Av. General Delgado. **O Convento**, Rua da Graça, tel. 329461. **A Bohemia**, Av. 1 de Mayo 13, tel. 24878. **Patrimonio Bar**, Lg. Luis de Camoês. **CASTELO DE VIDE**: **Dom Pedro V**, Praça D. Pedro V, tel. 91236. **O Canapé**, Sítio do Canapé, tel. 90108. **CONSTÂNCIA**: **Casa de Pasto Odete**, Pr. A. Herculano, tel. 99109. **O Trovador**, Rua da Misericórdia 2, tel. 99440. **Os Falcões**, Rua L. de Camões, tel. 99099. **Entre Ríos**, Montalvo, tel. 99222. **FÁTIMA**: **Grelha**, Rua Jacinta Marto 76. **Dom Gonçalo**, Rua Jacinta Marto 100. **PORTALEGRE**: **O Escondidinho**, Trav. Cruzes 1, tel. 22728. **Poeiras**, Praça República 13, tel. 21862. **Painel**, Av. Liberdade 61, tel. 21039. **O Retiro**, Estrada Penha, Tel. 24398. **SANTARÉM**: **O Mal Cozinhado**, Campo Emilio Infante da Cámara, tel. 23584. **O Castiço**, Campo da Feira, tel. 332709. With fados and folkloristic program. **Café Central**, Rua Guilherme de Azevedo 32, tel. 22303. **O Ilhéu**, Rua do Comércio 46, tel. 65204. **Retiro do Zé Pedro**, Rua do Mercado 12, tel. 25353. **Vitória**, Rua Visconde de Santarém 21, tel. 22573. **Rafael**, Rua 1. Dez. 3, tel. 26517. **Portas do Sol**, Jardim das Portas do Sol, tel. 29520. Terrace with a pretty garden. **TOMAR**: **Bela Vista**, Fonte do Choupo 6, tel. 312294. **Beira Río**, Rua A. Herculano, 1/3, tel. 312806.

Sights / Museums

ABRANTES: **Museu do Castelo**: 10am-12:30pm and 2pm-5:30pm, closed Saturdays. **ALPIARÇA**: Casa dos Patudos: Wed-Sun 10am-12:30pm and 2pm-5pm. **ALTER DO CHÃO**: **Castelo**, Tue-Sun, 9am-1pm and 2pm-6pm, closed Mondays. **Coudelaria de Alter**: 9:30am-midday and 2pm-4:30pm. **CARTAXO**: **Museu Rural e do Vinho**, Tue-Fri 10:30am-12:30pm and 3pm-5:30pm, closed Mon. **CASTELO BRANCO**: **Jardim do Paço Episcopal**: 9am until sundown, closed Mon. Museum currently being renovated. **Museu Etnográfico**: 9am-12:30pm and 2:30pm-5:30pm, closed Mon. **CASTELO DE VIDE**: **Synagoge**, **fortress**: daily 9am-5:30pm. **CRATO**: **Museu Municipal**: 9am-12:30pm and 2pm-5pm. **GOLEGÃ**: **Museu Martins Correia** 9am-12:30pm and 2:30pm-5pm, closed Mondays. **Museu Carlos Relvas**: 11am-12:30pm and 3pm-6pm, Sun 3pm-7pm, closed Mon

FÁTIMA: **Museu das Aparições**: May-Oct 9am-8pm, Nov-Apr 9am-6pm. **Stalagtite caves of Santo António**, **Alvados** and **Mira de Aire**: Oct.Mar: 9am-6pm, Apr-May 9am-7pm, Jun and Sept 9am-8pm, July and Aug 9am-9pm. **PORTALEGRE**: **Casa Museu José Regio**: 10am-12:30pm and 2pm-5pm. **Museu Municipal**: 10am-12:30pm and 2pm-5:30pm. **TORRES NOVAS**: **Burg**: 8am-5pm, im Sommer 9am-6pm. **Roman ruins Vila Cardílio**: always open. **Artificial caves of Lapas**: key in house Nr. 16. **Museu Carlos Reis**: Largo do Salvador, 10am-12:30pm and 2pm-5:30pm, closed Mondays. **SANTARÉM**: Churches of **Santa Clara**, **Marvila**, **São Nicolas**, **Misericórdia**, **Graça** and Archeol. Museum in S. **J. de Aporão**: 9am-12:30pm and 2pm-5:30pm, closed Mon and holidays. **TOMAR**: **Christ the Knight Monastery**: 9:30am-12:30pm and 2pm-5pm, in summer until 6pm. **Museum Luso-Hebraico / Synagoge Abraham Zacuto**, Rua Dr. J. Jacinto 73, 9am-1pm and 2pm-6pm, closed Mondays.

Tourist information

ABRANTES: **Tourist Office**: Lg. 1 de Maio, tel. 22555, Mon and Fri: 9am-6:30pm; Tue-Thu: 8.30am-8pm, Sat-Sun 9:30am-12:30pm and 2pm-5:30pm. **ALTER DO CHÃO**: **Tourist Office**: Palácio do Alamo, tel. 62053, 10am-12:30pm and 2pm-6:30pm. **CASTELO BRANCO**: **Tourist Office**: Rua do Passeio Público, tel. 21002. **Post**: Largo da Sé. **CASTELO DE VIDE**: **Tourist Office**: Rua Bartolomeu A. da Santa 81/3, tel. 91361, 9am-12:30pm and 2pm-5:30pm, summer until 7pm. **CONSTÂNCIA**: **Tourist Office**: 9am-12:30pm and 2:30pm-5:30pm, closed weekends. **ENTROCAMENTO**: **Tourist Office**: Av, Dr. José Neves, tel. 719229. **FÁTIMA**: **Tourist Office**: Av. D. José Alves Correia da Silva, tel. 531139. **MARVÃO**: **Tourist Office**: R. Dr. António Matos, tel. 93226. **PORTALEGRE**: **Tourist Office**: Estrada de Santana 25, tel.21815, fax:24053. **SANTARÉM**: **Tourist Office**: R. Capelo e Ivens 63, tel. 391512. Tue-Fri: 9am-7pm. Sat, Sun, Mon and holidays: 9am-12:30pm and 2pm-6pm. **TOMAR**: **Tourist Office**: Av. Cándido Madureira, tel. 313237, Mon-Fri 9:30am-12:30pm and 2pm-6pm, Sat and Sun 10am-1pm and 3pm-6pm. **TORRES NOVAS**: **Tourist Office**: Largo dos Combatentes, tel. 24910, Mon-Fri 9:30am-12:30pm and 2:30pm-5:30pm, Sat 10am-12:30pm, closed Sundays.

COSTA DA PRATA
THE SILVER COAST

RIA DE AVEIRO

COIMBRA

THE SOUTHERN SILVER COAST

ALCOBAÇA

BATALHA

The Costa da Prata, or Silver Coast, extends some 120 miles (200 km) between Cape Carvoeiro and Porto. Broad beaches of fine white sand backed by long chains of sparsely-vegetated dunes face the west without the slightest protection. The Atlantic breakers rolling into shore are often accompanied by dangerous currents. Vacationers here seek refuge from the merciless winds and the burning sun in the small striped cabanas that stand in long lines along the beach, a feature typical of Atlantic resorts.

Inland consists, pine forests alternate with other delightful landscapes such as the Ria de Aveiro, the National Park of Buçaco, or the State Forests of Leira. The traditional trades of fishing and salt production have long since been overtaken by the lucrative tourist trade; but this has remained enough under control that you can still find solitary stretches of beach without too much trouble.

You can find history and culture here, as wel. Venerable Coimbra is the heart and soul of the region; and to the south are Alcobaça and Batalha, two of the most important medieval monasteries of Portugal.

Preceding pages: An audience watches the nets being hauled in (Torreira). Left: Colorful moliçeiros in the lagoon by Aveiro.

RIA DE AVEIRO

The Ria de Aveiro is a labyrinth of water courses and marshlands separated from the sea by a 30-mile (50 km) spit of land. Six rivers empty into this lagoon. Wherever there's not actually water, there's a salina or a rice paddy. These shallow waters provide the ideal habitat for *moliço*, a kind of algae that the locals use as fertilizer. They harvest it in long flat-bottomed, brightly-painted boats known as *moliçeiros*. The entire area is protected as a habitat for migratory birds.

The most important town in the Ria is **Aveiro**, Portugal's second-largest fishing port after Matosinhos. In the 10th century, the land here was still underwater, but Mumadona, the woman who founded Guimarães, already mentioned the salinas of Aveiro in her will. In the 14th century, Pedro I ordered the settlement to be surrounded by a defensive wall, and granted it the rights to hold an annual market that is still held to this day every March. Aveiro's good fortunes ended abruptly in 1685 when a fierce storm dammed up the entrance to the harbor. During the French occupation more than a century later, French commander Oudinot had the passage to the ocean cleared for business and shored up with broken stones from the old city wall. The salinas around Aveiro are still in operation, but the main sources of income now are tourism, fishing, and the extraction of clay from the Ria. The latter is processed into tiles for floors and walls in the industrial suburb of Cacia, where another main industry is the drying and canning of cod.

Several canals pass through Aveiro. On one side of the main canal is the **Praça Humberto Delgado**, lined with beautiful Art Nouveau façades. Behind it lie the streets of the old fishermenn's quarter, which extends to the São Roque Canal; this district is the center of Aveiro's night life. The best restaurants are around **Largo do Mercado**, the market square. A wide avenue connects it to the train station, which is luxuriously decorated with tile paintings by Colaço.

The older part of town is on the other side of the canal. The two main sights here are the **Catedral de São Domingo**, a Gothic edifice with a Baroque façade, and the **Convento de Jesús**, a monastery founded in the 15th century which has served as the City Museum since 1911. The portrait of St. Johanna by Nuno Gonçalves that hangs here warrants particular attention. Johanna was the daughter of Afonso V, and is the patron saint of Aveiro. She was a famous beauty, and it caused quite a stir when she opted to enter the convent rather than marry Henry IV of Castile. She died here in 1480. Her sarcophagus, in a Baroque tomb by João Antunes, is located in the church chancel, where painted tiles illustrate scenes from her life.

In summer, you can take a five-hour boat excursion from Aveiro to the villages on the northern sandbank that divides the Ria from the sea: Gafanha, Barra, São Jacinto, and Torreira. The sandbank, some 1,635 feet (500 m) wide and 12.5 miles (20 km) long, forms a unique double beach. On the inland side, the calm, shallow, warm waters are particularly suitable for swimming with small children. Between the two seams of sand are the dunes of São Jacinto, a nature preservation area. The road that leads out to the spit of land is lined with restaurants, campgrounds, forests with picnic spots, and a Pousada. On summer weekends, of course, the road is hopelessly congested with traffic.

Sleepier and quieter are the villages on the other side of the Ria. In **Bico**, the harbor of **Murtosa**, fishermen and *moliçeiros* still work in relative solitude. An ethnographical museum in town has an exhibition describing the traditions and tribulations of these professions.

At the northernmost end of the Ria lies **Ovar**, which is surrounded by several beaches: Furadouro, Areinho, and Monte Branco. The little town is famous for its carnival festivities and its Easter processions. The parish church is tiled right up to the ceiling, and the local museum has a noteworthy collection of African art. In the **São Francisco Monastery**, there's a display of Baroque ecclesiastical treasures.

Nearby is the castle complex of **Santa Maria da Feira**, one of the most important in Portugal. In the Middle Ages, a fortress was built here on the foundations of a Roman temple; and here, in 1127, the allies in the Battle of São Mamede congregated to found the nation of Portugal. The mighty wall and ceremonial tower were added in the 14th century.

Further inland lies **Arouca**, which is surrounded by hills. Its famous sight is the **Cisterciean Monastery of São Pedro**. The building has undergone numerous facelifts over the centuries. It has many interesting features, including a museum with sacred art and Portuguese paintings, the choir stalls of the church, and ornately carved *talha dourada* altars. An urn of ebony and silver contains the remains of St. Mafalda, daughter of Sancho I, who died in the monastery in 1252.

One long branch of the Ria extends southwards from Aveiro to Mira. A narrow road leads through pine and euca-

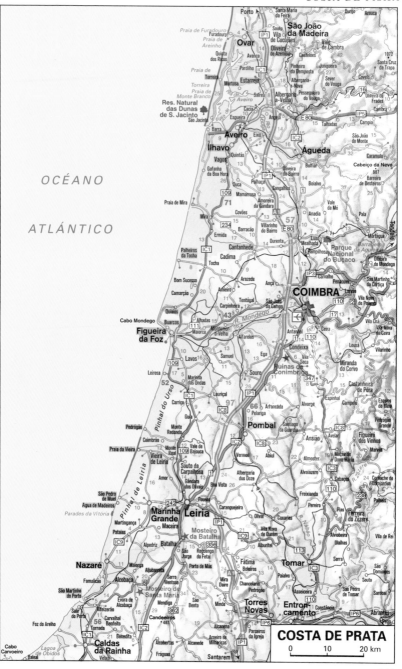

COSTA DE PRATA

0   10   20 km

lyptus forests, with a number of sandy paths which will bring you to solitary spots even in high tourist season.

Ílhavo, the region's largest town, and the home port of many fishermen and merchant mariners, boasts a handsome 18th-century church and a shipping museum that has been open since 1937. One of its sections is devoted to crystal and porcelain from the long-standing local manufacture of Vista Alegre.

In days of yore, little fishing settlements known as *gafanhas* established themselves in the dunes south of Ílhavo. They grew into the villages we see today. **Vagos** still had a port in the Middle Ages; today, it is surrounded by fertile alluvial plains. The most important local event is the annual pilgrimage on August 15 to a chapel standing in the middle of a pine forest. The superb beach of **Mira** is one

Above: Boats are still pulled up onto the shore with oxen along the Silver Coast (Mira). Right: The old Palace of Buçaco is today a luxury hotel.

of the region's most-frequented. The town's reputation as a fishing village is, however, a thing of the distant past. Along the coastal promenade are only a few of the wooden sheds, *palheiros,* that fishermen used for protection, for their animals, or to store equipment.

A road – in poor condition, but generally empty of traffic – leads south from Mira through more pine and eucalyptus groves. If you go by the inland route, you'll traverse the wine region of La Bairrada. The **Pousada de Santo Antonio**, north of Agueda, has a great view of the vineyards in the Vouga Valley.

Buçaco

The **National Park of Buçaco**, which begins near the spa of **Luso**, lies in a sylvan mountainscape with wonderful old trees. From the summit of the Cruz Alta (1,795 feet/549 meters), you can see the ocean on a clear day. The forest once belonged to the bishop of Coimbra, who gave it to the Carmelites in 1628.

The monks built a monastery and planted an exotic garden with more than 1,000 species from South America, Crete, Goa, Italy, and Lebanon. Delightful paths meander through the park, leading off to chapels and small fountains. In 1887, the monastery was torn down to make way for the palace that still stands today. Only the church was spared.

The **Palace** was the last architectural undertaking of the Bragança Dynasty. It was supposed to serve as a summer residence for Carlos I, who commissioned the Italian Luigi Manini to draw up the plans. Some of the best Portuguese painters were also called in on the job, Carlos dos Reis, João Vaz, and Veloso Salgado. Colaço created the famous tile paintings. This eclectic construction contains virtually all the major stylistic elements from the past, Byzantine, Romanesque, Manuelistic, and even Classical. Today, the palace is a luxury hotel, exuding a hint of the opulent decadence characteristic of the late 19th century.

COIMBRA

Coimbra, the old university town on the Mondego River, was once a small Roman community known as *Aeminium*. Its function was to defend the ford over the river which connected the road from Braga to Lisbon. In the 5th century, after the Swabians leveled the Roman town of Conímbriga 10.5 miles (17 km) further south, *Aeminium* took over the other town's name, bishopric, and significance.

Under the Visigoths, Coimbra minted its own coins. In 716, the Moors conquered the area, and held it until the 11th century. In 1064, after Coimbra had been passed from hand to hand for decades, Count Henry finally took over. His son, Afonso Henriques, made Coimbra the epicenter of his military campaigns, and declared it the capital of his self-proclaimed kingdom. It remained the capital of the Burgundian Dynasty and the seat of the royal court until the Avis Dynasty took power in 1385.

The heart of the lower city is the **Largo da Portagem**, next to the Santa Clara Bridge. The square is lined with hotels, restaurants and sidewalk cafés. A pedestrian street leads to **Praço do Comércio** where market was held in the Middle Ages. Surrounded by tall houses and the Romanesque **Church of São Tiago**, it is probably the most atmospheric square in Coimbra. The adjoining streets have kept up the tradition and ambience of an old market town, with small, old-fashioned shops, little bars, and simple but good restaurants.

The Augustine monastery **Convento de Santa Cruz**, consecrated in 1131 and today the artistic and historic nucleus of the town, once functioned as the first theological seminary of the country. The monastery's church, completed in 1131, stands in the southern wing of the complex. 400 years after its completion, it received a new Manuelistic façade decorated with numerous sculptures – the

work of Boytaca and Diego de Castilho – and the two-story **Claustro de Silêncio** (Silent Cloister). In the center of the cloister, which is decorated with bas-reliefs, is a splendid Renaissance fountain. During the reign of Manuel I, a sculpture school opened here that produced several great artists, notably Chanteréne, who designed the royal tombs of Afonso Henriques and Sancho I in the monastery church. João III continued extending the building and added the cloister **Jardim da Manga**, with a small domed construction in which there are four round chapels. These days, the monastery is used by the town administration.

The **Arco de Almedina** (in Arabic *al medina* means city), a gateway through the medieval city wall, leads to the steep and narrow streets of the upper city. Atop the first hill is the **Old Cathedral** (Sé Velha), a Romanesque fortified church built around 1160. Its northern portal, the

Porta Especiosa, was added in the 16th century. Inside, its three aisles are surmounted by barrel vaults. The main altar is in Flemish style. In the Gothic cloister, you can see the tomb of the first Christian conqueror of Coimbra, Sisnando.

Behind Sé Velha, the mountain continues up to its peak. Located here are the University; the **New Cathedral** (Sé Nova) built in the 16th and 17th centuries with a Baroque façade, which has functioned as Cathedral since 1772; the Romanesque **Church of São Salvador**; and the **Museu Nacional del Machado de Castro**. The latter is situated in the former bishop's palace, which was revamped in the 16th century. The original building was erected in the 12th century over the Roman *porticus*, which can still be seen on the ground floor. The exhibitions include Roman, Visigoth, and Arabic finds, as well as Portuguese paintings, porcelain, sacred art and crèches by Machado de Castro. From an elegant loggia on the second floor, you have a splendid view over the roofs of the Old Town.

Above: View of the upper city of Coimbra, with the old University, from Rio Mondego.

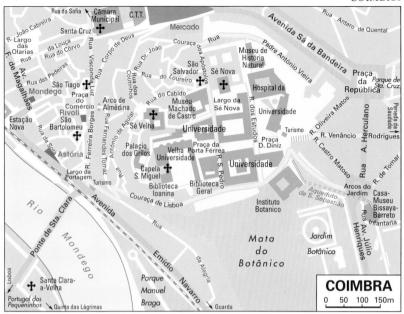

Since the 16th century, Coimbra has basked in its reputation as the country's leading center of higher learning; it was, in fact, the only one until 1911. In 1537, João III moved the University from Lisbon (where Dom Dinis had founded it in the 13th century) to Coimbra, and put one wing of his castle at its disposal. In 1555, he entrusted the Jesuits with the curriculum. Renovated in the 17th and 18th centuries, the **Old University** remains an impressive building for its ample size. The manneristic **Porta Férea** (the "Iron Gate," built in 1634), with the University's coat-of-arms embedded into the paving stones before it, leads into the huge courtyard. An elegant free-standing stairway leads up to the **Aula Magna**, the Capelos Hall. This was originally the royal throne room, and the portraits of all the Portuguese kings hang here. Off to the side, the slener, 111-foot (34 m) Baroque belltower built in 1733 stands over the ensemble. It is the highest point in town, and can be seen from all over.

On the east side of the plaza is an ob-

servatory, and to the west a Manuelistic portal forms the entrance to the **University Church of São Miguel** (16th century), which houses a small museum of religious art. Its neighbor is the most impressive building of the complex, the **Biblioteca Ioanina** (1716-1723), one of the most splendid libraries in the world. It was constructed during the reign of João V in Baroque style and was patterned on the Court Library in Vienna. It is lavishly decorated with ceiling and wall frescoes, and furnished with expensive inlaid furniture. About 150,000 old books, the oldest of which dates from the 13th century, are kept here, and are accessible to students to this day.

Needless to say, the presence of 20,000 students in Coimbra leaves an indelible mark on the city. Of course, they no longer wear the black outfits they used to sport in the old days, but streets, bars, cafés, and restaurants always seem filled with joyful young people. Graduation ceremonies are held every year in May with the *Queima das Fitas*, a ritual burn-

ing of the colored ribbons on the students' costumes and briefcases which originally denoted different departments. What used to be a fairly short event is now a festival lasting several days. Colleges that still maintain their old traditional feeling are on **Rua da Sofia**, which leads out of the lower city. Here, too, are the churches Carmo, Graça, São Pedro, and Santa Justa, all built during the 16th and 17th centuries and all – except for Santa Justa – originally college churches.

Near the University is the 16th-century **aqueduct**, built by Felipe Terzi, that once supplied the town with water. Next to it lies the **Botanical Garden**, laid out by the Marquis de Pombal in the 18th century. Another place worth dropping in to see is **Santa Cruz Park**, which extends behind the hill bearing the Old Town. It has a beautiful, romantic fountain decorated with tiles. A little further

Above: The Arco de Almedina leads to the upper city of Coimbra. Right: Romantic Gothic vaulting in the Café Santa Cruz.

on, the rise of **Penedo da Saudade** has long been a favorite haunt of students with a leaning toward melancholic poetic inspiration; their verses are engraved in stone in the little park. Fado music is also part and parcel of Coimbra, province of the students and their nocturnal haunts. Nowadays, this bittersweet music has become a tourist attraction served up in special establishments. Genuine fado, according to the experts, can only be heard in Lisbon.

On the left bank of the Montego, right beside the bridge, stands the former monastery church of **Santa Clara-a-Velha**, which was founded in 1286 and recently restored. St. Isabel, the wife of King Dom Dinis, was buried here in 1336. After a flood destroyed much of it, a new Convent of the Poor Clares, **Santa Clara-a-Nova**, was erected a little higher up the mountain in 1612. It commands a wonderful view over the river and the concatenated houses of Coimbra's old city.

This bank of the river is also where one finds the "Miniland" **Portugal dos**

Pequeninhos, where all the nation's most important architectural monuments have been rebuilt on a small scale. Beyond it, somewhat hidden from sight, is the **Quinta das Lágrimas**, the Estate of Tears, where Ines de Castro was murdered on orders of Afonso IV. It is a romantic park, with artificial "ruins" (a popular conceit of the period); at its "Love Fountain," *Fonte dos Amores*, the Lusiades of Camões document the more romantic sides of popular legend.

Around Coimbra

Through the picturesque town of **Penacova**, which looks down from its rise of land over the Mondego Valley, you come into the secluded valley itself and to the monastery of **Lorvão**, which the bishop of Coimbra founded in the 6th century to serve as the cultural nucleus of the region. Princess Theresa, the daughter of Sancho I (13th century) retired to this secluded place after her marriage to Alfonso IX of Leon had been an-

nulled by the Pope. Her mortal remains, and those of her sister Sancha, are in two silver shrines on the altar of the monastery church. The monastery itself has become a psychiatric institution and cannot be visited.

Downstream from Coimbra, the Mondego River leaves its narrow, forested valley and flows deliberately through a wide irrigated plain. The imposing silhouette of **Montemor-o-Velho** rises from the rice paddies and corn fields. Up to 6,000 people with their belongings could seek refuge in the fortress during the Middle Ages. It had four hospitals and four monasteries. Only a single church remains, however: **Santa Maria de Alcáçova**, redone in Manuelistic style in the 16th century. The fort itself provides the dramatic backdrop for an open-air theater festival held each summer. Farther to the south, near the town of **Condeixa**, is the excavation site of **Conímbriga**. The old Roman settlement was destroyed by the Swabians in 486, and was completely forgotten until 1930, the year in which digging began. Some of Portugal's most important and well-preserved ruins came to light: patrician houses with fine mosaics, baths, the remains of a forum, an inn, and the network of streets. A museum was established to display some of the finds and explain the workings of the Roman town, which is still not completely excavated.

SOUTHERN COSTA DE PRATA

One of the most popular vacation spots in Portugal is the long sandy bay between Buarcos and **Figueira da Foz**. Hotels, apartment houses, restaurants, discos, and a casino have gathered along the road that follows the coastline. A film festival attracts crowds to the area every fall. The region's other sources of income after tourism are fishing, the harbor itself, cellulose, and small industries.

The Serra do Boa Viagem closes off the northern end of the bay. The village of **Quiaios,** an old fishing village with Phoenician roots that has only recently been sniffed out by tourists, lies in the protective arms of the mountains. Preserved here is the typical landscape of beachside forests, mills, and little white houses. The traditional garlic sausage made of pork loin is still sold by the old measurement of a handspan. There are a number of beautiful lagoons sprawled out between pine trees and dunes a little farther to the north between Cabo Mondego and Mira. Some original pile houses can still be seen in **Palheiros da Tocha**, a fairly crowded vacation town.

To the south, behind a chain of dunes, miles of beach stretch between the sea and huge pine forests all the way to Nazaré. The forest was first planted in the 13th century during the reign of Dom Dinis, who was already thinking in terms

Right: This idyllic beach scene is atypical of Figueira da Foz; more common are agglomerations of cabanas for vacationers.

of the resin and logging industries, and of ways of shoring up the dunes. Only a few poorly signposted roads cut through the forest, and strangers to the place usually find the beach by accident rather than by design. Pedrógão, Praia de Vieira, and São Pedro de Muel are among the better-known resorts. Between them are a web of small access roads that lead to secluded sections of beach.

Leiria, which lies on the banks of the Lis, is about 12.5 miles (20 km) inland. The river was navigable up to the town until 1912 when its mouth silted up and it dug itself a new bed a little way to the south. Leiria evolved in the shadow of the **Castelo**, which was completed in 1135 by Afonso Henriques. Dom Dinis also resided here for a while. The building's metamorphosis into a Renaissance palace took place during the 16th century under João I. Some parts of this were reconstructed in the 20th century. Of the royal rooms, only a Gothic window and an elegant gallery with a broad vista of the town remain. A similar fort from the 13th century is located about 12.5 miles (20 km) to the south in Porto de Mós.

In the 15th century, Leiria had a sizable Jewish community. The Jews had a major influence on the town's economic life, with their paper mills and printing shops. The massive Renaissance Cathedral towers over the old town center; while the regional museum offers a sampling of local art treasures. Smaller and more exclusive is the museum in the priests' seminary, which displays old tiles, religious carvings and sculptures, and paintings from the 16th century.

Besides the logging, resin, and paper industries, Leira and the surrounding villages and towns are known for glassmaking. This all began in **Marinha Grande** in the 18th century, thanks to an Englishman. The factory and glassblowers' school documents the evolution and success of this local industry in their own museum.

Not far from Leiria and Marinha Grande is the resort of **São Pedro de Muel**, which lies on a 1,960-foot (600 m) stretch of bay enclosed by beautiful rock formations. The sea here is wild and unpredictable; the lifeguards often raise the yellow warning flag or the red one that prohibits swimming altogether. Above the town stands the house of the poet Lopes Vieira, now a museum. It includes a small 18th-century chapel decorated with marine motifs.

The beaches to the south of **São Pedro** are long and fairly secluded. **Agua de Madeiros**, with an inn and a good beach restaurant, is even accessible on foot from São Pedro. A little fresh-water spring which flows to the beach makes this an ideal spot for families with small children. The beach of **Paredes da Victória** is equally quiet. Beginning here and extending some 6 miles (10 km) southwards is a wonderful, pristine sand coastline at the foot of a steep cliff, where hardly anyone bothers to come. The village of **Pataias** is a short distance inland.

It is surrounded by dunes up to 440 feet (135 m) high, which are under special conservation order: they are not the product of drifts, but rather consist of layers of ancient Pliocene sand.

Nazaré is the most famous resort along the Silver Coast. Its broad bay begins in the south with the foothills of the Pederneira mountains and ends in the north with a 360-foot (110 m) cliff on top of which lies the district of Sítio; a funicular connects the two parts of town. The lookout balconies of Sítio offer a unique panorama of the bay, the beach, and the sea of houses. A tiny chapel, lined from top to bottom with tiles, recalls the miracle that once took place here: the mayor of Porto de Mós was out hunting in the fog when he accidentally rode his horse over the cliff; but he was saved when the animal's hind hooves took root in the rock.

The strength of the tides here has prevented Nazaré from ever being used as a harbor. As in the old days, the fishermen haul their boats up onto specially

reserved sections of beach, either using oxen or, more often nowadays, with the help of a tractor.

The coast becomes rockier south of Nazaré, but one still finds pretty beaches along the way. In **São Martinho do Porto** the forest reaches all the way down to the waterline. The elliptical bay, its opening to the sea measuring only 654 feet (200 m), is an ideal natural harbor. In the Middle Ages, the town was known for its shipbuilding, an industry that lasted until 1923. There was room for as many as 80 ships in the harbor back then, but the bay has since sanded up and the water is now too shallow.

ALCOBAÇA

The little town of Alcobaça grew up at the confluence of the Alcoa and Baça rivers; it boasted a Moorish fortress as

Above: Waiting for baptism in front of the Monastery of Alcobaça, one of the largest monastery complexes in Portugal.

early as the 10th century. In the Middle Ages a bay connected it with Nazaré so that the fruit grown by the Cistercian monks could easily be shipped away. The monastery was founded after a vow Afonso Henriques took before fighting the Moors near Santarém in 1147. But there were other reasons as well. First, the king needed the Cistercians, with their motto (borrowed from the Benedictines) *ora et labora* – pray and work – to resettle the land reconquered from the Moors. Secondly, founding the monastery fulfilled the obligations to Pope Innocent II which had arisen with the declaration of Portugal's independence. In 1153, the King laid the cornerstone of the church; the **Monastery of Santa Maria** was officially consecrated in 1252. The abbey became the most important of the 18 Cistercian monasteries in the country. Its lands extended from São Pedro de Muel to São Martinho do Porto, and from Aljubarrota to Caldas da Rainha, and included 13 towns and three sea ports. In 1269 it also established a theological seminary. The monks cultivated the land, drained marshes, and established the basis of today's agricultural wealth of the region. The 1755 earthquake and the French occupation in 1808 heavily damaged the buildings. After secularization, the monastery was turned over to the 13 communities; in 1930, it was declared a national monument.

The monastery was rebuilt several times. In 1725, the Gothic façade was given a Baroque facelift. The interior of the church, the largest in Portugal, is nevertheless still in simple Gothic style. The tombs of Pedro I and Inés de Castro are in the wings of the transept. The two lovers lie face to face, so that when they rise on Judgment Day they will be able to look each other in the eye. Surrounded by a host of quasi-Mannerist angels, the magnificent tomb sculptures, wrought in the 13th century by an unknown master, are accounted among the greatest masterpieces of Gothic funerary art. On the base of Pedro I's sarcophagus is a depiction of the life of St. Bartholomew, and in a rosette at its head are 18 scenes from the life and death of Inés. This tomb rests on stone lions, symbols of royal power; while that of Inés de Castro is supported by the figures of monks doing penance.

The transept has four side chapels. In one of them are life-sized terra-cotta figures depicting scenes from the life of St. Bernard. The tombs of Afonso II and Afonso III are also here, but their wives and children are buried in the adjoining sepulchral chamber. Opening off the aisle around the main altar are nine chapels. Behind it is the Renaissance sacristy, designed by João Castilho. Unfortunately it was severely damaged in the 1755 earthquake.

The **Claustro de Silêncio** (Cloister of Silence) dates to Dom Dinis. In the 16th century, the Castilho brothers added a second story in Manuelistic style. Particularly noteworthy is the spring-house in front of the refectory, where the monks used to wash after their labor in the fields and gardens before going to eat. In the dining hall, you can still see the stairway to the chancel where a monk used to read aloud to his fellow monks during meals. Behind this hall is the enormous kitchen. Its 60-foot (18 m) ceiling and gigantic tiled chimney give an idea of the scale on which this kitchen prepared food every day. The chapter room, the dormitory, and the cellar are also original. The terracotta figures of Portuguese kings that ornament the Royal Hall were made by the monks; on the walls, the history of the monastery is illustrated in painted tiles.

BATALHA

On the edge of **Aljubarrota** is a small chapel built by Nuno Alvares Pereira on the spot where he hoisted his banner on August 14, 1385 and dedicated it to St. George. The battle, in which 7,000 Portuguese defeated a Castilian army of 17,000 by luring them into wolf traps hidden in the bushes, ushered in the Avis Dynasty. In gratitude for the help of the Virgin Mary, João I built the Dominican monastery **Santa Maria da Batalha** (of the Battle) in **Batalha**. An equestrian statue of the victor stands on the broad square in front of the complex.

Twelve of the best architects in Portugal worked on the complex for more than 150 years. It's fairly easy to distinguish the different construction periods. During the rules of João I and Duarte, Afonso Domingues and the Irishman Huguet built the church, the **Claustro Real** (Royal Cloister), the Founder's Chapel, and the chapter room. The tall church, with its double row of windows, seems simple compared to the Flamboyant façade and cloister. The influence of the French high Gothic is particulary obvious in the funneled portal, decked out with six archivolts with figures of Apostles, and in the **Capela do Fundador** (Founder's Chapel), which begins on a square

ground plan and rises to an octagonal cupola with ribbed vaulting.

In his novella *The Vaulting*, Herculano tells of some of the difficulties encountered during construction: the plans of the architect Domingues originally called for a ribbed vaulting over the chapter room with a span of 62 feet (19 m). But the old architect went blind, so Huguet took on the project and changed the plans, which seemed to him technically impossible. Domingues insisted, however, that although he was blind, he should still be permitted to carry out his version of the chapter room, and the roof was built under his supervision. To prove that he did not fear the roof collapsing, he had himself locked into the chapter room for three days and three nights without bread or water after the job was completed. Unfortunately, his aged body could not withstand the strain, and he

Above: The fabulous ornamentation of the Claustro Real (Royal Cloister) in the Monastery of Batalha is worth long contemplation.

died shortly after; but his construction has successfully stood the test of time, as you can see today. After Domingues' death, Huguet had the Capela do Fundador built (1426-1434), with its filigree rosettes. It contains the tombs of João I and Filipa and her children, one of whom was Henry the Navigator.

Huguet also designed the **Capelas Imperfeitas** (Unfinished Chapels) during the reign of King Duarte. Under Manuel I, this construction was turned into a masterpiece of Manuelism. Seven burial chapels surround an octagonal central room with a portal 50 feet (15 m) high, decorated with wonderful stone carvings by Boytaca. The mighty central dome was never completed. During the reign of Afonso V, Martin Vasques and Fernão de Évora designed the **Claustro de Dom Afonso V** and the second cloister.

Otherwise, Batalha is a simple town where visitors can enjoy a Pousada, pleasant cafés and restaurants, and a market held on the broad square in front of the monastery.

COSTA DE PRATA
Accommodations

ÁGUEDA (034): *LUXURY:* **Palácio de Águeda**, Quinta da Borralha, tel. 601977, fax: 601976. *BUDGET:* **Parreira**, Passadouro, tel. 666326. *CAMPING:* **Rossio**, tel. 666327. **ALCOBAÇA** (062): *MODERATE:* **Santa María**, Rua Dr. F. Zagalo, tel. 597405, fax: 596715. *BUDGET:* **Mosteiro**, Av. J.de Deus 1, tel. 42183. **Corações Unidos**, Rua F. A. Brandão 39, tel. 42142. *CAMPING:* **Municipal**, tel. 42265. *TURISMO RURAL:* **Palacete Fonte Nova**, Estr. de Fonte Nova, tel. 598300. **Casa da Padeira**, Aljubarrota, Tel/fax: 508272. **AROUCA** (056): *MODERATE:* **São Pedro**, Ev. Reinaldo de Noronha, tel. 944580. *TURISMO RURAL:* **Quinta do Boco**, tel. 944169. **AVEIRO** (034): *MODERATE:* **Jardim Afonso V**, Praceta Afonso V, tel. 26514, fax: 24133. **Imperial**, Rua Dr.Nascimento Laitão, tel. 222141. **Alboi**, Rua da Arrochela 6, tel. 25121, fax: 22163. **Santa Joana**, Av. Dr. L. Peixinho 227, tel. 28604. *BUDGET:* **Beira**, Av. J.Estevão 18, tel. 24297. **Europa**, Rua Dr. M. Sacramento 143, tel. 21666. **Palmeira**, Rua da Palmeira 7, tel. 22521. *CAMPING:* **São J.Orbitur**, tel. 48284, fax: 48122. **BATALHA** (044): *LUXURY:* **Pousada de Mestre A. Domingues**, tel. 96261, fax: 96260. *MODERATE:* **São Jorge**, Casal da Ameiria, tel. 96210. **Batalha**, L. da Igreja, tel. 767500, fax: 767467. *TURISMO RURAL:* **Quinta do Fidalgo**, tel. 96114, fax: 767401. **Casa do Outeiro**, Lg. Carvalho do Outeiro, tel. 96806. **CANTANHEDE** (031): *MODERATE:* **Gandárez**, Rua Jaime Cortesão 6, tel. 422712. *CAMPING:* **Praia da Tocha**, tel. 442343. **COIMBRA** (039): *LUXURY:* **Tívoli**, Rua João Machado, tel. 26934, fax: 26827. **Astória**, Av. Emidio Navarro 21, tel. 22055, fax: 22057. Classically stylish, right on the L. Portagem. *MODERATE:* **Rívoli**, Pr. do Comércio 27, tel. 25550. **Mondego**, Lg. das Ameias 4, tel. 29087. *BUDGET:* **Alentejana**, R. Dr. A. Henrique Seco, tel. 25924, fax: 405124. **Domus**, R. Adelino Veiga 63, tel. 28584. *CAMPING:* **Municipal**, Pr. 25 de Abril, tel. 701497. *TURISMO RURAL:* **Casa dos Quintais**, Carvalhais de Cima, tel. 438305. **FIGUEIRA DA FOZ** (033): *LUXURY:* **Clube Vale de Leão**, Buarcos, tel. 23057. **Atlántida Sol**, Marginal Oceánica, Buarcos, tel. 21997, fax: 21867. **Nicola**, Rua B. Lopes 59, tel. 22359. *MODERATE:* **Sottomayor**, Rua dos Lusiadas, tel. 29455, fax: 22420. **Tarmagueira**, Marginal do Cabo Mondego, tel. 22514, fax: 21067. **Pena Branca**, Rua 5 de Outubro 42, Buarcos, tel. 23665. *BUDGET:* **Moderna**, Rua 8 de Maio 61, tel.

22701. **Astória**, Rua B. Lopes 45, tel. 22656. **Universal**, Rua Miguel Bombarda 50, tel. 26228, fax: 22962. *CAMPING:* **Municipal**, tel. 33033, fax: 28549. **Foz do Mondego**, tel. 31496. **Gala Orbitur**, tel. 31492. *TURISMO RURAL:* **Casa da Azenha Velha**, Caceira de Cima, tel. 25041. **ÍLHAVO** (034): *LUXURY:* **Arimar**, Av. Mário Sacramento 113, Tel/fax: 322131. *MODERATE:* **Barra**, Av. F. Lavrador 18, tel. 369156, fax: 360007. *BUDGET:* **Galera**, Av. Manuel Maia, tel. 322081. **Jardim**, Forte da Barra, tel. 361745. *CAMPING:* **Praia da Barra**, tel. 369425, fax: 323244. *TURISMO RURAL:* **Paço da Ermida**, Ermida, tel. 322496. **LEIRIA** (044): *LUXURY:* **Lis**, L. A. Herculano 10, tel. 814017, fax: 25099. **Ala dos Enamorados**, Vale Gracioso, Azóia, tel. 817961, fax: 25099. *MODERATE:* **Ramalhete**, Rua Dr. Correia Mateus 30, tel. 812802, fax: 25099. **São Francisco**, Rua de São Francisco 26, tel. 823110, fax: 812677. **São Luís**, Rua H. Sommer, tel. 813197, fax: 813897. *BUDGET:* **Alcoa**, Rua R. Cordeiro 24, tel. 32690. *TURISMO RURAL:* **Quinta das Silveiras**, Azóia, tel. 823784, fax: 823291. **LUSO-BUÇACO** (031): *LUXURY:* **Buçaco**, tel. 93101, fax: 93609. *MODERATE:* **Eden**, Rua Emidio Navarro, tel. 939171, fax: 930193. **Alegre**, Rua Emidio Navarro, tel. 939251, fax: 930256. *BUDGET:* **Portugal**, Rua Dr. Marinho Pimenta, tel. 939158. **Lusa**, Rua Dr. Costa Simões, tel. 939207. *TURISMO RURAL:* **Quinta da Tapada do Luso**, Estr. dos Moínhos, tel. 939281. **Vila Aurora**, tel. 930150. **Vila do Duparchy**, Rua José Duarte Figueiredo, tel. 939120. **Solar da Vacariça**, Vacariça, tel. 939458. **MARINHA GRANDE** (044): *LUXURY:* **Nobre**, Rua A. Herculano 21, tel. 568770. *MODERATE:* **París**, Estr. de S. Pedro de Moel, tel. 505584. *CAMPING:* **Praia da Vieira**, tel. 695334. **MIRA** (031): *MODERATE:* **A Canhota**, Rua Dr. A. José de Almeida 104, tel. 451448. **Arco Iris**, Av. do Mar, tel. 471202. **Maçarico**, Av. Arrais Batista Cera, tel. 47114. **Senhora da Conceição**, Av. Cidade de Coimbra, tel. 471645. *BUDGET:* **App. Quinta da Lágoa**, tel. 458688, fax: 458180. *CAMPING:* **Dunas de Mira**, tel. 472173, fax: 458185. **Orbitur**, Mira, tel. 471234. **MONTEMOR-O-VELHO** (039): *MODERATE:* **Abade João**, Rua Combatentes da Grande Guerra 15, tel. 689458. **MURTOSA** (034): *LUXURY:* **Pousada da Ria**, Bico do Muranzel, tel. 48332, fax: 48333. **Riabela**, Torreira, tel. 48137. *MODERATE:* **Alber-Tina**, Tr. Arrais Faustino, tel. 48306, *BUDGET:* **A Mansão**, Bunheiro, tel. 46000. *CAMPING:* **Praia da Torreira**, tel. 48397.

NAZARÉ (062): *LUXURY:* **Mar Bravo**, Pr. Sousa Oliveira, tel. 551180, fax: 533979. *MODERATE:* **Oceano**, Rua dos Pescadores 8, tel. 561161. **Miramar**, Rua Abel da Silva, Pederneira, tel. 561333, fax: 561734. **Praia**, Av. Vieira Guimarães 39, tel. 561423, fax: 561436. **Dom Fuas**, Av. Manuel Remigio, tel. 561351, fax: 561500. *BUDGET:* **Beira Mar**, Rua dos Lavradores, tel. 561358. **Ribamar**, Rua Gomes Freire 9, tel. 551158. *CAMPING:* **Valado Orbitur**, Tel. 561111, fax: 561137. **Vale Paraíso**, tel. 561546. *TURISMO RURAL:* **Quinta do Campo**, Valado dos Frades, tel. 577135, fax: 577555.

OLIVEIRA DE AZEMÉIS (056): *LUXURY:* **San Miguel**, Parque La Salette, tel. 681049, fax: 685141. *MODERATE:* **Albergaria do Campo**, Rua de São Miguel, tel. 682745, fax: 682385. *BUDGET:* **Anacleto**, Av. António José Almeida 310, tel. 682541. **Casa das Pedras**, Cidacos, tel. 682723. *CAMPING:* **La Salette**, tel. 674373. *TURISMO RURAL:* **Casa de Cidacos**, Cidacos, tel. 62723.

SÃO MARTINHO DO PORTO (062): *LUXURY:* **São Pedro**, Lg. V. Fróis 7, tel. 98328. *MODERATE:* **Concha**, Lg. V. Fróis, tel. 989220. **Carvalho**, Rua M. Bombarda 6, tel. 989605. **Parque**, Av. Marechal Carmona 3, tel. 989505, fax: 989105.

SÃO PEDRO DE MUEL (044): *MODERATE:* **Pérola do Oceano**, tel. 599157. **Mar e Sol**, tel. 599182, fax: 15529. Modern building over the bay. **Agua de Madeiros**, tel/fax: 599324. Stands alone on the next beach south; pleasant, beautiful location. **Miramar**, tel. 599141. **Verde Pinho**, Rua das Saudades, tel. 599233. *BUDGET:* **D. Fernando I** 19, Rua D. Fernando I. 19, tel. 541449. *CAMPING:* **São Pedro de Moel**, Orbitur, tel. 599168. fax: 599148. **Parque do Inatel**, tel. 599289. fax: 599550.

VIEIRA DE LEIRIA (044): *LUXURY:* **Estrêla do Mar**, José Loureiro Botas 18, tel./fax: 695404. **Ouro Verde**, Rua D. Dinís, Praia de Vieira, 697156. *BUDGET:* **Pensão Clara**, Rua Padre Franklin 12, tel. 695128.

Restaurants / Cafés

ALCOBAÇA: **Corações Unidos**, Rua Frei António Brandão 39, tel. 42142. **Trindade**, Pr. D. Afonso Henriques 22, tel. 42397.

AVEIRO: **A Cocinha do Rei**, Rua Dr. Manuel das Neves 65, tel. 26802. **Galo d'Ouro**, Travessa do Mercado 2, tel. 23456. **Centenario**, Pr. do Mercado 9, tel. 22798. **Salpoente**, Canal S. Roque 83, tel. 382674. **Alho Pôrro**, Rua da Arrochela, 23, tel. 20285. **O Moliceiro**, L. do Rossio 6. **O Chafariz**, L. do Peixe 3, tel. 27479.

COIMBRA: **Riviera**, R. do Brasil 310B, tel.

715512. **Dom Pedro**, Av. E.Navarro 58, tel. 29108. **Adega Paço do Conde**, Rua Paço do Conde 1. **Trovador**, L. da Sé Velha 15, tel. 25475. A Lanterna, L. da Sota 6, tel. 26729. **Café Sta. Cruz**, Pr. 8 de Maio.

BARS: **Aqui há Rato**, L. da Sé Velha 20. **Califa**, Rua da Matemática 20. **Noites Longas**, Rua Garrett 9. **De Sjoelbak**, Rua do Brasil 93. **Via Latina**, Rua Garrett 1, Discothek.

FIGUEIRA DA FOZ: **Tasca do Zé**, Pr. Velha, tel. 22449. **Sereia do Mar**, Av. do Brasil 59, tel. 26190. **Piano-Bar**, Casino da Figueira, Rua B. Lopes, tel. 22041. **Vale do Leão**, Buarcos, tel. 33057. **Agostin Grill**, Vila Verde, tel. 25296. **Tamargueira**, Quinta da Tamargueira, tel. 22514. **Branco e Negro**, Rua da Fonte 91.

LEIRIA: **Casarão**, Cruces de Azóia, tel. 871080. **Eurosol**, Rua José Alves Correira da Silva, tel. 812201. **Solar do Alcaíde**, Av. 25 de Abril, Lote 12, tel. 35248. **Marqués**, Av. Marquês de Pombal, Lote 1, tel. 25493.

LUSO-BUÇACO: **Palace Hotel**, tel. 93101. Toll for driving into the park, which can be redeemed if you eat. Free for pedestrians. It's about 600 m to the palace itself.

MARINHA GRANDE: **Nobre**, Rua A. Herculano 21, tel. 52226. **A Aldeia**, Travessa Vieira de Leiria 5, tel. 566404.

MONTEMOR-O-VELHO: **Ramalhão**, Rua Tenente Valadim 24, tel. 68435.

NAZARÉ: **Arte Xábega**, Calçada do Sítio, tel. 552136. **Beira Mar**, Av. da República 40, tel. 551458. **Mar Bravo**, Pr. S. Oliveira 75, tel. 51180. **Adega Oceano**, Av. República 51, tel. 561311.

OLIVEIRA DE AZEMÉIS: **São Miguel**, Parque da Salette, tel. 681049. **Diplomata**, Rua Dr. Simões dos Reis, tel. 62590.

SÃO PEDRO DE MUEL: **A Concha**, Rua Duquesa da Caminha 16, tel. 599150. **Pérola do Oceano**, tel. 599157. **Brisamar**, Rua Dr. Nicolau Bettencourt, tel. 599250. **Gato Preto**, Praia Agua de Madeiros, tel. 599186.

Sights / Museums

ÁGUEDA: **Casa-Museu Fund. Pinheiro**, P. Dr. A. Breda, Tue, Thu, weekends 3pm-6pm. **Casa-Museu de Etnografía**, Mour. del Vouga, 10am-midday and 2pm-5pm, closed Mon

ALCOBAÇA: **Cloister** 9am-6:30pm. **ALJUBARROTA**: **Military museum**, Tue-Fri 2pm-5pm, Sat, Sun 10am-noon and 2pm-5pm, closed Mon. **AROUCA**: **Museu de Arte Sacro**, 9am-midday and 2pm-5pm, closed Mon. **AVEIRO**: **Museu de Aveiro**, Rua de Santa Joana Princesa, 10am-12:30pm and 2pm-5pm, closed Mon. **Hunting and Fishing Museum**, Parque Municipal, Sat and Sun 2pm-5pm. **BATALHA**: **Monastery**,

9am-1pm and 2pm-6pm. **CARAMULO**: **Museum**, daily 10am-1pm and 2pm-6pm. **COIMBRA**: **Museu Machado de Castro**, L. Dr. José Rodrigues 2, 10am-5pm, closed Mon. **Museu da Igreja**, Capela da Universidade 1, 10am-midday and 2pm-5pm, closed weekends. **Museu Académico**, Pr. D. Dinís, 9:30am-midday and 2pm-5pm, closed weekends and holidays. **Casa-Museu Bissaya Barreto**, Rua da Infantería 23, Tue to Fri 3pm-5pm; Sat, Sun 10am-midday and 3pm-5pm, closed Mon **Museu Antropológico**, Bairro Sousa Pinto, 2pm-5:30pm, closed weekends. **University**: 9:30am-12:30pm and 2pm-5pm. **Sé Velha**, 9:30am-12:30pm and 2pm-5pm. **Igreja Santa Cruz**, 9-midday and 2pm-6pm. **Santa Clara-a-Nova**, 9am-12:30pm and 2pm-5:30pm. **Portugal dos Pequenitos**, 9am-7pm, In winter 9am-5:30pm. **CONDEIXA**: **Conímbriga**, **Roman excavations** 9am-1pm and 2pm-6pm (in summer 8pm), museum: 10am-1pm and 2pm-5pm (in summer 6pm). **ESTARREJA**: **Egas Moniz Museum**, Casa do Marinheiro, 9am-noon and 1:30pm-5pm, closed Mon and Tue **FIGUEIRA DA FOZ**: **Museu Municipal**, Cámara Municipal, 9am-12:30pm and 2pm-5:30pm, closed Mon. **Casa do Paço**, Rua 5 do Outubro. Bishop's Palace with tile collection. **ÍLHAVO**: **Museu Histórico de Vista Alegre**, porcelain factory: 9am-12:30pm and 2pm-4:30pm, closed Mon. **Museu Marítimo**, 9am-12:30pm and 2pm-5:30pm, Sun and Tue 2pm-5:30pm, closed Mon. **LEIRIA**: **Fortress**, 9am-6:30pm, in winter until 5:30pm. **LORVÃO**: **Cloister**: 9:30am-12:30pm and 2pm-5pm, closed Mon and Tues. **MONTEMOR-O-VELHO**: **Fortress**: 10am-12:30pm and 2pm-8pm, closed Mon. **MURTOSA**: **Museu Etnográfico**, 9am-12:30pm and 2pm-5:30pm, Thu and Sun 2pm-5:30pm, Fridays closed. **NAZARÉ**: **Museu Etnológico**, Rua Fuas Roupinho, Sítio, 11am-2pm and 2:30pm-6pm, in winter 10am-1pm. **OLIVEIRA DE AZEMÉIS**: **Regional museum**, Rua A. Alegria 119, 9:30am-12:30pm and 2pm-5pm, closed weekends. **Casa-Museu Ferreira de Castro**, Ossela, 2pm-5pm. **OVAR**: **Museum**, Rua H. Salgado, 10am-noon and 2pm-6pm. **Museu São Francisco**, Rua G. Freire, 10am-noon and 2pm-6pm.

Tourist information

ÁGUEDA: **Tourist Office**: L. Dr. Elisio Sucena, tel. 601412. **ALCOBAÇA**: **Tourist Office**: Pr. 25 de Abril, tel. 42377, May to Sep 9am-7pm (in winter 5pm), Sat and Sun 10am-1pm and 3pm-6pm. **AROUCA**: **Tourist Office**: Pr. Brandão de Vasconcelos, tel. 601412. **AVEIRO**: **Tourist Office**: Pr. da República, tel. 23680. **Boat rides on the Ria**, Jun 15 - Sep 15, central canal, daily 10am. **BATALHA**: **Tourist Office**: L. Paulo VI, tel. 96180,

10am-1pm and 3pm-7pm, Sat/Sun 6pm. **COIMBRA**: **Tourist Office**: L. da Portagem, tel. 25576. Avenida Narro 6, tel. 26813; 9am-7pm, Sat, Sun 9am-12:30pm and 2pm-5:30pm. **Bus station**: Av, F. Magalhães. **Post office**: Av. Fernão Magalhães 223. **Hospital**: Pr. Prof. Mota Pinto, tel. 403939. **ESTARREJA**: **Tourist Office**: Pr. F. Barbosa, tel. 41737. **FIGUEIRA DA FOZ**: **Tourist Office**: Av. 25 de Abril, tel. 22610, 9am-midnight (winter 9am-12:30pm and 2pm-5:30pm). **Post office**: Rua M. Bombarda. **Riding**: Quinta das Rolas, Quiaios, tel. 910694. Quinta do Montalto, Quiaios, tel. 910404. **LEIRIA**: **Tourist Office**: Jardim L. de Camões, tel. 32748, fax: 33533, 9am-7pm, Sat, Sun 10am-1pm and 3pm-7pm.
MARINHA GRANDE: **Tourist Office**: Av. José Henriques Varela, tel. 59152. **Riding**: Centro Hípico, Atalaias, Ameirinha, tel. 613836. **MONTEMOR-O-VELHO**: **Tourist Office**: Rua dos Combatentes, tel. 68187. **MURTOSA**: **Tourist Office**: Praia da Torreira, Av. Hintze Ribeiro, tel. 48250. 9am-9pm (in winter 9am-5pm Mon to Fri). **Bicycle rental**: Videoclube São Paio, Rua Enrique Taveres / L. do Mercado, tel. 48667. **NAZARÉ**: **Tourist Office**: Av. da República, tel. 561194. **OLIVEIRA DE AZEMÉIS**: **Tourist Office**: Pr. José da Costa, tel. 64463. **OVAR**: **Tourist Office**: Rua Elias Garcia, tel. 572215.Branch offices in Esmoriz (Jul 1 – Sep 30.): Av. 29 de Março, tel. 753084 and Furadouro (Jul 1 – Aug 30) Av. Central, Mon-Fri 10am-1pm and 3pm-7pm, Sat 10am-3pm. **PENACOVA**: **Rent a Kayak**, tel. 039-478385. (Bus from Coimbra to Penacova is included). **POMBAL**: **Tourist Office**: L. do Cardal, Town Hall, tel. 23230; 10am-1pm and 3pm-6pm, Sat, Sun until 5pm, closed Thu. **PORTO DE MÓS**: **Tourist Office**: On the Park, Mon to Fri 10am-1pm and 3pm-7pm, Sat, Sun until 6pm. **SÃO MARTINHO DO PORTO**: **Tourist Office**: Av. 25 de Abril, tel. 989110.
TONDELA: **Tourist Office**: Pr. Maior, Mon-Thu 9am-midday and 2pm-5pm, Fri 9am-midday.

Festivals

ALCOBAÇA: *S. Bernardo*, last week in August. **BATALHA**: 14/15 August. **COIMBRA**: Mid May *Queima das Fitas*; June 24, St. John's, first week in July *Rainha Santa* festival. **FIGUEIRA DA FOZ**: June 24, St. John's; in September intl. film festival. **LEIRIA**: Annual market, May 1-25. **MONTEMOR-O-VELHO**: **Citemor**, Theater festival, Jul/Aug, performances in the fortress. **MURTOSA**: S. Paio pilgrimage, Torreira, Sep 3-9. **POMBAL**: *Nossa Senhora do Cardal*, last week in July. **VAGOS**: Pilgrimage on Whit Monday and in the last week of August.

PORTO AND THE DOURO VALLEY

PORTO

THE COAST SOUTH OF PORTO

ALONG THE ATLANTIC

NORTH OF PORTO

ALONG THE DOURO

Porto is the second-largest city in Portugal. Its bustling business district consists of an unsightly collection of industrial complexes and oil refineries. Cramped living conditions and poverty exist cheek-by-jowl with a romantic portside, lively streets, pretty parks, numerous museums, and several Baroque churches, all in the city center. For many, Porto is the epitome of authentic, down-to-earth Portugal. One saying goes: "They pray in Braga, study in Coimbra, spend money in Lisbon, and earn it in Porto."

History

On the left bank of the Douro, where today Vila Nova de Gaia lies with its wine-cellars, there was once a Greek trading post known as *Cale*, "the Beautiful." Later the Romans built their road from Braga to Lisbon through this area, and they named the settlement on the right bank of the river *Portus*. The Swabians occupied Porto in the 5th century, and built the first city wall of *Portucale Castrum Novum* up on the hill. The Moors arrived in the year 716, but were

Preceding pages: The train station of Porto was done up in azulejos in 1930. Left Bold feats of diving off the Dom Luís Bridge in Porto.

forced out in 825. The Spanish Khalif of Omayad succeeded in restoring Islamic rule to the harbor town in 997; their occupation, however, was short-lived. In 1050, the knights of Gascogne reconquered Porto, and made it the capital of the County of Portucale. Fernão I replaced the old Swabian defensive wall with a larger one in the 14th century.

When João I married the British noblewoman Philipa of Lancaster in Porto in 1386, the town became the seat of the royal family and began establishing trade links with England. Prince Henry "the Navigator" was born here. He did a great deal to foster the city's existing seafaring tradition, building the first caravels that were used for the 1415 expedition to Ceuta. For the sailors' provisions, local farmers were required to salt and pickle all their cattle; they were only allowed to keep the offal, *tripas*, which cannot be preserved properly. This gave rise to the local specialty *tripas à moda do Porto*, tripe with beans and ham, and the people of Porto are derogatorily known as *tripeiros*.

In 1703, the Methuen Treaty became effective. It was named after the British ambassador who signed it, the brother of a wealthy textile manufacturer. The treaty guaranteed lower import tariffs for British cloth, in exchange for lower ta-

161

riffs on Portuguese wine exported to Britain. The ships that arrived in Porto laden with woolens went back with a cargo of Porto wine aboard. Within a century, wine production in the area rose from 7,000 barrels a year to 44,000 barrels. Until 1756, when the Marquis de Pombal founded the Douro Wine Company, the wine trade was entirely in British hands. The price of the wine was increased in order to tap into the English profit margin, and the Marquis had the cheap wine taverns in Porto closed, giving rise to a popular rebellion that was brutally put down by the military.

The profits from the wine trade and gold from Brazil amply filled the city's coffers during the 18th century. It was during that period that Porto was built up to look as it does today: it grew well beyond the old defensive walls, and the center of town shifted to Praça de Liberdade, a process which involved tearing down entire blocks of houses. Veritable palaces sprang up as residences of the prosperous bourgeoisie, and churches and monasteries were built or tailored to suit contemporary tastes.

Pombal installed military governors at the city's helm, first Almada and then his son. Their Italian architect, Nicolo Nasoni, changed the face of Porto: he was responsible for the Clérigos and Misericórdia Churches, the Bishop's Palace, the Prelates' Palace, the Quinta de Bonjoi, the Freixo Palace, and many more.

When the French took over the town in 1809, there was a mass exodus over the pontoon bridge to Vila Nova de Gaia. The bridge couldn't hold up to the onslaught, and more than 5,000 people drowned. A memorial relief on the Dom Luis I Bridge recalls this *Tragedia da Ponte das Barcas.*

Industrialization in Porto during the 19th century spawned a powerful middle class and a corresponding rise in liberal thought. The first liberal rebellions began as early as 1820. In 1833, the Miguelists

surrounded the city with an army of 70,000, but had to turn back when Pedro IV promulgated liberal laws. This formed the basis for the Republican movement whose first uprising took place in Porto in 1891, but was bloodily put down.

The arrival of the railway in 1877 finally connected the city with Portugal's interior and with the capital. Gustave Eiffel built the first railway bridge across the Douro, and ten years later one of his students added the ingenious Dom Luis I double bridge to it. The bridge's two levels connect Porto's upper and lower towns with Vila Nova da Gaia. The first highway bridge was built in 1963, and in 1993 the town inaugurated yet another railway bridge.

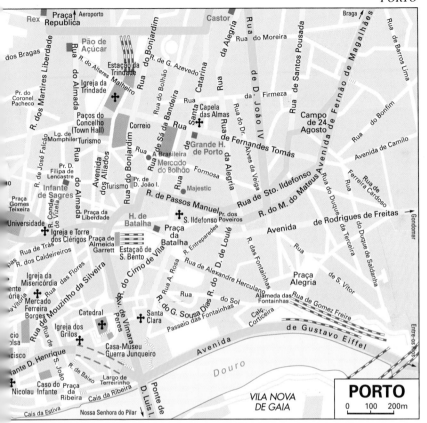

The City Center

Porto's inner city is spread out on a steep granite slope that overlooks the Douro. Its narrow streets and dense houses form a contrasting ensemble of ostentatious buildings, banks, Baroque churches covered in blue tiles, and more or less dilapidated quarters where poverty is rampant. There are elegant shops, lively markets, parks overrun with street kids, and dark, incommodious courtyards. The romantic ambience of the portside often ends in havens of misery.

The **Praça da Liberdade**, dominated by an equestrian statue of Dom Pedro IV, is at the heart of the city. The wide **Avenida dos Aliados** begins here, a street lined with stately office buildings and banks. It ends at the grandiose City Hall, which was built in 1920. Right beside it is the tourist office.

The main shopping streets, some for pedestrians only, also begin at Praça da Liberdade, and lead upward through the city. **Rua de Sá da Bandeira** boasts the covered market **Mercado do Bolhão**, and **Rua da Santa Catarina** leads by the brilliantly painted **Capela das Almas** (Chapel of the Poor Souls) and the turn-of-the-century café **Majestic**.

To the south of the commercial zone is the train station **Estação São Bento**, which was built at the beginning of the 20th century on the foundations of an old Benedictine monastery. In 1930, Jorge

163

Colaço tiled the interior with *azulejos* that depict highlights from the history of Portugal. Adjacent **Praça da Batalha** is lined with movie theaters, pubs, and the 18th-century **Igreja São Ildefonso**; the latter is of particular interest as Colaço also did the tiling on the outside, painted with scenes from the life of the church's patron saint.

Southwest of Praça da Liberdade stands another important church, **São Pedro dos Clérigos** (1732-1748), a Baroque masterpiece by the Italian Nicolo Nasoni, who is also buried here. It has an oval ground plan and a free-standing tower, whose height of 248 feet (76 m) makes it the tallest in Portugal and a hallmark of the town. Those who take the challenge of the 225 steps will be rewarded with a panoramic view of Porto. To the west, by the triangular **João Chagas Park**, sprawls the university

Above: A delicatessen in Porto with an ornate tile façade. Right: Night view of the Cathedral and the Torre dos Clérigos, Porto.

complex. Across from it to the northwest are the 17th-century **Carmelite Church** and the 18th-century **Carmo Church**. Student life sets the tone of the streets around here, with lots of cafés, bars, and galleries. The studios of the **Arvore Artists' Cooperative**, housed in the **Quinta das Virtudes**, an 18th-century palace, have been making a name for themselves for the past 30 years.

Another 18th-century edifice, the **Caranças Palace**, stands to the west of the Old Town. It was originally built by Jewish jewelers, but was later promoted to royal residence. Today, it houses the **Museu Nacional de Soares dos Reis**, named after its first director and one of the leading 19th-century sculptors in Portugal. His works, and those of Teixera Lopes, are exhibited in the museum, as well as Portuguese paintings from the 16th century to modern times and ceramics from the 19th and 20th centuries. Not far from here is the **Jardim do Palácio de Cristal**, a luxuriant, flowery park in the midst of which stands the **Crystal**

Palace, a futuristic construction that raised quite a furor at the time of its completion in 1865, and now serves as a sports arena. West of the park is the **Maceirinha Palace** with the **Museu Romântico**, which replicates the atmosphere of an upper-middle-class residence of the 19th century. One of the rooms is where the Italian king Carlos Alberto died in 1849 while in exile. The tasting hall of the port wine institute **Solar do Vinho do Porto** is also in this building, offering visitors a choice of more than 200 vintages.

The Old Town

The actual old town of Porto stretches between Praça da Liberdade and the river. On the windy hill of Penha Ventosa is the **Cathedral**, which watches over the picturesque Barredo district. On the broad square before it, **O Terreiro**, stands a pillory (*pelourhino*), although no one ever had to suffer here, as it was erected in the 19th century as a strictly decorative item in neo-Pombalic style. The Cathedral was originally a Romanesque defensive church of the Cluny monks. Over the centuries, a number of architects added to it, most recently the great Nasoni, who did the Baroque loggia. The interior, however, still sports its early Gothic arches; the main altar was designed by the Frenchman Claude Laprade in the 18th century. A unique feature is the pure silver sacramental retable in the Chapel of the Holiest of Holies. A relief by Teixeira Lopes in the baptismal alcove shows the baptism of Christ. In the chapel to the right of the altar are the Renaissance sepulchers of the Brandão Pereiras, a wealthy family of merchants. They brought a number of great European artists to Portugal in their day, and maintained good contact with no less a figure than Albrecht Dürer. The 17th-century **Root of Jesse Altar** in the left-hand nave, which depicts the lineage from the 12 kings of Judea to the Holy Family, is one of the finest works in the church.

165

The Gothic cloister, paneled in *azulejos* in the 18th century, is decorated with religious and mythological motifs. The remains of a Jewish cemetery were discovered beside it.

Work on the **Archbishop's Palace**, south of the Cathedral, started in 1771 under the direction of the German architect Ludwig, who designed the monastery of Mafra for João V. Southeast of the Cathedral is the **Museu Guerra Junqueiro**, housed in a Baroque palace that was most probably built by Nasoni. The museum has a collection of furniture, ceramics, silver, and tapestries donated by the widow of satiricist Guerra Junqueiro (1850-1923). The **Igreja de Santa Clara**, on the other side of Avenida Peres, is one of the city's most beautiful churches. It was originally built in Gothic times, but was renovated in the 18th century with *talha dourada* altars.

Above: Hustle and bustle on the Cais da Ribeira. Right: Keeping an eye on the tourists for a change (Ribeira district).

Descending the Colegio stairway from the Cathedral, you come to another 18th-century church, the **Igreja dos Grilos**, built by Baltasar Alvares in the austere style preferred by the Jesuits. Nowadays the complex houses a priests' seminary and the **Museum of Religious Art**.

The warren of streets around the Cathedral are full of little shops, bars, and an open market. On Rua do Infante Henrique, which runs down to the river, are the Gothic **Igreja São Francisco** and the Stock Exchange. Like many other churches in town, this one was rebuilt in the 18th century, and became the most splendid one of Porto. The interior is more like a ballroom than a house of worship; more than 200 kilograms of gold dust were used for the ornamentation. As for the Stock Exchange, the **Palácio de Bolsa**, it is the very symbol of Porto's 19th-century mercantilism. You can visit its elegant salons, some of which boast frescoes by Soares dos Reis, and one spectacularly decorated in Moorish style, but only with a guided tour. A memorial to Henry the

Navigator stands in the garden diagonally opposite the **Caso do Infante**, the house where he is believed to have been born.

Behind the Exchange, in another Nasoni masterpiece, is the **Museum of Ethnography and History**, where one can examine folk costumes, furniture, religious objects, and musical instruments from the region. Particularly impressive are the replicas of a wine-cellar and a rustic kitchen. Somewhat further east, on the same street, is the restored, cast-iron **Ferreira Borges Covered Market** (1883); it's used today for exhibitions.

In Rua das Flores is yet another work by Nasoni: the **Misericórdia Church**. The famous picture known as *Fons Vitae*, by an unknown artist of the beginning of the 16th century, hangs in the sacristy. The Source of Life is shown as the blood of Christ, which gives the picture a very powerful shade of red. King Manuel I and his family are shown at the bottom of the painting.

If you walk south through the narrow streets at the edge of Porto's city center – streets lined in many places with extremely decrepit houses – you come to the river and the former **Harbor District of Ribeira**. The vibrant heart of this area is **Praça da Ribeira**; in this area, people still live as much on the streets as inside their homes. One street leads down to the river over what seems to be an endless series of stairs, the **Escadas dos Guindais**, along the remains of the 14th-century Fernandine city wall. By the riverbank, on the **Cais da Ribeira** and **Cais da Estiva**, locals and foreigners rub elbows; street vendors haggle with the tourists; and there are row upon row of bars, old-fashioned stores, souvenir shops, fish restaurants, and establishments with sometimes dubious clientele. Fast-flowing and dirty, the Douro here passes through a bottleneck of granite cliffs. Daring children jump from the Dom Luis I Bridge into the river for a few pennies from the crowd of spectators.

They then swim downstream to the next pier, where you can embark on excursion boats for short local tours or trips of several days to the Spanish border.

Outlying Districts

Leaving Porto's town center going north on the busy Rua Cedofeita, you come to the oldest church in town, **São Martinho da Cedofeita**, which translates as "quickly done." Afonso Henriques erected this simple Romanesque building in the 12th century, after the Moorish general Almansor had destroyed its Visigothic predecessor.

Avenida da Boavista takes you from here to a modern shopping area also known as Boavista that is centered around Praça Mouzinho de Albuquerque. Nearby is the Antonio de Almeida Foundation, named after a doctor and statesman who led the 1910 revolution and later became President of the Republic. His former residence, located in a pretty park, today displays, in addition to its

stately furnishings, the comprehensive coin collection of the doctor himself. The home of the poet and businessman Fernando de Castro, a little farther to the north, has also been turned into a museum, this one exhibiting paintings and works of religious art.

If you leave the center by following the river westward, you will come to the Miragaia district, which means "look toward Gaia," that is, over at the picturesque port wine cellars on the other side of the Douro. The **Museum of Transportation**, with its impressive collection of old tramways, can be found on the bank of the river. A few miles downstream, the Douro opens into the ocean.

Porto's beach consists of a long sand bar on the southern bank of the river, which shuts off a large section of the mouth of the Douro. It can be reached either by boat from town or by road

Above: A port wine cellar in Vila Nova de Gaia. Right: Tastings are open to any- and everyone.

through Gaia. **Fort São João** has watched over the entrance of the harbor since the 16th century. The town's night life is concentrated in the area, an agglomeration of bars, discos, and extravagant pubs. On the Atlantic side is the suburb of **Foz do Douro**, which is part residential neighborhood and part resort, with big hotels and many restaurants along the ocean-front promenade. The beach ends at the so-called "cheese castle," the **Castelo do Queijo**, which was built as a defense against pirates.

Porto has grown well beyond its limits during the past few decades. The city itself has 350,000 inhabitants, but Greater Porto is more like 1.5 million. By now it has extended east to reach **Gondomar**, a town traditionally known for its handicrafts, in particular woodworking and filigree jewelry. To the north Porto has swallowed the industrial suburb of **Matosinhos**, with the harbor of Leixões – a zone with the nation's heaviest concentration of industry: the petrochemical industry, heavy industry, textiles, leather, and food processing. But even here, there's an old town center where the **Igreja Bom Jesús de Bouças** stands, an edifice built by Nasoni, with a gigantic *talha dourada* altar.

THE COAST SOUTH OF PORTO

Vila Nova de Gaia is arranged like an amphitheater along the granite slopes on the left bank of the Douro. All the major port wine producers have their headquarters here, and most still bear the English names of their founders. The cellars where the select wines age for up to 40 years are hewn into the rock near the river, which guarantees a steady temperature throughout the year. Most of them can be visited, and some even have sidewalk cafés along the bank of the river. The fringe benefit of a pause at one of them is the incomparable view: Porto lying on the opposite side of the Douro, a picturesque sea of houses that sweeps up a steep slope, the *rabelo* boats, which were once used to transport the wine barrels, and the **Dom Luís I Bridge**, built 1881-1885, with its double-decker roads that carry a continuous rush of traffic. The upper lane leads directly to the **Monastery of Nossa Senhora do Pilar**, which was most probably built by Filipo Terzi in the 16th century. This former Augustine convent has an elegant domed church on a round ground plan, and an unusual cloister, also circular, from the 17th century.

Further uphill, in the town, stands the house of Teixeira Lopes, a student of Soares dos Reis. He was considered one of the most important figures in the intellectual life of Porto at the turn of the century. His sculptural work can be seen throughout the city, and some items have been neatly exhibited in the pleasant ambience of his house.

To the west, downstream from Gaia, is the fishing village of **Afurada**, where, as one might expect, some excellent fish

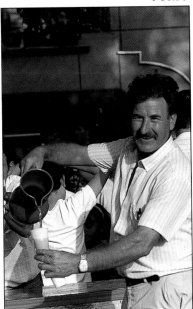

restaurants have opened. This marks the beginning of the people of Porto's favorite recreation area; in summer, they crowd the beaches all the way to the Ria of Aveiro. Especially popular is the first beach on the Atlantic, the beach of **Lavadores**, which adjoins the sand bank. To the south are the beaches of **Madalena** and **Valadares**. From **Miramar** onwards, the local railway line from Porto runs nearer and nearer to the coast. On the barren cliff stands a Baroque chapel, **Senhor da Pedra**.

The area also has a golf course. It's worth stopping off in Granja for a look at the *azulejo* decoration of the train station. **Espinho** is a modern resort with crowded beaches, countless apartment blocks, and a checkerboard street pattern.

Visibly smaller, and with an old town center, **Esmoriz**, which lies somewhat farther to the south on a lagoon, is more atmospheric. Among the traditional craftsmen in town, the coopers who manufacture the port wine barrels are the most famous.

THE ATLANTIC NORTH OF PORTO

The good beaches for outings to the north begin after **Leça da Palmeira**, where one finds **Leça do Balio**, a monastery once belonging to the Knights Hospitaller. All that is left is the early-Gothic fortified church, with its beautiful capitals, some tombs, and a baptismal font.

Around Labruge and Vila Châ, the beaches gradually become cleaner and less crowded. The resorts of Vila do Conde and Póvoa de Varzim straddle the mouth of the Ave River. **Vila do Conde** is a friendly town with a handsome old section. Of particular interest is the **Church of São Francisco**, which was once part of the monastery of Santa Clara. It stands on an elevation looking over the river. The splendid Gothic **Burial Chapel**, with a ribbed vaulting, has a skillfully sculpted tomb containing the remains of Afonso Sanches, an illegitimate son of Dom Dinis. The burial statues showing him and his wife Teresa date back to the 16th century. The water supply for the monastery came from Póvoa de Varzim over a 4-mile (7 km) aqueduct. In the district of Caxinas there's an interesting **Oceanographic Museum**; while in the former fishing village of **Azurara**, south of Vila da Conde, stands a beautiful Manuelistic church. The local women are famous for lace-making, and their handicrafts are sold everywhere.

Póvoa de Varzim is the most important seaside resort on this section of the coast. It has the usual restaurants, wide beaches, huge hotels, apartment houses, and a gambling casino, but along the jetty behind the pentagonal citadel there are also a number of smaller, cosier places. The regional **Ethnographical Museum** is located in the **Palaço dos Carneiros**.

There are some noteworthy Romanesque churches nearby. Most beautiful of these are the 12th-century chapel of **Rates** and **São Cristóvão** in Rio Mau.

PORTO AND THE COAST
Accommodations

ESPINHO (02): *LUXURY:* **Solverde**, Valadares, tel. 726666, Fax: 726236. **PORTO** (02): *LUXURY:* **Infante de Sagres**, Pr. D. Filipa de Lencastre 62, tel. 2008101, Fax: 314937. **Grande Hotel da Batalha**, Pr. da Batalha 116, tel. 2000571, Fax: 2002468. **Castor**, R. das doze Casas 17, tel. 570014, Fax: 566076. *MODERATE:* **César**, R. da Boavista 667, tel. 314984. **Grande Hotel de Porto**, R. de Santa Catarina 137, tel. 2008176, Fax: 311061. **Bolsa**, R. Ferreira Borges 101, tel. 2026768, Fax: 318888. **Apartamentos Turísticos Nau**, R. dos Abraços 16, tel. 576231, Fax: 561216. **Rex**, Pr. da República 117, tel. 2083709. **Miradouro**, tel. 570717, Fax: 570206. **Pão de Açúcar**, R. do Almada 262, tel. 2002425, Fax: 310239. *BUDGET:* **União**, R. Conde de Vizela 62, tel. 2003078. **Douro**, Pr. Parada Leitão 41, tel. 2081201. **Estoril**, da Cedofeita 193, tel. 2005152. **França**, Pr. Gomes Teixeira 7, tel. 2002791. *CAMPING:* **Prelada**, R. Monte dos Burgos, tel. 812616. **PÓVOA DE VARZIM**: *LUXURY:* **Sto. André**, Aver-o-Mar, tel. 681881/2/3. **S. Félix**, Laúndos. tel. 612176. *BUDGET:* **Luso-Brasileiro**, R. dos Cafés, tel. 615161. **Torre do Mar**, Aver-o-Mar, tel. 613677. *CAMPING:* **Rio Alto**, Estela, tel. 615699. **VILA NOVA DE GAIA** (02): *LUXURY:* **Casa Branca Praia**, R. da Bélgica 98, Praia dos Lavradores, tel. 7813516, Fax: 7813691. **Gaiahotel**, Av. da República, tel. 7814242, Fax: 7814573. *MODERATE:* **Davilina**, Av. da República, tel. 307596, Fax: 307571. **Sobreiro Grosso**, R. Américo de Oliveira, Grijó, tel. 7644896. *BUDGET:* **Orla Marítima**, R. dos Combatentes 78, tel. 7116080. *CAMPING:* **Salgueiros**, tel. 7810500. *TURISMO RURAL:* **Casa do Mosteiro**, Grijó, tel. 7640008.

Restaurants / Cafés

ESPINHO: **O Convívio**, R. 15 No. 270, tel. 724654. **Churrascaria Graciosa**, Largo da Graciosa, tel. 720470. **Sãozinha**, R. 16 No. 380, tel. 726707. **Retornado**, R. 23, Ecke Av. 2, tel. 722580. **PORTO**: **D'Tonho**, Cais da Ribeira 13-15, tel. 2004307. **Churrascão do Mar**, R. João Grave 134, tel. 696382. **O Escondidinho**, R. de Passos Manuel 144, tel. 2001079. **Mesa Antiga**, R. Santo Ildefonso 208, tel. 2006432. **Gambamar**, R. Campo Alegre 110, tel. 692396. **Aleixo**, R. da Estação 216, tel. 570462. **Taverna do Bebobos**, Cais da Ribeira 21, tel. 313565. **Filha da Mãe Preta**, Cais da Ribeira 40, tel. 315515. **Casa Victorina**, Cais de Ribeira 44. **Mondari**, Rua do Cimo de Vila 147. **Porto à Noite**, Rua da Arrabida. Home cooking with homey atmosphere. *CAFÉS:* **A Brasileira**, R. Sá da Bandeira. **Café Majestic**, R. Santa

Catalina 112. *BARS*: **Meia Cave**, Pr. da Ribeira 6. **Ribeirinha**, R. São João 70. **Academia**, R. de São João 80. **Mercado**, R. de São João 36. **Quando-quando**, Av. do Brasil 60. **O Muro**, Muro de Bacalhoeiros 87. **Cova funda**, R. da Lada 30. **Solar do Vinho do Porto**, R. de Entre Quintas 220. **Ogesto**, Rua dos Caldeireiros. **FOZ DO DOURO**: **Don Manoel**, Av. de Montevideu 384, tel. 6170179. **Varanda da Barra**, R. Paulo Gama 470, tel. 685006. **VILA NOVA DE GAIA**: **Casa Branca**, R. da Bélgica 98. Praia dos Lavadores. tel. 7810269. **Quinta de São Salvador**, R. Silva Tapada 200, Quebrantões, tel. 3702575. **LEÇA DA PALMEIRA**: **O Chanquinhas**, R. de Santana 243, tel. 9951884. **MATOSINHOS**: **Bom Abrigo**, R. Sant Catarina 243, tel. 995255.

Sights / Museums
MATOSINHOS: **Casa Museu Abel Salazar**, São Mamede de Infesta, 9:30am-12:30pm and 2:30pm-6pm, Sun 10am-6pm, closed Mon. **PORTO**: **Cathedral**: Terreiro da Sé, 9am-midday and 3pm-5pm. **Palácio da Bolsa** (the Stock Exchange): R. Ferreira Borges, in winter: Mon-Fri, 9am-midday and 2pm-5pm, closed weekends. From May to Sep: Mon-Fri 10am-5:30pm, Sat, Sun 10am-midday and 2pm-5pm. **Igreja dos Clérigos**: Mon-Sat 10:30am-midday and 3pm-6pm, Sun 10:30am-1pm. **Torre dos Clérigos**: Mon-Sat 10:30am-midday and 3:30pm-5pm, Sun 10:30am-midday and 3pm-5pm, closed Wed. **Igreja São Francisco**: Mon-Sat 9am-midday and 2pm-5pm, closed Sun. **Igreja de Santa Clara**: Mon-Fri 9:30am-11:30am and 3pm-6pm, Sat 9am-midday, closed Sun. **Igreja da Misericórdia**: Mon-Sat 8am-midday and 3pm-5pm, Sun 8am-midday. **Igreja do Carmo**: 9am-midday and 3pm-5pm. **Igreja das Carmelitas**: 8am-12:30pm and 4pm-7pm. **Igreja de Cedofeita**: 9am-12:30pm and 4pm-7pm, Sun 9am-12:30pm. **Igreja de São Bento da Vitória**: 4pm-7pm, Sun 9am-midday. **Igreja de S. Pedro de Miragaia**: 4pm-7pm, Sun 9am-midday. **Igreja de S. Nicolau**: 9am-12:30pm and 4pm-7pm, Sat and Sun 9am-12:30pm, closed Tue. **Casa do Infante**: Mon and Fri 9am-midday and 2pm-pm. **Museu Nacional de Soares dos Reis**: Palácio dos Carranças, currently closed (renovations). **Casa-Museu Guerra Junqueiro**: currently closed. **Museu Romântico**: Entre-Quintas 220, Quinta da Macieirinha, 10am-midday and 2pm-5pm, closed Sun and Mon. **Casa António Carneiro**: R. Antonio Carneiro 363, 10am-midday and 2pm-5:30pm, closed Sun and Mon. **Fundação Antonio de Almeida**: R. Tenente Valadim 231, Mon-Sat 2:30pm-5:30pm, closed Sundays. **PÓVOA DE VARZIM**: **Ethnol. Museum**: 10am-12:30pm and 2:30pm-6pm, closed Mon. **VILA NOVA DE GAIA**: **Museu Teixeira**

Lopes: R. T. Lopes 16, 9am-12:30pm and 2pm-5:30pm.

Shopping
PORTO: **Guitars**: R. Mouzinho da Silveira 165. **Silver filigree work**: R. das Flores. **Market**: R. Sá da Bandeira, Mon-Fri 8am-5pm, Sat 8am-1pm. **Flea market**: near the Cathedral every 2nd and 4th Saturday of the month, mornings. **Flowers**: Pr. da Liberdade, Sun morning. **Handicrafts**: Pr. da Batalha. **Coin and Stamp market**: Pr. do João I., Sun mornings. **Wine and second-hand stores** (*garrafeiras*): **Campo Alegre**, R. de Campo Alegre 1598. **Januario**, R. do Bonjardim 352. **Super Garrafeira**, R. Coelho Neto 95.

Festivals
PORTO: June 24, St. John's and city festival with *rabelos* regatta. **PÓVOA DE VARZIM**: Easter processions, Sunday before Palm Sunday, Palm Sunday, Good Friday, Easter Sunday; June 28/29, São Pedro; Sept 15.

Tourist information
ESPINHO: **Tourist Office**: R. 6, 709, Tel. 720911, summer: daily 9am-9pm, winter Mon-Fri 9:30am-12:30pm and 14-5:30pm. **Market**: Mon, flea market every first Sunday of the month. **Hospital**: tel. 721141. **Casino**: Hotel Solverde. **PORTO**: **Offices of tourism**: R. Clube Fenianos 25, tel. 312740. (I.C.E.P.): Pr. de D. João I. 25, Tel 317514, Mon-Fri 9am-6:45pm, Sat 9am-3:45pm, Sun 10am-12:45pm. **Post office**: Pr. Gen. Humberto Delgado. **Bus stations**: Rodoviaria Norte, Pr. Filipa de Lancastre, tel. 2003152. Rodoviaria Sul, R. A. Herculano, tel. 2006954. Rodoviaria Internacional, Pr. Galiza 96, tel. 693220. **Train stations**: *Long distance*: Estação de S. Bento, Pr. Almeida Garret, tel. 2002722. *Local traffic*: Estação da Trindade, R. Alferes Malheiro, tel. 2005224. **Ferries**: ENDOURO, R. da Reboleira 49, tel. 324236, Fax: 317260. **Car rental**: Budget, Airport. Avis: Guede de Acevedo 125. Europcar: Camões 93. Hertz, Santa Catarina 899. Inter-Rent, Bolhao 182. **PÓVOA DE VARZIM**: **Tourist Office**: Av. Mousinho de Albuquerque 160, tel. 614609. **Golf course**: Sopete, 8 km. **Train station**: R. Almirante Reis. **Clinic**: tel. 615111/615555. **Post office**: Lg. Elísio da Nova. **Car rental**: Avis, Ag. Bom Despacho, tel. 615592. Hertz, Ag. Rondatur, tel. 683686. **VILA NOVA DE GAIA**: **Tourist Office**: Av. Diogo Leite, Santa Marinha, tel. 301902. **Port wine cellars**: Sandeman, L. M. Bombarda 3, 9:30am-12:30pm and 2pm-5pm, Oct-Apr, closed on weekends. Romariz, R. Barão Forrester, 3pm-11pm. Vasconcellos, R. Barão Forrester 73, 9am-8pm. Taylor's, R. do Choupelo 250, 10am-6pm. Cálem, Av. D.Leite 26-42. **Boat rides**: Mare Alte, Av. R. Pinto, departure 11am, noon, 3pm, 4pm, 5pm (three-bridges tour).

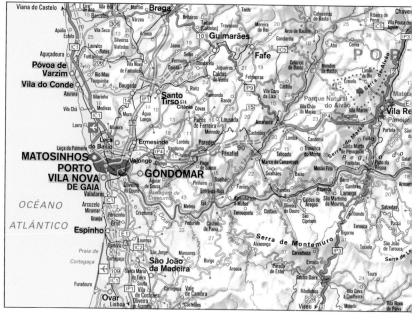

ALONG THE DOURO

One delightful excursion from Porto leads downstream along the Douro. The entire course of the river can be followed all the way to the Spanish border either by train, by boat, or by car. The best season for this trip is fall, when the leaves of the vineyards have donned their brightest colors and the harvest has begun. Drivingthrough the Douro Valley also crosses a great variety of landscapes.

The actual region where port wine is grown, a region of endless terraced vineyards dotted with the odd, white manor, begins about 60 miles (100 km) from Porto. The father inland you go, the more arid and thinly settled the land. As the river nears the border, it carves its way deep into the granite bedrock, forming the most bizarre nature spectacle.

Toward the beginning of the trip, one should take a few side trips to the east of Porto to some of the churches and monasteries. They are off the main stretch before the confluences of the Tâmega and Paiva Rivers. The Benedictine cloister of São Bento in **São Tirso** 20 kilometers to the northeast of Porto was originally founded in the Visigoth days. Once Romanesque, the construction underwent a complete facelift in the Baroque era. The showpiece of this complex, which is covered with woodcarvings, is the two-story Renaissance cloister with figurative capitals.

The Cluny monastery of **São Salvador** stands in **Paço de Sousa** to the east of Porto and to the south of the highway near the town of Parades. It, too, is of Romanesque birth. Inside, the stone, Gothic sarcophagus carried by four lions belongs to Egas Moniz, the teacher and armorer of Afonso Henriques. The life of this famous Portuguese figure, a symbol of loyalty, has been chiseled into the sides of the tomb. The portrayal, though no longer in mint shape, can be deciphered: When the king of Castile besieged Guimarães, Egas Moniz went to negotiate with him. The Castilian promised to raise the siege if the Por-

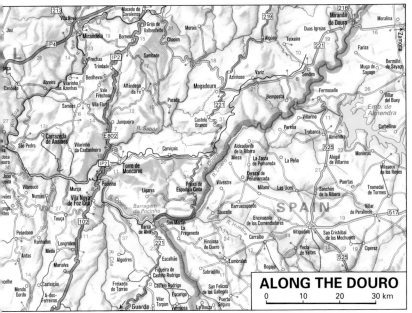

tuguese would renounce secession. When Afonso Henriques broke the pact by declaring himself king of an independent Portugal, Moniz went to the king of Castile as a penant, wearing a noose around his neck. He was generously pardoned.

In **Eja**, just before Entre-os-Rios in the Douro Valley itself, there are two other little churches that are purely Romanesque, and higher up the mountain is São Salvador. A Celtic *castrum*, Monte Mozinho, was excavated not far from here.

On the Tâmega and Paiva Rivers

The Tâmega River flows in one of the most pretty side valleys of the Douro. It is reached by passing through **Penafiel**, a village dominated by the ruins of a 14th-century fortress. The local vineyards grow the grapes from which the refreshing, spritely *vinho verde* is made.

Amarante, another picturesque town, lies on both banks of the river. An 18th-century bridge connects the busy riverside promenade, enlivened by cafés and bars, with the old monastery. A café has set up tables and chairs on the plaza facing the monastery. A steep staircase leads alongside the church to an elevation offering a wonderful view of the little town and the river banks.

The façade of the **monastery church** is a proud Renaissance affair that is topped off by a royal gallery where the kings of that epoch have been immortalized: the sponsor, João III, Dom Sebastião, the Cardinal and King Henrique, and Filipe I. The church has been named after the saint buried here, São Gonçalo, a 12th-century hermit who was considered the patron of fertility. His nameday in June is celebrated with phallus-shaped cookies. Young girls pray to him for a husband, and childless parents for children. The monastery, which has two cloisters, nowadays houses a museum of modern art. The most interesting works exhibited here are those of the Cubist painter Souza Cardoso.

Another detour can be made at this point to **Travanca do Monte**, site of a

173

Benedictine monastery, a Romanesque church, and a fortified tower that dates back to the Moorish period. More Romanesque churches can be found near the town of **Marco da Canaveses**, namely in Boelhe and Taboado.

The Paiva flows from the south into the Douro. Before that it winds its way for a solid 100 kilometers along the foot of the Serra de Montemuro mountains. Its valley exudes the calm and slowness of a region that has had little contact with the great wide world. Modest villages such as **Vila Nova de Paiva**, the spa of **Carvalhosa**, and **Castro Daire** at the upper end of the river, are pretty places for summer outings, with forests, vineyards, vegetable fields, meadows, streams, little mills, and humble Romanesque churches. The river is clean, and provides numerous opportunities for swimming, fishing, and other aquatic

Above: Vineyards near Peso da Régua in the midst of the port wine region. Right: Harvesting the grapes along the Douro.

sports. In **Gralheira** near Souselo, a village that looks down onto the Paiva from a slight elevation, one still finds a few of the old thatched stone houses, that were once typical of the whole region. The main town in the valley is **Castelo de Paiva**. It has a very special flair thanks to a host of elegant 17th- and 18th-century palaces with opulent sprawling gardens and parks.

Port Wine Country

In a region that gets only one-half to one-third of the precipitation commong along the Atlantic coast, at a point where the Douro's deep-etched course is protected by steep hills, are the great vineyards of the Douro Valley, extending up the slopes and over into the side valleys. The port wine region extends right up to the Spanish border. Its heart is between Mesão Frio and Tua. And sailing peacefully down the river leaves one with an unforgettable impression of this land that has so long been cultivated and cared for by human hands. It leaves no doubt, too, that wine-growing has always been a lucrative business. As opposed to the adjoining regions, this landscape of vineyards has not been as actively settled. The traveler passing through will not find all those little villages that make a trip across northern Portugal so entertaining.

The ebb and flow of the wine business over the centuries has concentrated the arable parcels in the hands of a few noblemen. About 50 large and 20 to 30 small producers now control the entire port wine market. Many of them have English names, as it was the British who helped the wine on its way to fame and fortune in the 18th cenutry. They generally took over the production and shipping tiers of the business. For practical purposes, the fresh grape must was carried on rafts and the typical *rabelo* boats to the place where it could later be transported abroad, namely Vila Nova da

Gaia. Regulations promulgated by the local powers-that-be stipulate that a vintner has to be settled in Gaia in order to call his wine "port."

The railway line from Porto into the northeast shares a bit of its way with the Douro. The panorama between Cinfães and Pocinho, a section lasting about two and a half hours, has few rivals in Portugal. The ship takes takes several days to cover the distance between Porto and Barca de Alva on the Spanish border, an exciting undertaking, with a number of locks, some of which are as high as 30 meters. The road, for those who are driving, follows a course high over the valley, dropping only sporadically down to the bank of the river. There are few bridges crossing the Douro, but the dams are for the most part passable. It is wise to decide beforehand on which side of the river one would like to drive.

Besides all the visual thrills along the way, there are also many opportunities to tickle ones taste buds: It's also time to learn to distinguish between port wines,

from the graceful white one to the heavier table wines. A few glasses of *vinho verde* and some of the local gourmet specialties, especially fish from the river, trout or lamprey, can turn the journey into a veritable gastronomical experience.

The villages cannot be compared to those of French or German wine-growing regions; you'll note that only a few port wines are actually aged and sold in the area. Nevertheless, some places do warrant a visit, such as **Mesão Frio** on the leeward side of the Serra de Marão, which is considered the western border of port wine country. It still has its old defenses on view, and the Town Hall located in a former Franciscan monastery is also worth seeing.

Between Peso da Régua and Pinhão, the road follows the southern bank of the Douro; after that, the road leaves the river, and only boat and train travelers can enjoy the grandiose panorama. There are hardly any villages; only wineries with such famous names as Sandemann, Ferreira, Croft, or Calem.

North of Peso da Régua, the valley of the Corgo, one of the most beautiful side valleys of the Douro, wends its way up the mountainside. Every square meter of the carefully terraced slopes is planted with vineyards. The best and most expensive port wines, the wines of **Santa Marta de Penaguião**, are cultivated here.

The moniker means "Guião's penance," which draws on a legend telling how the wine came to the Douro Valley. The French Duke Guillon had a chapel devoted to St. Martha burned down. She had opposed his plans to cultivated plants brought from France. After the deed, St. Martha appeared to him, and ordered him to work the land himself. The repentant duke rolled up his sleeves and set about the task. Soon his plants were producing the finest wines in the land. In order to complete his penance, he dedicated his

Above: The romantic Palace of Solar Mateus.
Right: Many Portuguese women can still carry great burdens on their heads.

wine to the saint, who in turn forgave him and blessed it.

Vila Real

The little town with a royal name, **Vila Real**, presides over the left bank of the Corgo. It's a lively place, graced with beautiful plazas and elegant palaces. Two of its sons are a source of local pride: Diego Cão, who discovered the estuary of the Congo River, was born here; and the 19th-century novelist Castelo Branco, who lived here for a while and set some of his stories in the town. The former hospital, which looks more like a palace thanks to its Baroque double stairway, serves as Town Hall these days.

The Gothic Cathedral, its Romanesque buttresses taken over from an earlier building on this site, used to be the church of a Dominican monastery. The Baroque **Capela Nova**, also called the Clérigos Church, stands out in the midst of the pedestrian zone. The alleys of the town exude an atmosphere from the last century. But cheek-by-jowl is the modern section of Vila Real with the newly-founded university and attractive shopping opportunities.

About 2.5 miles (4 km) west of town is a very special gem, the recently renovated Parish Church of **Vila Marim**. It was built in 1006, and boasts Portugal's most beautiful frescos, which have also been restored in the past few years. Behind it stands the 4,250-foot-high (1,300 m) **Serra de Alvão**, which has been declared a nature conservation area.

The village of **Bisalhães** is known for its black pottery. In **Agarez**, however, the traditional handicraft is linen weaving. If you want to visit the weavers at work you will have to ask your way, but the effort is worth it. The women who work in the back rooms of their houses as they have for centuries, processing the flax, spinning it into threads and then weaving it, are proud of their art.

Another must on this itinerary is a visit to the **Solar de Mateus**, the palace of the Counts of Mangualde, 2.5 miles (4 km) east of Vila Real. This former headquarters of the Mateus winery has now gone into the hands of the state, and is used as a music school and concert hall. A double entry ticket allows you to visit the park and take a tour through the exclusively furnished building, which ressembles a Rococo castle, and testifies to the wealth of a great 18th-century family. A stroll through the ornamental garden alone is also possible. The playfully pruned hedges, the luxuriant flowers, a pond, and a floral tunnel all give a feeling of magic, especially before the backdrop of the fairytale castle with its massive coat of arms and double staircase.

Panóias is signposted nearby, a mysterious heathen sacrificial spot dedicated to the Egyptian god Serapis. A large Roman settlement is thought to have existed here at one time, and the shrine belonged to it. Beyond the last house of the village are some bulky rounded rocks. Stairs and nooks have been carved into them. The geometrically perfect round and square holes suggest that they might have been covered with lids, and served to catch the blood of the victims.

South of the Douro

If taking the route that runs to the south of the Douro from Castelo de Paiva, one crosses a number of pretty places: Tarouquela, Cinfães, São Martinho de Mouros, and the spa of Caldas de Aregos. The **Monastery of Santa María de Cárquere** near **Resende** is a reminder of the miraculous healing of Afonso Henriques' crippled legs. His teacher Egas Moniz founded it as a gesture of gratitude for this bit of divine intervention.

Lamego earned its fame as the place where the *cortes*, that is the estates assembly, met in 1143 to elect Afonso Henriques king of Portugal. It is about 6 miles (10 km) south of the Douro and is one of the most attractive destinations along the way. At the end of town, a pil-

177

grim's stairway leads up to the Baroque mountain shrine **Nossa Senhora de Remédios**. The pilgrimage church was built in the middle of the 18th century, but the double stairway, with its 680 steps decorated with blue tiles, was added in 1960. It was patterned after Bom Jesus in Braga. The 14 stations of the cross, each with a Baroque chapel standing on separate ledges, are filled with thousands of pilgrims on the day of the Virgin of Remédios in September.

On one hill lie the ruins of a medieval **fortress** that was first built by the Moors. An attractive street in the old part of town leads up to it. A chapel tucked away in the row of houses has an inscription stating that the first cathedral of Lamegos stood on the spot in 435. Both hills give a good view over the town: the central Avenida with cafés, villas, and large shading trees, at the end of which stands

Above: The tile paintings of Colaço in the train station of Pinhão depict wine-growing.
Right: The eastern Douro Valley.

the Bishop's Palace with a good museum. It displays archeological finds and the sarcophagi of among others the Countess of Barcelos, Flemish Gobelins from the 16th century, paintings, tiles, and furniture. There are even some complete Baroque chapels taken from monasteries that were not destroyed during the era of secularization. The five altar panels of Grão Vasco are also exhibited, among them the one called "the Creation of Animals," which includes a gentle white unicorn. Vasco painted them for the main altar in the cathedral.

The statue in front of the museum represents one of the most important men in Portuguese history, Miguel of Portugal, the bishop of Lamego. It is said that his personal petition in Rome resulted in the Pope's acceptance of Portugal's independence.

Work on the powerful **Cathedral** began in 1129, but only the tower has survived from those days. The façade is pure and simple Gothic. The interior was redone during the Renaissance and even more thoroughly during the Baroque period. Behind the fortress is a small Romanesque church, **Santa María de Almacave**. It stands on a tract of land that was once used by the Arabs as a cemetery, hence the name, which derives from *al-mokab*, the "district of the dead."

The town is filled with pleasant cafés and restaurants, where one can enjoy local specialties. Among those are smoked hams and sausages, that seem to hang in all stores.

A steep street leads from Lamego down to the Varosa River and the church of **São Pedro de Balsemão**. This three-naved, Visigothic construction dating to the 7th century is one of the oldest churches on the Iberian Peninsula. The choir and the horseshoe arches so typical of Visigothic architecture, are still in their original shape. The 17th-century wooden ceiling, decorated with birds and flowers, forms an unusual, if striking, contrast.

The Eastern Douro Valley

The villages to the east of the Douro are usually a few kilometers away from the river itself. Until the Douro was properly regulated and dammed up, floods were fairly frequent and devastating. The banks are so steep in many places, that they offer no space for a road. Only the train penetrates the quiet valley in some places.

Pinhão, on the north bank of the river, is famous for its train station that was panneled in tiles by Colaço. They tell the story of the region and its wine-making. The next station is **Tua**. Here the rails fork off to the north into the pretty Tua Valley. If one begins early enough in Porto, one can complete a breathtaking return trip that ends with a bus ride from Mirandela.

Terra Quente, or "hot land," is what the people call the area around **Carrazeda de Ansiães**, perhaps because of its thermal springs. The landscape is already very dry. Besides vineyards, there are also a few almond groves, and in autumn the earth is burnt to a crisp brown color. South of the Douro, from Lamego to the east, is **Armamar**, which features a few interesting churches. The two medieval churches of the Cistercian monasteries of Tarouca and **Salzedas** are especially worth stopping for, however. In São João of Tarouca is the sarcophagus of the Count of Barcelos, a 14th-century work, and the sepulchers of the illegitimate sons of Dom Dinis.

For a good bout of swimming, one has to make a detour over **Moimenta da Beira**: The **Vilar storage lake** here is fed from the clear and refreshing waters that spring in the Leomil and Serra da Lapa mountains.

Saao João da Pesqueira is nestled in the beautiful craggy territory high up over the Douro. The **Chapel of São Salvador de Mundo** is perfectly situated for a plunging view of the river and its flanking vineyards. A handful of palaces recall the port wine wealth of some noble families.

179

Near the Border

Last stop on the Douro line is **Pocinho**. Very close by is the town of **Vila Nova de Foz Côa**, where a new dam was being built until October 1995. Archeologists discovered a slew of Paleolithic rock carvings estimated to be over 20,000 years old, the oldest in Europe. Controversy on whether or not the dam project should be continued ended when the new Socialist government vetoed further work and ordered an investigation into the historic value of the carvings. Equally interesting are the Celtic excavations of Citânia de Taja, its Parish Church with strange, leaning columns, and luxurious manors.

Torre de Moncorvo was always a well-defended border town, with its massive fortress and fortified church. But the actual border is beyond **Barca de Alva**. The train tracks are covered in grass nowadays, but the tiny village does come alive every time a Douro ship ties up at the pier and belches forth a throng of tourists on the search for a perfect photo subject. A special treat awaits at **Freixo de Espada à Cinta**. The octagonal "Cock Tower" there is said to have served at one time as a royal residence. As for the Parish Church, it boasts a painting by the great Basque artist Grão Vasco, and is considered one of the finest examples of Manuelistic architecture in the country.

After Barca de Alva, the Douro turns northward and separates Portugal from Spain for about 60 miles (100 km). Five more dams interrupt its flow for the production of electricity on both sides of the border. One can hardly imagine the former power of this river, which dug its way into a landscape of canyons some up to 300 meters deep. The climate in these ravines is a lot milder than on the harsh summits, which has given rise to interesting ecosystems with very special vegetation, bird life, and small mammals.

THE DOURO VALLEY
Accommodations

ALIJÓ (059): *LUXURY:* **Pousada do Barrão de Forrester**, Rua J. Rufino, tel. 95215, Fax: 959304. *BUDGET:* **Oasis**, Av. Sá Carneiro, tel. 95334.

AMARANTE (055): *MODERATE:* **Amarante**, Murtas-Madalena, tel. 422106/7, Fax: 425949. *BUDGET:* **Silva**, Rua Cândido dos Reis 53, tel. 423110. *CAMPING:* **Municipal**, Quinta da Cerca de Baixo, tel. 432133. *TURISMO RURAL:* **Casa do Zé da Calçada**, Rua 31 de Janeiro, Cepelos, tel. 422023. **Casal de Aboadela**, Aboadela, tel. 441141. **Casa da Obra**, Fregim, Tel/Fax: 425907.

ARMAMAR (054): *TURISMO RURAL:* **Quinta da Barroca**, Queimada, tel. 95757, Fax: 95756.

CASTELO DE PAIVA (055): *LUXURY:* **Casa de S. Pedro**, Sobrado, tel. 65647/65468, Fax: 65510. *MODERATE:* **Castelo D'Ouro**, Sobrado, Amaro da Costa 44. *TURISMO RURAL:* **Quinta do Lameiro**, Escamarão, Souselo, Tel. 69495.

CELORICO DE BASTO (055): *TURISMO RURAL:* **Casa do Barão de Fermil**, Fermil, tel. 361211 or 02-680778. **Casa do Campo**, Molares, tel. 361231. **Quinta da Vila Pouca**, Codeçoso, tel. 432451, Fax: 321766.

CINFÃES (055): *TURISMO RURAL:* **Casa de Rebolfe**, Porto Antigo, Tel. 562334 oder 02-813482. **Quinta de Miragaia**, Lugar de Travanca, Tel. 68214 or 02-578059.

LAMEGO (054): *MODERATE:* **Império**, Trav. dos Loureiros 6, tel. 62742. **S. Paulo**, Av. 5 de Oct. 22C, tel. 63114/5. **Solar do Espírito Santo**, Rua A. Herculano, tel. 64386/63450. **Parque**, Parque de Na. Sra. dos Remedios, tel. 62105/6 Fax: 65203. *BUDGET:* **Solar da Sé**, Largo da Sé, tel. 62060. **Silva**, Rua Tras da Sé 26, tel. 62929.

TURISMO RURAL: **Casa de Cimo de Vila**, Samodães, tel. 665044/96150. **Casa dos Pingueis** and **Casa dos Varais**, Cambres, tel. 23251. **Quinta de Marrocos**, Valdigem, tel. 23012. **Quinta da Timpeira**, Penude, tel. 62811, Fax: 65176.

MARCO DE CANAVESES (055): *MODERATE:* **Torre de Nevões** (Hotel village), Tabuado, tel. 522354/522755, Fax: 522354. **Quinta das Agros**, Sande, tel. 581473, Fax: 581465. **Marco**, Rua Dr. Sá Carneiro 684, tel. 522093/523403.

TURISMO RURAL: **Casa de Telhe**, Soalhães, tel. 522481 oder 02-671770. **Casa da Boavista**, Livração, Tel/Fax: 530262.

MÊDA (079): *TURISMO RURAL:* **Solar de Longroiva**, tel. 84167.

MESÃO FRIO (054): *MODERATE:* **Panorama**, Av. Conselheiro Alpoim 525, tel. 99236.

MONDIM DE BASTO (055): *CAMPING:* Parque de Campismo, tel. 381650.

PESO DA RÉGUA: *TURISMO RURAL:* **Quinta de Sta. Eufémia**, Parada do Bispo, Régua, tel. 24820.
PINHÃO (054): *MODERATE:* **Ponto Grande**, Rua Central 103-105, tel. 72456. *BUDGET:* **Douro**, Largo da Estação, tel. 72404. *TURISMO RURAL:* **Casa das Pontes**, Quinta da Foz, tel. 72353/72521 or 02-2004867, Fax: 72354. **Casa de Casal de Loivos**, tel. 72149.
RESENDE (054): *MODERATE:* **California**, Rua Dr. Francisco Carneiro, tel. 97252/62. *BUDGET:* **Quinta da Granja**, tel. 97502. *TURISMO RURAL:* **Casa do Fundo da Aldeia**, Caldas de Aregos, tel. 875290 or 02-7622371. **Quinta do Carujeiro**, Miomães, Caldas de Aregos, tel. 875214. **Quinta do Ribeiro**, Lugar do Ribeiro, tel. 97113/97447.
VILA REAL (059): *MODERATE:* **Mira Corgo**, Av. 1 de Maio 76-78, tel. 25001/2/3, Fax: 25006. **Cabanelas**, Rua D. Pedro de Castro, tel. 323153, Fax: 74181.
BUDGET: **O Vizinho**, Av. Aureliano Barrigas, tel. 22881/71027. **Aquariu's**, Rua Miguel Torga, tel. 23787. **Encontro**, Av. Carvalho Araújo 76-78, tel. 322532. **Countinho**, Trav. de S. Domingos 33, tel. 22039. *CAMPING:* **Municipal**, Quinta da Carreira, Tel. 24724.
TURISMO RURAL: **Casa das Quartas**, Abambres, tel. 22976/74430/24520. **Casa Agricola da Levada**, Timpeira, tel. 322190, Fax: 23955. **Casa das Cardosas**, Folhadela, tel. 331487.

Restaurants / Cafés

AMARANTE: **Zé da Calçada**, Rua 31 de Janeiro 81. **São Gonçalo**, Praça da República, tel. 422707. **Nazareth**, Rua 31 de Janeiro. **Estoril**, Rua 31 de Janeiro.
CINFÃES: **Encosta do Moínho**, Gralheira, tel. 571159.
VILA REAL: **Aquariu's**, Rua Miguel Torga, tel. 23787. **Escondidinho**, Rua Teixeira de Sousa. **Transmontano**, Rua Teixeira de Sousa, tel. 23540. **Excelsior**, Rua Teixeira de Sousa.

Sights / Museums

AMARANTE: **Monastery São Gonçalo / Museum**: daily 10am-midday and 2pm-5pm.
LAMEGO: **Regional Museum** 10am-12:30pm and 2pm-6pm. **Castle**: 10am-midday and 3pm-5pm, closed Mondays.
TABUAÇO: **Quinta Panascal** offers tours through the vineyards and cellars. Weekdays 10am-7:30pm.
VILA REAL: **Mateus**,palace and gardens daily 9am-1pm and 2pm-7pm.

Festivals

AMARANTE: Apr 29: *Feira do Cavalinho*, first Saturday in June, *Pilgrimage of S. Gonçalo*.

Sept 7/8: *S. Gens Pilgrimage* in Freixo de Cima. 2nd Sunday in July: *Pilgrimage of Sa. do Marão* in Teixeira. Sept 23/24 S. *Bartolomeu* in Campelo.
CASTELO DE PAIVA: Aug 3/4: *Pilgrimage of S. Domingos da Serra* Sept 14-16: pilgrimages. Around June 24: *Town fest of S. João and S. Pedro*, June, popular festival and *vinho verde* festival.
CELORICO DE BASTO: 3rd weekend in July: town festival and *Santiago Pilgrimage*. November 25: *Sta. Catarina* in Britelo.
LAMEGO: Sept 6-8: Pilgrimage to Na. Sra. dos Remédios, known as *Romaria de Portugal*.
MARCO DE CANAVESES: Friday after the Ascencion: *Pilgrimage of Na. Sa. da Livração* in Toutosa.
MESÃO FRIO: Nov 30: *Santo André*, festival and market (10 days long).
MIRANDA DO DOURO: July 25: *São Tiago*.
MONDIM DE BASTO: 1rst Sunday in September: *Na. Sa. da Graça Pilgrimage*; July 25: *São Tiago*.
VILA REAL: 2nd Sunday after Easter: celebration of the day of the ill. Corpus CHristi procession. June 13: town festival. June 29: *Feira dos Pucarinhos e Bordados* (potters' and crafts market). Last Sunday in August: *St. Ana Pilgrimage in Campeã*. June 29: São Pedro.

Transportation

Trains from Porto to Marco de Canaveses over Pinhão and Pocinho (change trains in Régua). Trains to Mirandela in Tua; busses from Mirandelato Porto; day-long round trips are possible.

Tourist information

AMARANTE: **Tourist Office**: Alamêda de Teixeira de Pascoães, tel. 432259, daily 9:30am-12:30pm and 2pm-7pm. **Parque Aquático**: Estr. Vila Meá, daily 11am-8pm.
CINFÃES (055): **Tourist Office**: 561297/ 561757. **Market**: on the 10th and 26th of each month.
LAMEGO (054): **Tourist Office**: Av. Visconde Guedes Teixeira, tel. 62005, Fax: 63758, 9am-12:30pm and 2pm-7pm, Sa/So only till 5:30pm. **Market**:Fridays. **Boat rides** on the Douro: Companhia Turística do Douro, Quinta de Tourais, tel. 331020, Fax: 65176.
MARCO DE CANAVESES: **Tourist Office**: tel. 534101/2. **Market**: Mondays.
PINHÃO: **Boat rides** to the ford of Bagauste just before Régua, Mondays, Wednesdays, and weekends, Info: Companhia Turística do Douro, Quinta de Tourais, Lamego, tel. 054-331020, Fax: 65176.
VILA REAL (059): **Tourist Office**: Av. Carvalho Araújo, tel. 322819, 9:30am-12:30pm and 2:30pm-5pm, in summer until 7pm. **Car rentals**: NUROCAR, Rua dos Quinchosos, ent. 26, loja 5, tel. 321733. **Market**: Tuesdays.

PORTUGAL'S
MOUNTAIN HEART

GUARDA / SERRA DA ESTRÊLA
VISEU AND THE DÃO
SERRA DO AÇOR AND SERRA
DA LOUSÃ
BETWEEN THE ZÊZERE AND
THE TEJO

The inland territory of the Beira between the Douro and Tejo Rivers is Portugal's most mountainous area. The region between the Mondego and the Zêzere is cordoned off by the Serra da Estrêla, the Serra do Açor, and the Serra da Lousa. These mountains are of granite and deeply furrowed by river valleys, which often makes travel somewhat difficult.

The rainy northern slopes have a dense and rich vegetation, with numerous varieties of oaks, chestnut trees, as well as bushy forests. The southern side is drier, and the most one finds here are pines and eucalyptus trees. The tree line begins at about 4,265 feet (1,300 m).

The roads, for those driving, are narrow and winding, villages are fairly rare. The main attraction for the traveler in these parts consists of picnic places, riverside swimming pools, hiking trails, and lookout platforms. The air, too, with its dizzying aroma of thyme and broom, and the sturdy local cuisine, should not be left out of the list of lures. Among the specialties are goat cheeses, fish from the rivers, bread, and rich meat dishes.

Preceding pages: Shepherds in the Serra da Estrêla taking a break. Left: The cool waters of the lakes and streams of the Serra da Estrêla are a favorite on hot summer days.

GUARDA AND ITS ENVIRONS

Guarda was founded by King Sancho I at the end of the 12th century. It lies at an elevation of 3526 feet (1075 m), which makes it the highest town in Portugal. In order to ensure the defense of this territory, Sancho I had a string of forts built and forced thieves and highway robbers to settle the region. The cornerstone of the Romanesque cathedral was also laid during his reign. A memorial statue has been erected to him in front of the Cathedral on Praça de Camões. Dom Dinis continued supporting this little community by building a wall around it, and moving the bishop from Egitania – which was later called Idanha-a-Velha – to here.

Modern Guarda is a lively provincial town whose economy derives from the food processing industry, its educational institutions, and from being a regional administrative center. The **Cathedral** and the ruins of the old fortress lie at its highest point. The former was originally a fortified church built between the 14th and 16th centuries. In spite of later additions and renovations, it has maintained its simple Gothic character. The western portal and a part of the altar room were redone in Manuelistic style by the architect Boytaca. The *pièce de resistance* is the Renaissance altar piece by João de

185

SERRA DA ESTRELA

0   10   20   30 km

Rouão (Jean de Rouen). Its gilding, however, was done in the 18th century. Anyone making his way up to the roof of the Cathedral will be rewarded with a comprehensive view of Guarda and its green surroundings.

The oldest part of town adjoins the Cathedral. It is enclosed in the remains of the city wall, which at one point grows into the **Feirros Tower**. The candidly elegant granite façades of the houses and palaces are decorated with flowers and the coats of arms of the noble families that once lived here. Next to the Old Town is the *juderia*, where Jews fleeing from Spain at the end of the 15th century found refuge until they were also expelled from Portugal. Many of them were forced to convert, but went on practicing their religion in secret. In the more remote mountains, far from anything ressembling a human community, many Jews continued holding their *conversos* well into the 18th century.

The **Regional Museum** has been moved into the former priests' seminary of the Bishop's Palace, a building dating to the 15th and 16th centuries. It documents the growth and evolution of the region since the Paleolithic days, has a section devoted to folklore, and the top floor exhibits a collection of modern paintings. Another sight well worth indulging the eyes in is the church **Igreja São Vincente** (18th-century), which is heavily decorated with *azulejos*.

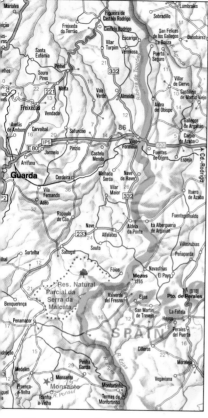

The area extending north of Guarda to the Douro and east to the Spanish border consists of arid mountains. The villages are generally sleepy, having long lost their defensive function. **Trancoso** is a perfect example, a peaceful community with clean air. It is also where Dom Dinis married Isabel of Aragón. The stout defensive wall, with its five towers, the tower of homage, and four gates, still dates to that period. Equally old is the annual animal market, which attracts people from beyond the region. Trancoso also has a significant Jewish community. One can also visit the house of the rabbi, which is popularly known as *gato preto*, meaning "black tomcat," and suggests, most probably, the lion of Judea.

Powerful fortresses also rise over **Penedono** and **Marialva** to the north of Trancoso. **Pinhel**, a small village on a mountain, specializes in wine-making. The two towers of a fortress built by Dom Dinis in the 14th century form its hallmark. **Almeida** has a very complete star-shaped citadel in typical Vauban style of the 18th century. Napoleon's army clashed with Wellington's here. The place seemed impregnable until the arsenal blew up, forcing the British and Portuguese to surrender. One can walk along most of the bastions, except where a modern Pousada has anachronistically opened for business.

The fortified hill of **Castelo Rodrigo**, which features 13 defensive towers, can be seen from a great distance. A Moorish cistern has been found in it, and one can still visit the ruins of the palace where the traitor Cristóvão de Moura once lived. He helped the Spanish king Felipe II slide into the Portuguese throne.

The more accessible **Figueira de Castelo Rodrigo** was granted market rights in the 19th century. On the edge of town is the Cistercian **Monastery of Santa María de Aguiar** (13th century), which is in private hands. It features a three-aisled Gothic hall church, an ornate chapter room, and a loggia with Tuscan columns. And if you are still not tired of visiting forts, **Vilar Formoso** at the border has a few more: Castelo Born and Castelo Mendo, which were supposed to keep the Spaniards at bay. The town also has a beautifully tiled train station.

South of Guarda, in the valley called Cova da Beira, the worthy old town of **Belmonte** sweeps picturesquely down to the Zêzere River from the side of Mount Esperança. It owes its fame to Pedro Alvares de Cabral, the discoverer of Brazil, who was born here. His family's coat-of-arms adorns the tower of homage of the old fortress. Its members are all buried in the early Gothic Santiago Chapel, but the great explorer himself lies in Santarém.

Belmonte had quite a sizable Jewish community until the 18th century, a fact that contributed to the town's wealth. Nearby is the mysterious **Centum Cellas Tower**, which, as the name indicates, once had a hundred cells. Its origins are Roman, and some think that it was once upon a time used as a jail.

Another fortified hill stands to the west of Guarda near the highway. The fort of **Celorico de Beira**, whose cornerstone was laid in the 10th century, was destroyed by the French in the 19th century. The ruin is still in the process of falling apart. The Old Town's narrow streets have lost none of their medieval quality. The town's claim to fame is a soft cheese, the *queijo da serra*, which is made between December and May, and tastes best when fresh. Market is held every second Friday, and the local farmers usually have the cheese on their stalls.

Above: The Judería – old Jewish quarter – of Guarda. Right: Pasturelands coaxed out of the rocky surface of the Serra da Estrêla.

SERRA DA ESTRÊLA

The monumental granite range **Serra da Estrêla**, the highest in mainland Portugal, with peaks nearing the 6,500-foot (2000 m) mark, has been declared a nature conservation area in its entirety. Boars, wolves, and rare birds of prey are among its points of interest. Its visual attractiveness lies in its variety of landscapes, deep, steep valleys, rocky summits, quiet hiking trails, clean streams, and small villages with pretty restaurants. Getting there, however, is no easy task. The narrow and tortuous roads are used not only by thousands of vacationers and locals, but also by logging trucks. Rain and fog are no strangers to the place either. In winter there is often enough snow to allow a few ski lifts to run. The two largest Portuguese rivers, the Mondego and the Zêzere, arise in the Serra, which they also frame in the north and south.

Little roads leave from Guarda and crisscross the northern part of the Serra,

188

ultimately leading to **Cabeça Alta**, a peak at an altitude of 4,208 feet (1,287 m) and a number of handsome mountain villages, such as the medieval **Linhares**, whose fortress guarded the Mondego crossing in days of yore. The church owns a few paintings by Grão Vasco. The most exciting event in town, however, is the paragliding competition held every August.

Access to the higher western part of the range begins in Gouveia and Seia. Just beyond Seia, near the village of São Romão, is the nature park with rock formations that look a little like human heads, hence bear such nicknames as "old man's head" and "baldy." The southern route goes through Lapa dos Dinheiros and Lorigã, to regions that have suffered major forest fires. The second mountain road winds its way over hairpin turns and serpentine stretches to **Sabugueiro**. It passes by the storage lake **Lagoa Comprida**, which is at 5,232 feet (1,600 m), and then skirts the Torre, Portugal's highest point at 6,517 feet (1,993 m). The

way to the Zêzere Valley leads one through the ski resort of **Penhas da Saúde**.

The drive downward is also very impressive, with spectacular views of the plain and **Covilhã**. This modest little town was Portugal's most important trading post for wool in the 17th century until the Methuen Treaty of 1703 allowed the import of British textiles, which drastically affected the native market. The Romanesque **Chapel of São Martinho** and the **Church of Santa María Major**, which is adorned with beautiful *azulejos*, are both worth a visit in Corvilhã.

If you would rather go on a round trip, then turn north before Penhas da Saúde and drive straight through the former glacial valley to **Manteigas**. The spa **Caldas da Manteigas**, with its hot sulphurous springs, lies about a mile (2 km) to the south. About 4 miles (6 km) from town is the **Poço do Inferno**, the "Fountain of Hell," a high waterfall that pours down into a natural basin. Another road meanders its way up to the high plateau called Penhas Dorados, the Golden Rock,

where there is an observatory, a rest station, and vacation homes. The granite formations here also have peculiar forms and corresponding names, such as *cabeça do velho*, "head of the old man." Two miles (3 km) further, at an altitude of 4,905 feet (1,500 m), is the *Pousada São Lourenço*. The way down is on a road that swings gently through a hilly, agricultural landscape, back toward the northern edge of the range and **Gouveia**. In town is the tourist office where one can find information about the fauna, flora, hotels, and inns of the nature park.

VISEU AND THE DÃO

Viseu is an important market town in the middle of a large wine-growing area. It stands at the intersection of the old highways from Guardia to Aveiro, and from Vila Real to Coimbra. The Lusita-

Above: Folk dances in the Serra da Estrêla.
Right: Piódão, a remote little village in the Serra do Açor.

nian warrior Viriato is said to have hidden here in the 2nd century B.C. The Romans had to hire the services of a treacherous assassin in order to end his resistance. A memorial to Viriato has been placed on the edge of town. The Old Town grew within the limits of the former Roman quarter, and is surrounded by its own set of walls, which Afonso V had built over the Roman foundations. The Romanesque **Cathedral**, which was altered in the 16th century, stands on the edge of the Old Town. In 1640, the old façade was replaced with a Baroque one, and the blend of styles was repeated inside. The Manuelistic vaulted ceiling rests on Romanesque columns, and the two-story cloister has clear Renaissance features. A museum of religious art is in the side rooms of the Cathedral, showing among other works by Machado de Castro, and enamelware from Limoges.

In the former Bishop's Palace, the "Palace with the three steps," as it is popularly called, is a **museum** devoted to the works of Grão Vasco, who is considered by the experts as one of the finest painters in the 16th century. The "great Basque," whose actual name was Vasco Fernandes, was born in 1480 in Viseu. His father was a Basque immigrant. Vasco founded the local art school, which became one of the best known in Portugal. The depiction of St. Peter as the first Pope, and a landscape with the Cathedral of Viseu are seen as his masterpieces.

Viseu is surrounded by a number of spas, such as **Vouzela**, **Oliveira de Frades**, **São Pedro do Sul**, whose healing waters were already known to the Romans. To the north is the popular climatic health resort **Carvalhal**. And still further north, at the foot of the Serra de Montemuro, lies a pretty medieval town called **Castro Daire**. The Town Hall and the museum are both located in the **Palace Casa da Cerca** (18th century). The community church has a noteworthy *talha dourada* altar and a coffered ceiling.

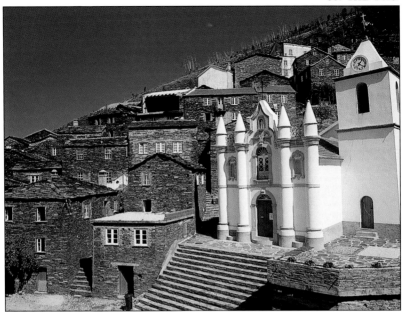

Castro Daire is an excellent base for excursions into the neighboring Montemuro mountains, to the Valley of the Douro, and into the mountains around Moledo. The area has hiking trails, riverside pools, old mills, and pristine landscapes. The Paiva Valley is particularly attractive. The charming early Romanesque **Chapel of Ermida da Paiva** is just 3 miles (5 km) west of Castro Daire.

A single mountain crest rises out of the hilly landscape southwest of Viseu: the Serra do Caramulo, whose highest peak reaches an altitude of 3,512 feet (1,074 m). The barren summit contrasts sharply with the luscious vegetation at lower altitudes. **Caramulo** itself is a health resort featuring parks and a private museum. It has a host of paintings by artists ranging from Grão Vasco to Picasso, and a large collection of automobiles.

The main attraction in the simple but pretty little villages to the south of Viseu, between the Dão and the Mondego, is the locally produced wine. The **Palace of the Anadia Princes** in **Mangualde**, whose 18th-century tile paintings are exquisitely done, should not be left out.

The comely **Santa Comba Dão**, which lies high over the Dão near its confluence with the Mondego, has one skeleton in its closet. It is the birthplace of the late dictator Oliveira Salazar (1889-1970), who ruled Portugal with an iron hand for much of the 20th century.

SERRA DO AÇOR AND SERRA DA LOUSÃ

Oliveira do Hospital was named after a hospital operated by the Knights of St. John that stood here during the Middle Ages. The town is ideal as a base for excursions into the charming valleys on the northern edge of the Açor and Lousã mountains. The **Alva River** runs through the prettiest one. It flows out of the mountains near Sandomil, passing by small villages and lovingly cared-for gardens. The Alva provides an exquisite backdrop for more than 18 miles (30 km) before feeding the Fronhas storage lake.

It then meets up with the Mondego. Each of the villages along the way seems to have evolved according to the same pattern, namely around a small main plaza with a bar, a *pelourinho*, and a fountain, one or two manors that have seen better times, and a Baroque church. Along the river bank where the Y-shaped bridge crosses two small rivers in **Ponte das Tres Entradas** is a camping site. **Avô**, **Coja**, and **Arganil** have enjoyable restaurants and bars. Vegetation in the valley is luscious and green. Higher up are **Lourosa**, with a pre-Romanesque church, and **Aldeia das Dez**, with the remains of Baroque palaces.

Few travelers ever make their way into the more remote regions of the **Serra do Açor** mountains. The higher one goes, the more unadulderated appear the villages. The common building material is dark slate, but here and there a small

church all in white shines like a gem. The most beautiful village of all is **Piódão**.

The **Serra da Lousã** is a little closer to Coimbra and hence seems more connected to the world of the present. **Lousã** itself has long been a summer escape for the middle class. Its industrial development started early with the opening of Portugal's first paper mill in the 19th century. Some of the opulent villas still seen in town date from that period. About 2 miles (3 km) away, high up in the Serra, are the ruins of the **Arouce** fortress, romantically set in the middle of a forest. Only the reverential tower remains standing. A little further up the mountain, the pilgrimage chapel **Ermida da Piedade** glows in the forest. For swimming one can follow the **Ceira River** up the mountain from the village of **Góis**. At one point it feeds a handful of small lakes.

The romantic atmosphere of the villages up here tends to blind one to the harsh realities of life. In most places only a half-dozen houses are inhabited by members of the older generation.

Above: Weaving is one of the more common handicrafts. Right: Monsanto looks over a wide landscape from its elevated location.

BETWEEN THE ZÊZERE AND THE TEJO

To the southeast of the Serra da Estrêla lies a region of thinly settled, mellifluous hills, with isolated valleys and orchards. As one heads eastward, the landscape becomes drier and more steppe-like. The little town of **Fundão** is located here, just to the south of Covilhã at the foot of the Gardunha range, whose peaks rise up to 4,012 feet (1,227 m). Hiking trails begin at the lovely village of **Alpedrinha**.

The "holy mountain," **Monsanto**, one of the most beautiful pieces of real estate in Portugal, rises out of the flatlands near Spain. On its summit, embraced by menacing granite rocks, is a reconstructed medieval fortress. From this spot one can see the Serra da Estrêla and into Spain. In 1938, Monsanto won a competition for "Portugal's most Portuguese village." The prize, a silver weather vane, is on the church steeple. The village, which is built of granite – that includes the modern Pousada – hangs on to the side of the mountain at a dizzying height. At night the fortress and the rocks are illuminated. The apparent proximity of the stars and the stillness of the area only help increase the magic. Long before our time Monsanto was used as a cultic site.

To the south of the mountain lies **Idanha-a-Velha**, which the Romans called *Egitania*. About a dozen houses, a dilapidated manor, a pretty plaza with a *pelourinho*, are all that remain of this town that was the first bishopric of the region in Roman and Visigothic days. The hard-working traveler will be able to make out the remains of the fortress, the city wall, the cathedral, the local oil press, and several churches.

The road to the border leads through **Penha García**, another mountain village sitting at the foot of a fort, and then to **Monfortinho**. This popular health resort only provides a few hotels for overnight stays. Everything is nicely tended to, and its pools, tennis courts, and golf courses complete the picture of an attractive place to enjoy one's vacation.

SERRA DA ESTRÊLA
Accommodations

ARGANIL (035): *MODERATE:* **Arganil**, Av. das Forças Armadas, Tel: 22959, Fax: 23123. **Piquenique do Paço**, Largo do Paço, Coja, Tel: 92156. *BUDGET:* **Canário**, Rua Oliveira Matos 13, Tel: 22457. **Flor do Alva**, Coja, Tel: 92152. *CAMPING:* **Municipal**, Sarcedo, Tel: 22706. **AVÔ** (038): *BUDGET:* **Italva**, Ponte das Tres Entradas, Tel: 57685. *CAMPING:* **Ponte das Tres Entradas**, Tel: 57684, Fax: 57685. **Coja**, Tel: 035-92359. *TURISMO RURAL:* **Bõa Vida**, Vila Cova do Alva. Pretty villa on a slope.
BELMONTE (075): *LUXURY:* **Belsol**. Quinta do Rio. E.N. 18. Tel: 912206, Fax: 912315. *MODERATE:* **Altitude**, Rua A. Cabral 33, Tel: 911170. *CAMPING:* **Parque de Valhelhas**, Tel: 48160.
CARAMULO (032): *LUXURY:* **Pousada de S. Jerónimo**, Tel: 861291, Fax: 861640.
CASTRO DAIRE (032): *BUDGET:* **Morgado**, Vila Pouca, Tel: 33287. *CAMPING:* **Termas de Carvalhal**, Tel: 32803. *TURISMO RURAL:* **Casa Campo das Bizarras,**, Tel: 36107, Fax: 32044.
COVILHÃ (075): *LUXURY:* **Turismo**, Tel: 324545, Fax: 324630. **Fonte Nova**: Dominguiso, Tel: 959778, Fax: 959339.
MODERATE: **Santa Eufémia**, Sitio da Palmatoria, Tel: 313308, Fax: 314184. *BUDGET:* **A Regional**, Rua das Flores 4, Tel: 322596.
CAMPING: **Parque do Pião**, Tel: 314312.
FUNDÃO (075): *LUXURY:* **Samasa**, Rua Vasco da Gama, Tel: 71608, Fax: 71809. **Est. da Neve**, Calçada de São Sebastião, Tel: 52215, Fax: 71809. *MODERATE:* **Fundão**, Rua Vasco de Gama, Tel: 52051. *CAMPING:* **Parque Quinta do Convento**, Tel: 53118. *TURISMO RURAL:* **Casa dos Maias**, Praça do Município 11, Tel: 73286. **Casa do Barreiro**, Largo das Escolas, Tel: 57120. **Casa da Comenda**, Alpedrinha, Tel: 57161.
GÓIS (035): *CAMPING:* **Municipal**, Tel: 97128.
GOUVEIA (038): *MODERATE:* **Gouveiá**, Av. 1 de Maio, Tel: 491010, Fax: 41370. *BUDGET:* **Estrêla do Parque**, Rua da República 36, Tel: 42171. *CAMPING:* **Parque Curral do Negro**, Tel: 491008. *TURISMO RURAL:* **Casa da Rainha**, Rua Direita 68, Toural, Tel: 42132. **Casa Grande**, Paços da Serra, Tel: 43341. **Quinta da Tremõa**, Nespereira, Tel: 42087. **Casa da Capela**, Rio Torto, Tel: 46423.
GUARDA (071): *LUXURY:* **Turismo**, Av. Coronel O. Carvalho. Tel:223366, Fax:223399. **Felipe**, Rua Vasco da Gama 9, Tel: 212658, Fax: 221402. *MODERATE:* **Aliança**, Rua V.da Gama 8, Tel: 222235, Fax: 221451. *BUDGET:* **Beira Serra**, Rua Infante D. Henrique, 35, Tel:212392. **Guardense**, Rua S.Pinto 13, Tel: 211311.

CAMPING: **Orbitur**, Tel: 211406. *TURISMO RURAL:* **Solar do Alarcão**, Rua D. Miguel de Alarcão 25, Tel: 24392. Elegant, in the midst of the Old Town. **Quinta da Ponte**, Faia, Tel: 96126. **Quinta de S. José**, Aldeia Viçosa, Tel: 96210. **Quinta do Pinheiro**, Covadoude, Tel/Fax: 96162.
LOUSÃ (039): **Parque de Bungalows A.C.M.**, Foz de Arouce, Tel: 991539. *TURISMO RURAL:* **Casa da Quinta da Saudade**, Rua Dr. Pires de Carvalho, Tel: 991240.
MANTEIGAS (075): *LUXURY:* **Pousada de São Lourenço**, Penhas Douradas, Tel: 982450, Fax: 982453. **Berne**, Quinta de Santo António, Tel: 981391, Fax: 982114. *MODERATE:* **Estrêla**, Rua Dr. Sobral 3, Tel: 981288. **Serradalto**, Rua 1 de Maio, Tel: 981151. *TURISMO RURAL:* **Casa de São Roque**, Rua de Santo António 51, Tel: 981125.
TERMAS DE MONFORTINHO (077): *LUXURY:* **Astória**, Tel: 44205, Fax: 44330. **Fonte Santa**, Tel: 44105, Fax: 44343.
MODERATE: **Martins**, Tel: 44246. **Portuguesa**, Tel: 44213. **Beira Baixa**, Tel: 44115.
MONSANTO (077): *LUXURY:* **Pousada**, Tel: 34471, Fax: 34481. *CAMPING:* **Barragem de Idanha-a-Nova**, Tel: 22793, Fax: 22723.
OLIVEIRA DO HOSPITAL (038): *LUXURY:* **Pousada de Santa Bárbara**, Póvoas das Quartas, Tel: 59551, Fax: 59645. **São Paulo**, Rua Prof. Antunes Varela 3, Tel: 52361, Fax: 52094. *CAMPING:* **Parque de São Gião**, São Gião, Tel: 51154. *TURISMO RURAL:* **Solar de Ervedal da Beira**, Ervedal da Beira, Tel: 641133, Fax: 641133. **Casa do Forninho**, Vila Franca da Beira, Tel: 54168. **Casa das Laranjeiras**, Gramaços, Tel: 52404.
SÃO PEDRO DO SUL (032): *LUXURY:* **Parque**, Termas de São Pedro do Sul, Tel: 723461, Fax: 723047. *MODERATE:* **Lafões**, Rua do Correio, Tel: 711616. **Avenida**, Rua Dr. Veiga Macedo, Tel: 723075. **Janelas do Rio**, Termas, Tel: 723013. Hotel village. *CAMPING:* **Termas**, Tel: 711793. Nice location on the River Vouga. *TURISMO RURAL:* **Quinta das Latas**, Freixo, Sta. Cruz da Tapa, Tel: 711855. With a swimming pool. **Quinta da Comenda**, Tel: 711101. Swimming pool. **Casa de Carvalhals**, Quintela, Várzea, Tel: 712865.
SEIA (038): *LUXURY:* **Est. de Seia**, Av. Dr. Afonso Costa, Tel: 22666, Fax: 22438. **Senhora do Espinheiro**, Lugar do Espinheiro, Tel: 22073. *MODERATE:* **Serra da Estrêla**, Rua Dr. Simões Pereira, Tel: 22573. *TURISMO RURAL:* **Casa da Ponte**, Alvoco da Serra, Tel: 93351. **Casa da Ribeira**, Alvoco da Serra, Tel: 94253, Fax: 7971172. **Casa das Tílias**, S. Romão, Tel: 20055. **Casa do Cruzeiro**, Sabugueiro, Tel: 22825. **Casa de Sofía**, Sabugueiro, Tel: 22825. **Solar das Oliveiras**, Girabolhos, Tel: 46691.

VISEU (032): *LUXURY*: **Grão Vasco**, Rua Gaspar Barreiros, Tel: 423511, Fax: 27047. **Maná**, Via Caçador, Tel: 472943, Fax: 478744. *MODERATE*: **Duque de Viseu**, Rua das Ameias 22, Tel: 421286. **Moínho de Vento**, Rua Paulo Emilio 13, Tel: 424116. *BUDGET*: **Pensão Viriato**, Largo Mouzinho de Alburquerque 24, Tel: 26510. *TURISMO RURAL*: **Casa dos Gomes**, São João de Lourosa, Tel: 461341. **Casa de Rebordinho**, Rebordinho, Tel: 461258. **Quinta de Baixo**, Marcozelos, Tel: 27631.

Restaurants / Cafés
ARGANIL: **Charles**, Av. José Augusto de Carvalho, Tel 22810. **O Telheiro**, Rua Oliveira Matos, Tel: 22655. **O Parque**, Sarcedo, Tel: 22820. **O Lagar do Alva**, Coja, Tel: 92460. **Príncipe da Alva**, Coja, Tel: 92159. **O Caçula**, S. Martinho da Cortiça, Tel: 455136. **O Fontinha**, Piodão, Tel: 93151.
CASTRO DAIRE: **O Braseiro**, Av. António Cerrado, Tel: 32026. **O Tosco**, Av. Marechal Gomes da Costa, Tel: 32693. **Canastro**, Av. Coronel António Serrado, Tel: 31134. **Encosta do Moínho**, Gralheira-Cinfães, Tel: 571159.
COVILHÃ: **A Cocinha d'Avô**, Quinta do Covelo, Tel: 331174. **Os Arcos**, Vale das Donas, Tel: 327077.
FUNDÃO: **Casa do Bico**, Estalagem da Neve, Tel: 52215. **Herminia**, Av. da Liberdade, Tel: 52537. **Mario's**, Rua Journal de Fundão 31, Tel: 52422. **Sol e Dó**, Av. da Liberdade, Tel: 52074.
GUARDA: **Beira Sierra**, Rua Infante D. Henrique 35, Tel: 212392. **Oliveira**, Rua do Encontro 1, Tel: 214446. **Belo Horizonte**, Lg. São Vicente 2, Tel: 211454. **Bom Gosto**, Quinta do Camalhão, Tel: 239378. **A Baronesa da Guarda**, Av. Dr. Afonso Costa, Bl. 4, Tel: 221901.
MANGUALDE: **Arco Iris**, Av. Comandante D. Henrique, Tel: 623075. **Zurão**, Rua Nova 56, Tel: 611073.
MANTEIGAS: **A Cascata**, Rua 1 de Maio, Tel: 982139. **Berne**, Quinta Santo António, Tel: 981351. **O Abrigo**, Bairro Alardo, Tel: 981271.
SANTA COMBA DÃO: **D. Julieta**, Rua Miguel Neves, Tel: 881755. **Rest. do Mercado**, Mercado municipal, Tel: 881846. **Santo Estevão**, Bairro Santo Estevão, Tel: 881749.
TRANCOSO: **O Museu**, Rua Coronel R. de Campos, Tel:91810. **S. Marcos**, L. Luis Alburquerque.
VISEU: **Casa dos Queijos**, Trav. Escadinhas da Sé 7, Tel: 22643. **Trave Negra**, Rua Loureiros 40, Tel: 21638. **A Parreira**, on the road to Lamego. **Retiro do Hilario**, Casa de Fados, Rua do Gonçalinho 42, Tel: 428425. **A Cocheira**, Rua Gonçalinho 84, Tel: 27571. **Feira São Mateus**, Largo Feira S. Mateus, Tel: 26992. **Verde Gaio**, Tra-

vessos de Baixo, Tel: 440146. **O Paradense**, Av. da Bélgica 83, Tel: 411628. Postigo da Sé, Largo do Pintor Gala. **Galeria 22**, Largo da Sé.

Sights / Museums
CARAMULO: Museu do Automóvil e Arte: 10am-1pm and 2pm-6pm, closed Mondays. **CASTRO DAIRE: Museum**: 9am-12:30pm and 2pm-5:30pm, closed Sundays. **GUARDA: Sé**: 9am-midday and 2pm-5pm, closed Mondays. **Museum**: 10am-1pm and 2pm-6pm, closed Mondays. **GOUVEIA: Museum**: 10am-12:30pm and 2pm-5pm, closed Mondays. **PINHEL: Museum**: daily 8am-6pm. **VISEU: Museu do Grão Vasco**, 10am-12:30pm and 2pm-5:30pm, closed Mondays and holidays. **Museu de Arte Sacra**, daily 10am-12:30pm and 2pm-6pm. **Museu Almeida Moreira**: 10am-12:30pm and 2pm-5pm, closed Mondays.

Festivals
CASTRO DAIRE: *Na. Sen. da Ouvida* Aug 3 **CELORICO DA BEIRA**: Pilgrimage *Sto. António do Río* June 13. **GUARDA**: June 24 and last weekend in July. **MANGUALDE**: *Feira dos Santos* first weekend in September.
VISEU: Town festival: June 13; *São Mateu*: 2nd weekend in September.

Tourist information
ARGANIL: Office of tourism: Cámara Municipal, Tel: 22850. **CARAMULO: Office of tourism**: Est. Principal, Tondela, Tel: 711320
CASTRO DAIRE: Office of tourism: 9am-12:30pm and 2pm-5:30pm, closed Sundays.
CELORICO DA BEIRA: Office of tourism: Rua Andrade Corvo, Tel: 72109. 9:30am-midday and 2pm-6pm. Closed Sundays and Mondays.
COVILHÃ: Office of tourism: Praça do Município, Tel: 322170, 9:30am-midday and 2pm-8pm. Closed Sundays.
FUNDÃO: Office of tourism: Av. da Liberdade, Tel: 52770.
GUARDA: Office of tourism: Praça Luís de Camões, Tel: 222251, Tue-Sat 9:30am-midday and 2pm-6pm. **Train station**: 5 km outside town.
GOUVEIA: Office of tourism: Av. 1 de Maio, Tel: 42185, 9:30am-12:30pm and 2:30pm-6pm, closed Sundays. **LOUSÃ: Office of tourism**: R. João de Cáceres, Tel: 993502.
MANTEIGAS: Office of tourism: Rua 1 de Maio, Tel: 98129.
NELAS: Office of tourism: Lg. Prof. Veiga Simão, Tel: 944348.
SEIA: Office of tourism: Rua do Mercado, Tel: 22272. **TRANCOSO: Office of tourism**: Mon bis Fri 9am-12:30pm and 2pm-5:30pm, Sat, Sun: 10am-midday and 2:30pm-4:30pm.
VISEU: Office of tourism: Av. Gulbenkian, Tel: 422014. **Market**: Tuesdays.

ENTRE-OS-RIOS
AND
TRAS-OS-MONTES

MINHO VALLEY / LIMA VALLEY
PENEDA-GERÊS
COSTA VERDE / BARCELOS
BRAGA / GUIMARÃES
THE NORTHEAST

Between the rivers and beyond the mountains – how better to describe the northern part of Portugal? The Minho, Lima, Cávado, Ave, and Tâmega irrigate northwestern Portugal, which is the wettest region on the Iberian Peninsula. The rivers and streams are for the most part clean, and have been dammed into a number of reservoirs, which are an El Dorado for swimmers, anglers, and hikers out to observe the fauna and flora of nature reserves. The numerous little communities in the valleys have their own specialties, forts, castles, and palaces that tell a thousand years of history.

THE MINHO VALLEY

The Minho forms the border between Spain and Portugal, but the land on both sides of the river seems to have been created by the same hand: houses built of granite, Baroque churches, elongated corncribs (*espigueiros*), stone crosses and pillories (*cruceiros* and *pelourinhos*), and the same tasty Albarinho wine. The two banks are frequently connected by ferries, but the only bridge is in **Valença do Minho**. It was built by Gustave Eiffel

Preceding pages: Valença do Minho, a fortified town on the Spanish border. Left: The pilgrimage church Bom Jesus do Monte in Braga.

in 1885 on the spot where the Roman road used to cross the river. Valença rests in the arms of a powerful fortified complex built in the 18th century. The few streets that fit into it are filled to the brim with people, cars, and street vendors. On weekends in particular, the Spanish come across the border on shopping sprees to buy towels and sheets, which are much cheaper than at home. Some degree of calm can be found on the fortified wall or the terrace of the Pousada. The view of the river valley is spectacular.

The other communities along the Minho are less overrun and therefore more contemplative. Upstream are a few health and vacation resorts, where one finds an attractive Romanesque church or two: the church of **Monçao**, the monastery church of the Mosteiro Longos Vales, São Fins in Friestas, or the chapel of Nossa Senhora de Orada on the northern tip of Portugal, which is dwarfed by a medieval fortified tower.

Vila Nova de Cerveira lies downstream from Valença. In spite of its relatively small size, it has achieved some fame thanks to the Arts Biennial held every second summer. In 1321, King Dinis I commissioned the fort and the buildings of the fortified ring to be built. One of Portugal's most beautiful Pousadas has been incorporated into one of

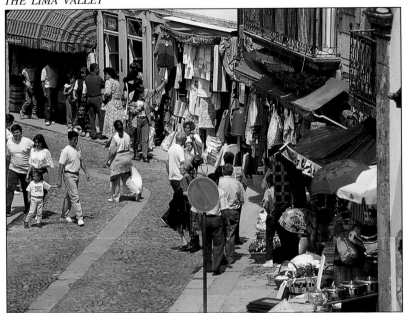

them. At this point the Minho is a wide, slow-moving river, dotted with picture-perfect islets. It pours into the sea near **Caminha**, where the Coura also converges with it. Caminha was an independent principality during the reign of Filipe II in the 17th century. The Town Hall, a Manuelistic noble palace known as **Paço das Pitas**, the clock tower of the old city wall, the Renaissance fountain on the main square, and the late-Gothic fortified church with splendid Renaissance portals and coffered ceiling are all witnesses of its erstwhile Golden Age.

THE LIMA VALLEY

The Lima rises in Spain and has carved itself one of the region's most beautiful valleys. The Romans called it *Lethe*, after the River of Forgetfulness in the underworld of Greek legend. When Julius De-

Above: Valença do Minho attracts many Spanish consumers looking for a good deal.
Right: Peace in the Valley of the Lima.

cius Brutus conquered the land, his legionaries refused to cross the river. He had to wade over to the other side alone and then call each of his soldiers by name to prove that his memory had not suffered.

As a vacation spot the valley provides many distractions, from long strolls to real hikes, angling, and swimming. It has good hotels and bed-and-breakfasts, and a large number of old manors, wealthy villas, rustic castles, and manor houses offering rooms for rent. The villages around here are all close to one another, and lure hikers with many establishments offering such local delights as homemade cheeses, hearty breads, the pork stew known as *sarrabulho*, and *vinho verde*, a young sparkling white wine. All streams are suitable for swimming, and some of the rivers have been dammed up as village pools.

The most important towns in the valley are **Ponte da Barca**, **Ponte da Lima**, and **Arcos de Valdevez**, which is on the Vez River. They are all picturesque little towns, a little sleepy at times, with medieval for-

200

tifications, Baroque churches, well-tended beaches along the river, Gothic bridges, and the standard *pelourinhos.*

A surprising sight is the perfect little Romanesque church on the side of the road in **Bravães** just before Ponte da Barca. It is all that remains of the Monastery of São Salvador that once stood here. The frescoes have been removed from the interior and transported for preservation to the museum in Lisbon. The only remaining artwork is the unusual portal decorated in naive style.

PENEDA-GERÊS NATIONAL PARK

Portugal's only National Park is a sickle-shaped territory with a surface area of 72,000 hectares that crosses two mountain ranges along the Spanish border. The Serra da Peneda constitutes the northern part, reaching a maximum altitude of 4,630 feet (1416 m). A road cuts through the mountains from north to south. Access in the north is from Mel-

gaço over Lamas de Mouro, and in the south over Arcos de Valdevez and Mezio. Megalith tombs, the fortress ruins of Castro Laboreiro, and the pilgrimage church Nossa Senhora da Peneda are among the most important sights awaiting the tourist. Mezio has a trail explaining to hikers the ins and outs of local nature.

A dammed section of the Lima River forms the southern border of these mountains. **Soajo** lies here, a delightful town where the *espigueiros*, those elongated corncribs, are arranged around the threshing floor exposed to the dry wind atop granite rocks. **Lindoso** also has *espigueiros* in addition to being a nice looking village with the ruins of an old fortress. Just below it is the reservoir of the same name, on the border with Spain.

The second half of the National Park continues in a southeasterly direction with the Serra Amarela and Serra do Gerês. Access is over Terras de Bouro, Vieira do Minho, and Montalegre. The Cávado River forms one edge of the park. A fine view over the forested mountain-

scape and its many lakes is from the Pousada do São Bento. A well signposted trail high over the river connects Cabril and Paradela, that is, the reservoirs of Salamonde and Paradela (a 5-hour hike). Farther up, far from human habitation, there are boars, deer, wildcats, foxes, and newly settled wolves. One comes across the odd herd of semi-wild horses. In the middle of the Park is **Caldas do Gerês**, a thermal bath that has been helping with liver illnesses since the days of Rome.

COSTA VERDE

Costa Verde, the Green Coast of Portugal, is the northernmost section of the country's 620-mile (1000 km) coastline, and has no less beautiful beaches than the more popular south, although the weather is not quite as stable. Little bath houses can be rented to defend against the brisk

Above: Corncribs on stilts (espigueiros) in Soajo in the Peneda-Gerês National Park. Right: The weekly market of Barcelos.

Atlantic winds. The resorts of Vila Praia de Âncora, Viana do Castelo, Esposende, and Ofir, offer a range of entertainment for all kinds of weather. Over the past few years some places have lost much of their original quality owing to uncontrolled building. On the other hand, there are still sections of the coast that are secluded and romantic, notably north of Esposende. The fish restaurants in **Esposende** and **Ofir**, two towns that face each other on the mouth of the Cávado, are considered among the best in Portugal.

The name **Vila Praia de Âncora** allegedly derives from a gruesome legend about the death of Queen Urraca in the 10th century. Her husband, Ramiro II, the King of Asturias, is said to have had her thrown in the ocean with an anchor around her neck for the crime of adultery.

Viana do Castelo, on the mouth of the Lima, combines the charm of the Lima villages with that of a coastal town. The main square is the vibrant heart of town, with its cafés and restaurants, the Gothic

Town Hall, and the *chafariz*, a large fountain dating back to the 16th century. The adjacent pedestrian zone has more cafés and historic buildings, and leads to the narrow streets of the Old Town. There's a lot to be seen here: monasteries, Baroque churches, the **Palace of Barbosa Maciel**, where the city museum keeps its extensive collection of furniture, porcelain, and art treasures. The Gothic Cathedral has a wealth of *talha dourada* works and Manuelistic decoration. The tourist office has been installed in the old hospital, and finally, there is the **Misericórdia Church** in unique Renaissance style, with fine 17th-century *azulejos*.

The colorful houses of the local fishermen and simple bars line the streets that head to the harbor. That's where one finds the great fortified complex shaped like a five-pointed star that Filipe I ordered built in 1589. On the other side of town, the pilgrimage church **Santa Luzia** greets from an elevated position. It was built in the 1920s, and is accessible by cable car.

BARCELOS

The famous rooster of **Barcelos**, who saved the life of a pious Galician pilgrim, has since become the symbol of all of Portugal. The gentleman in question had been condemned for a crime he had not committed. He swore to the judge that the roast chicken at his luncheon table would yet prove his innocence. Nevertheless, the innocent man was carried off to the gallows. But suddenly the chicken stood up and began crowing loudly. The judge, who was understandably shaken, ran out to the gallows and found the hanging defendant still alive, thanks to the support (from below) of São Tiago (St. James). After completing his pilgrimage, the man returned to the site of the miracle and donated a *cruceiros*, a cross inscribed with the whole story, and a drawing of the rooster. This cross can be admired in the open-air section of the archaeological museum. The same legend is found in many different versions along the pilgrim's road to Santiago de Compostela.

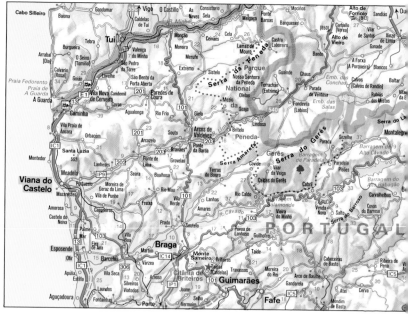

The artisans of Barcelos use this fabulous chicken as a model, and their *objets d'art* can be purchased at the weekly market, which is a lively affair at any rate. But fowl is not all that is produced in Barcelos. Earthenware, copper pots, wrought-iron work, baskets, straw hats, amusing and kitschy clay figurines, lace and woven cloth are all exhibited in the old watchtower of the city wall, next to the tourist information office.

The old town center within the walls is quite small. It begins right beside the Gothic bridge crossing the Cávado. The palace of the Dukes of Bragança, where the sire of the dynasty lived in the 15th century, once stood here. Ever since the 1755 earthquake the building has been a ruin. The **Museu Regional de Cerâmica** has moved into the lower floor. The main church in Barcelos is the **Igreja Matriz**, a Gothic structure in the heart of the Old Town. It is home to a carved statue of Mary, Barcelos' patron saint. Behind the city garden, on the north side of the Campo da Republica, is the church

Nossa Senhora do Terço, with walls covered in 18th-century tiles and a wooden coffered ceiling whose painting tells the tale of the Benedictine Order. Southwest of the Campo stands the Baroque chapel **Bom Jesus da Cruz**, which is abundantly decorated inside. Outside town are two more notable churches: the Romanesque fortified church of the monastery of **Abade do Neiva**, with a free-standing belltower; and the church of the convent of **Vilar de Frades**, which is in Manuelistic style.

BRAGA

The Romans called **Braga** *Bracara Augusta* and made it a provincial capital. Inscribed milestones of the former *Via Augusta* and other finds from the excavation site on the hill Collina de Maximinos are the silent witnesses of those bygone days. Braga is also seen as the first seed of Christianity in the west of the Iberian Peninsula. It was a bishopric as early as the 4th century. During the reign of the

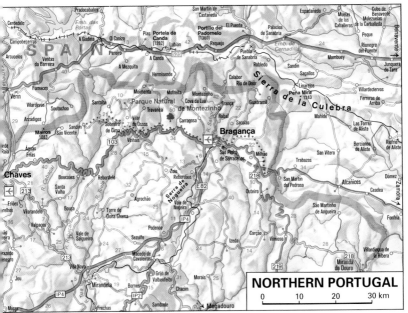

NORTHERN PORTUGAL

| 0 | 10 | 20 | 30 km |

Castilian king Alfonso VI in the 11th century, it served as the first capital of the County of Portucale, and remained an archbishopric and official residence of the country's leading church father until the 18th century. Nowadays it is the most important town in the north of Portugal. It has more than 100,000 inhabitants, a university, various institutions of higher learning, fair grounds, recreational parks, and modern shopping centers.

The historic heart of the city is transversed by wide, modern avenues. The old fortifications no longer exist, barring the reverential tower (1378) and the 18th-century city gate, the Porta Nova.

A stroll through town should begin at the main square, **Praça Municipal**, adorned with a fountain representing a pelican that stands before the Baroque Town Hall, and lead thereafter to the most beautiful churches of Braga. The first is southeast of the plaza, the **Misericórdia Church** in Italian Renaissance style, which boasts a painted wooden ceiling. To the north are **São Vincente**,

Santa Cruz, both with *talha dourada* altars, and the **Populo** Church, where the tile paintings show the history of the Augustine Order. A little farther on is the São Marcos hospital, which has its own Renaissance church. The proud Renaissance palaces give a strong flavor of Braga's wealth in the 16th century. The **Palace of the Coímbras** has its own chapel, and the **Palace of the Biscainhos** (west of the Town Hall) houses the city museum. The former Archbishop's Palace is located on Largo do Paço. It has been turned into a library and is the center of the new Minho University.

The Cathedral, **Sé Velha**, was consacrated in 1089, replacing a Visigothic construction that had been destroyed by the Moors in the 8th century. The southern portal is still in its original Romanesque style. The western anteroom was redecorated in the Renaissance period with luxurious grillework. Of particular interest in this three-aisled church are the altar, which depicts the Ascension, the 14th-century figure of Mary, the tomb of

the dauphin, the son of João I, and the Baroque high choir with its 15th-century pews. The Kings' Chapel, **Capela dos Reis**, adjoins the left-hand nave. The first duke of Portucale, Henry of Burgundy, and his wife Teresa are buried here in 12th-century tombs. A small museum displays the church treasure, some interesting ceramics, paintings, and religious sculptures. A climb up to the roof of the Cathedral is worth the effort, not only for the unique view of the city, but also to get a new perspective on some of the building's architectural fine points.

The significance of Braga as a bishopric is evidenced by a large number of churches, monasteries, and pilgrimage places in the surrounding area. The Visigoth bishop Frutuoso served as a missionary throughout northern Spain in the 7th century, and founded a number of monasteries. The **Igreja São Frutuoso**,

Above: A water fountain for the pilgrims making their way up to Bom Jesus do Monte in Braga. Right: In the Lower Town of Guimarães.

now on the edge of town, was built by the holy man as his own burial church. It is a simple, late Classical structure of impressive perfection. The crossing cupola and one side wing, however, still date back to the year 660. Inside, Corinthian columns support Moorish ogee arches. Experts think that the reason for this odd touch is that the church was rebuilt in the 11th century after being destroyed by the Arabs. São Frutuoso's grave is empty. His mortal remains are thought to be in the neighboring church of the Franciscan monastery of Montélios. But his bones are also being revered in Santiago de Compostela. Rumor has it that Archbishop Gelmirez moved them to his bishopric there in the 12th century.

There are three important places of pilgrimage in the mountains to the east of Braga. **Bom Jesus do Monte**, which looks over the urban sprawl from its 980-foot (300-m) perch, has become the town's hallmark. The 18th-century architect Carlos Amarante created a monumental double stairway, a Station of the Cross with 14 chapels ending at a wide esplanade adorned with allegorical fountains. Life-size figures depicting the Judgment of Christ stand in a semicircle. In the extensive gardens, one finds more chapels with scenes from the New Testament, a small lake, and even sports facilities.

Monte Sameiro has a 19th-century chapel in the midst of a lovely park used for Marian pilgrimages. Not too far is the Baroque church of **Santa María Madalena**. It stands on the crest of a hill near **Falperra** and a Roman excavation site.

The **Citânia de Briteiros** is on the same hill. An archaeologist named Sarmento unearthed a significant Celto-Iberian settlement at the end of the 19th century. Work until now has revealed a great deal, including a network of streets, foundations of round houses, fountains, a water supply and sewage systems, and the triple surrounding walls. Many household items belonging to the ap-

proximately 500 people who lived here about 3,000 years ago are exhibited in the Sarmento Museum in Guimarães.

GUIMARÃES

Guimarães is seen as the cradle of Portugal. Afonso Henriques, the man who led his soldiers against his own mother to achieve independence from Spain, was born here in 1111. The town was also the first capital of the new kingdom.

Guimarães is one of the most beautiful towns in northern Portugal. It has by and large kept its medieval atmosphere. Although only parts of the old city wall still exist, it is easy to trace its erstwhile path. The Lower Town is a network of narrow streets and handsome squares tightly lined with houses whose balconies gush forth with flowers. This contrasts with the Upper Town, where convents, palaces and corpulent administrative buildings pave the way to the Castle District.

Construction of the powerful **fortress** dates back to the 10th century. It was sponsored by Mumadona, a wealthy widow, who who had founded a convent here and wanted to defend it from the Moors. The great reverential tower is thought to be original, but the seven fortified towers and the massive ring wall all date back to Henry of Burgundy, that is, the 12th century. In the 19th century, the French architect Viollet-le-Duc, famous for his rebuilding of Carcassonne, was invited to restore the old fortress, which had suffered over the centuries.

The little church of **São Miguel** where Afonso Henriques was baptized stands between the fort and the palace. Near the latter are two statues honoring Guimarães' most important personalities. The one of Afonso Henriques (1880) is by Soares dos Reis, and the one of Mumadona (1960) by Alvaro de Brée.

The **Palace** of the Dukes of Bragança was built in the 15th century by another Afonso, the Count of Barcelos and first Duke of Bragança. It recalls its French models, in part even the châteaux of the Loire, though some rooms reveal typical

207

Manuelistic decorational elements. It lost its function as a ducal residence after the 16th century, and gradually became tattered by Father Time. Thorough renovation work at the beginning of the 20th century restored its old brilliance.

Rua Santa Maria leads from the Castle District down to the **Old Town**. The street is lined with cafés and restaurants, and a few structures of historic importance such as the **Carmo church**, which was once part of the São José Monastery, and the **Santa Clara Convent**, which is now used as the City Hall. The palaces of the nobility are spread out in the other streets of the district.

Praça de Santiago and **Largo da Oliveira**, which are only separated by the colonnade of the old City Hall, form together the heart of town. The Church of **Nossa Senhora da Oliveira**, on the square by the same name, was built on

the spot where the church of Mumadona's convent once stood. The first one was destroyed by the Moors. It was rebuilt in the 14th century by João I, who had vowed it should he win the Battle of Aljubarrota. The Manuelistic spire was added in 1523. The silver altar in the sacramental chapel is worth special note. It is the work of local silversmiths.

One should not fail to sit down for a coffee on **Praça de Santiago** and enjoy the view in peace and quiet. The Gothic pavilion in the center was built in 1340 by Afonso IV over the memorial stone for the victory against the Moors in the Battle of the Salado. The Oliveira Monastery once stood on the little street that connects Largo de Oliveira and the old city gate. The **Sampaio Museum** is now housed in what remains of it and displays religious artworks that were salvaged from the monasteries dissolved during secularization in the first half of the 19th century. Even a wing of the old monastery has been preserved in this museum. Rua Egas Moniz, the oldest street in town,

Above: Keeping the house spirits happy with floral decoration. Right: The old Roman bridge is the pride and joy of Chaves.

forks off diagonally opposite. Its pretty houses, now housing restaurants and bars, were built up against the city wall.

Extramuros, which means outside the wall of the Old Town, contains more churches and monasteries. The Gothic **Church of São Francisco**, which is completely paneled with tiles and has a wonderful two-story cloister, is considered the finest building in Guimarães. The **Santos Domingos Monastery**, with a Gothic church, houses the **Martins Sarmento Museum**, where, as mentioned, items excavated at the Celto-Iberian site of Citânia de Briteiros are on display.

South of the city is **Penha**, a mountain with a pilgrimage church and a large number of restaurants and cafés that welcome sightseers. On one of its slopes is the convent of **Santa Marinha da Costa**, founded by Dona Mafalda, the wife of Afonso Henriques. Only the church – a combination of Renaissance and Rococo – survived a major fire in 1951 intact. The rest of the convent has been made into an attractive Pousada.

THE NORTHEAST

The mountains in northeastern Portugal are generally lower and a little rounder. Forests and pasturelands give way to fields of wheat. The central community of the region is the thermal spa of Chaves, which is on the upper course of the Tâmega. Vidago, Pedras Salgadas, and Carvalhelos are also very popular health resorts. Anglers flock to the clean rivers and streams, and the remote mountains attract a steady flow of hunters. In Vidago there is a nostalgic turn-of-the-century hotel as well as a golf course.

Chaves was founded in the 1st century B.C. where the Roman road from Braga to Astorga crossed the Tâmega. Trajan's Bridge, named after its builder, still bears two old Roman milestones, with inscriptions telling a little about those days and honoring Emperor Flavius Vespasian. Rheumatic Romans already enjoyed the benefits of the healing waters of Chaves, which spring from the ground at a temperature of 73 °C. The fortress peering

over the town dates from the days when skirmishes with the Moors were frequent. The Dukes of Bragança kept adding to and changing it over the centuries. It now serves as an exhibition room for a military museum.

Otherwise Chaves is a busy little provincial town, whose life focusses on the main square. A regional museum has been arranged in the 15th-century **Palace of the Dukes of Bragança**. The originally Romanesque Community Church and the Baroque **Misericórdia Church** are both worth a visit. But by far the most beautiful church in the region is a few miles to the north in **Outeiro Seco**. It is purely Romanesque and in its original shape. Unfortunately, perhaps, its unique frescoes were taken down and transported to museums in Chaves and Porto.

Above: Poor soil and ancient cultivation means in the Tras-os-Montes region. Right: The Douro gorge near Miranda do Douro.

West of Chaves are the secluded ranges of Larouco and Barroso, and between them the two gigantic reservoirs of Alto Cávado and Alto Rabagão. They make up the eastern edge of the Peneda-Gerês National Park. Because of their remoteness, they tend not to be as overrun by tourists as the park.

Beyond the Rabaçal River begins the region called Tras-os-Montes. The earth is drier, even barren, the general atmosphere is pervaded by a feeling of remoteness and loneliness: villages are far apart from each other, and land parcels are a lot more generous than elsewhere. Many parts have not yet been discovered, and seem to have missed out on modern development. It is a tableau of mountains and countless streams rolling across the high plateau. Low precipitation is good for the cultivation of hardy olives and almonds, while the arid plains can only support sheep and goats. This solitary land, in particular the region around Macedo de Cavaleiros, attracts hunters and anglers from all Portugal.

The **Nature Park of Montezinho**, which covers 75,000 hectares and rises to an altitude of 4,843 feet (1,481 m), hugs the northern border. Meadows, glittering streams, oak and chestnut forests, pretty villages, and peaks of jagged slate contribute to its beauty. Above Montezinho is a little reservoir. Getting there on foot takes about an hour.

Rabal, França, Rio de Onor, Guadramil, Travanca, Moimenta, and Montezinho are villages that have not lost any of their traditional look. In Cova da Lua one frequently finds those typical slate-covered dovecotes known in Portuguese as *pombales*. Other villages still have community mills that tourists are invited to visit. Accomodations in the park area are guaranteed by a host of inns, rentable huts, camping sites, and private rooms.

Bragança, the dignified old ducal city, can be seen from a distance on the crest of a long hill. The Romans called it *Juliobriga*. The best view of the fortified complex is from the Pousada São Bartolomeu which stands on a slope of the Serra de Nogueira. The Old Town can be literally circled in a half hour on the outer ring wall, which was built by Sancho I in the 12th century. The stroll ends at the second ring wall and the reverential tower, which houses a military museum. This impressive construction, with its fantastic view from the merlons, is a must.

The Castle District is quiet and contemplative. Jewish families persecuted by the Spanish Inquisition found safe haven here in the 16th century. The Romanesque *domus municipalis*, an unusual building with an uneven pentagonal ground plan, served as an community and assembly house in the 12th century. The *pelourinho*, perched on a pig-shaped base, stands in the shadow of the wall.

Most of Bragança's churches are outside the ring wall, such as the **Cathedral** (Sé), a simple Renaissance structure, the **Misericórdia Church** of the **Monastery of São Francisco** (13th century), and a

few others that date back to the 16th century. Pedro I's secret marriage to Inês de Castro allegedly took place in the tile-covered **Church of São Vicente**.

The country is almost completely empty the farther east one goes. **Mogadouro**, which lies before the eponymous Serra, was built atop a Celtic *castrum*. The Roman, and later Moorish, fortifications were turned over to the Knights Templar in the Middle Ages before being given to the Távoras. When the Marquis de Pombal expropriated the nobles in the 18th century, all traces of the past were destroyed, and the little town behind the mountains slipped into oblivion.

Miranda do Douro, which is on the Spanish border, is somewhat livelier. The lengthy main street, which is lined with Gothic and Renaissance manors and palaces ends at the Cathedral. The place fills up with Spanish consumers, especially on weekends. The fortified walls over the deep Douro valley offer a great view of the river's canyonesque landscape, the *Arribes do Douro*.

ENTRE-OS-RIOS
AND TRAS-OS-MONTES
Accommodations

BARCELOS (053): *LUXURY:* **Condes de Barcelos**, Av. Alcaides de Faria, tel. 811061/2. *MODERATE:* **Dom Nuno**, Av. Nuno A. Pereira, tel. 815084/5. *BUDGET:* **Arantes**, Av. Liberdade, Tel. 811326. **O Galo**, Lugar da Peneda, Gamil, tel. 812683. *TURISMO RURAL:* **Quinta do Paço de Malta**, Durrães, tel. 058-971255. Swimming pool. **Quinta Sta. Comba**, Várzea S. Benio, tel. 832101. Swimming pool, riding. **Casa do Monie**, Abade do Neiva, tel. 811519.

BRAGA (053): *LUXURY:* **Parque**, Bom Jesus, tel. 676607, Fax: 676679. *MODERATE:* **S. Marcos**, Rua de S. Marcos 80, Tel/Fax: 77177/87. **Cairense**, Praçeta de Maximinos, tel. 616844, Fax: 612011. *BUDGET:* **João XXI**, Av. João XXI, tel. 61630, Fax: 616631. **Sul-Americano**, Bom Jesus, tel. 676615. **D. Sofia**, Largo S. João do Souto, Tel. 23160, Fax: 611245. *CAMPING:* **Parque da Ponte**, tel. 73355. *TURISMO RURAL:* **Casa dos Lagos**, Bom Jesus, tel. 676738. **Casa dos Castelos**, Bom Jesus, Tel. 676566, Fax: 617181.

BRAGANÇA (073) *LUXURY:* **Pousada S. Bartolomeu**, tel. 22493. *BUDGET:* **Sta. Isabel**, Rua A. Herculano 67, tel. 22427. *CAMPING:* **Municipal**, on the Sabo, tel. 26820. *TURISMO RURAL:* **Moinho Caniço**, Castrelos, tel. 23577.

ESPOSENDE/OFIR (053): *LUXURY:* **Parque do Rio**, Pinhal do Ofir, tel. 981521/2/3/4. *MODERATE:* **Suave Mar**, Av. Eng. Arantes e Oliveira, tel. 965445, Fax: 965249. **Acropole**, Praia São Sebastião, tel. 961941/42, Fax: 964238. *BUDGET:* **S. Remo**, Av. da Praia, Apulia, tel. 962585/6, Fax: 962586. *CAMPING:* **Fão**, tel. 981777. *TURISMO RURAL:* **Quinta do Matinho**, Forjaes, tel. 871167.

GUIMARÃES (053): *LUXURY:* **Pousada Santa Marinha**, road to the Penha, tel. 514453. **Pousada da Oliveira**, Largo da Oliveira, tel. 514157. *MODERATE:* **Das Trinas**, Rua das Trinas 29, tel. 517358. **Penha**, Penha, tel. 414245. *BUDGET:* **Vila Marita**, Lugar do Paço, S. João de Ponte, tel. 556997. *CAMPING:* **Penha**, tel. 414936/517451. *TURISMO RURAL:* **Casa dos Pombais**, Av. Londres, tel. 412917. **Casa do Ribeiro**, Lugar do Ribeiro, tel. 532881.

PENEDA-GERÊS NP: *LUXURY:* **Pousada São Bento**, Caniçada, tel. 57190. *MODERATE*: **Pedra Verde**, Cruz Real, Tabuacos, tel. 57444. Vacation village. *BUDGET*: **Pousadinha**, Paradela, tel. 56165. **Lopes**, Vieira do Minho, tel. 57172. *CAMPING:* **Lamas de Mouro**, tel. 051-45429, 42440. **Entre Ambos-os-Rios**, tel. 053-391289, Fax: 391496. **Rio Caldo**, Gerês, tel. 053-391271.

PONTE DA BARCA (058): *MODERATE:* **Os Poetas**, Jardim dos Poetas, tel. 43578. *TURISMO RURAL:* **Casa Nobre**, at the church, tel. 42129. **Quinta de Casais**, Bravães, tel. 42129. **Torre de Quintela**, Nogueira, tel. 42238.

PONTE DE LIMA (058): *LUXURY:* **Imperio do Minho**, Av. D. Luís Filipe, tel. 741510/1/2, Fax: 942567. *MODERATE:* **Solar das Arcadas**, Vitorino das Donas, tel. 731351, Fax: 732248. *BUDGET:* **O Limiano**, S. Gonçalo, Arcozelo, tel. 742365. **Solar do Pessegueiro**, Vitorino das Donas, tel. 731289. *TURISMO RURAL:* **Convento de Val de Peretras**, Arcozelo, tel. 742161, Fax: 947164. **Casa do Barreiro**, Gemieira, tel. 948137. **Quinta de Vermil**, Ardegão, tel. 761595.

VIANA DO CASTELO (058): *LUXURY:* **Pousada Santa Luzia**, tel. 828889, Fax: 828892. *MODERATE:* **Alambique**, R. Manuel Espregueira 86, tel. 823894. **Jardim**, Lg. 5 do Outubro 68, tel. 828915. *BUDGET*: **Magalhães**, R. Manuel Espregueira 62, tel. 823293. *CAMPING:* **ORBITUR**, Cabedelo beach, tel. 322167.

TURISMO RURAL: **Quinta da Boa Viagem**, tel. 835835, Fax: 836836. **Paço d'Anha**, Vila Nova de Anha, tel. 322459.

VILA NOVA DE CERVEIRA (051): *LUXURY:* **Pousada de D. Diniz**, Pr. da Libertade, tel. 795601/5, Fax: 795604. **Boega**, Quinta do Outeiral, Gondarém, tel. 795231. *MODERATE:* **Rainha Santa**, R. Herois do Ultramar, tel. 796227. *BUDGET:* **Balaustrada**, Gondarém, tel. 795438.

Restaurants / Cafés

BARCELOS: **Bagoeira**, Av. Dr. Sidonio Pais 495, tel. 811236. **Arantes**, Av. da Liberdade, tel. 811645. **Casa dos Arcos**, R. Duques de Bragança, tel. 811975. **Dom Antonio**, R. D. A. Barroso, tel. 812285. **Muralha**, Lg. das Calçadas, tel. 812042. **Solar da Franqueira**, Franqueira-Pereira, tel. 811293. **BRAGA:** **Churrasqueira da Sé**, R. D. Paio Mendes 25, tel. 23387. **Abade de Priscos**, Praça Mouzinho de Albuquerque 7, tel. 76650. **O Inácio**, Campo das Hortas 4, tel. 613225.Broa de Mel, Rua Cruz 288, Maximinos, tel. 614382. **Botafogo 2**, Rua Sto. André 11, tel. 611935. **BRAGANÇA**: **D. Fernando**, Cidadela 197 (castle district), tel. 26273. **Duque de Bragança**, castle distrct. **Solar Bragançano**, Pr. da Sé. **GUIMARÃES:** **Oriental**, Lg. do Toural, tel. 418923. **Mumadona**, Rua Serpa Pinto 260, tel. 414791. **Vira Bar**, Lg. Cond. do Juncal, tel. 414116. **O Burgo**, Rua Dr. Avelino Germano, tel. 516449. **Alameda**, Largo Cond. do Juncal, tel. 412372. **El Rei**, Pr. de São Tiago 19, tel. 419096. **Santiago**, São Tiago 17. **Solar do Arco**, Rua Sta. María 48, tel. 513072. Simple *Tascas* in Rua Egas Moniz.

PONTE DE LIMA: **Solar do Taberneiro**, on the Rio Lima, tel. 942169. **Império do Minho**, Av.

D. Luís Filipe, tel. 741510. **Madalena**, on the mountain, closed Thu, tel. 941239. **A Carvalheira**, Antepaça, Arcozelo, tel. 742316. **PONTE DA BARCA: Bar do Rio**, tel. 42582. **Varanda de Lima**, Campo do Corro, tel. 43469. **A Marisqueira I**, Rua das Maceiras, tel. 42514. **O Caçador**, Paço Vedro Magalhães, tel. 42106. **VIANA DO CASTELO: Os 3 Potes**, Beco dos Fornos, tel. 829928. **Alambique**, R. Manuel Espregueira 86, tel. 823894. **Espigueiro**, Quinta do Santoinho, tel. 322156. **Quinta da Presa**, Meadela, tel. 823771.

Sights / Museums
BRAGA: **Cathedral** and **Museum**: 9am-12:30pm and 2pm-5:30pm. **Museu Biscainhos**, **Museu Nogueira da Silva**, **São Frutuoso de Montélios**: 9am-noon and 2pm-5pm, closed Mon. **BRAGANÇA: Museu Militar** 9am-noon and 2pm-5pm, closed Thursdays. **Museu Abade de Baçal**, regional museum in the Bishop's Palace, Rua do C. Abílio Beça, closed Mon. **Cathedral**, **Treasure chamber**: 8:30am-6:30pm. **GUIMARÃES: Palace of the Duques de Bragança**: 9am-7pm (in winter 5:30pm). **Castle** 9am-12:30pm and 2pm-7:30pm (in winter 5:30pm), closed Mondays. **S. Miguel-Kapelle**: 10am-1pm and 2:30pm-7pm (in winter 5pm), closed Mon. **Igreja da Na. Sen. da Oliveira**: 7:15am-noon, 3:30pm-7:30pm. **Museu Martin Sarmento**: 9:30am-12:30pm and 2pm-5pm, closed Mon. **Museu Sampaio**: 10am-12:20pm, 2pm-7pm (in winter 5:30pm), closed Mon. **Museu da Arte Primitif**: 10am-1pm and 3pm-7pm, closed Sundays. **Citânia de Briteiros**: 9am-6pm. **MIRANDA DO DOURO: Museu do Terra do Miranda**: Tue-Sat 10am-12:15pm and 2pm-16.45, Sun 10am-12:15pm. **VIANA DO CASTELO: Museu Municipal**: Lg. S. Domingo, 9am-noon and 2pm-5pm, closed Mon.

Tourist information
ARCOS DE VALDEVES: Tourist Office: Av. das Tilias, tel. (058)-66001, Mon-Sat 9:30am-12:30pm and 2:30pm-6pm. **Market**: fortnightly Wednesdays. **BARCELOS: Tourist Office**: Lg. da Porta Nova, Torre de Menagem, tel. 811882/ 812135 (with handicrafts exhibition). **Market**: Thursdays. **Potters**: Mistério, in Galegos de Santa María, tel. 84227. **Coppersmiths**: Cobres Cunha, Rua da Madalena 8, tel. 811494. **BRAGA: Tourist Office**: Av. Combatente, Corner Av. Libertade, tel. 22550, 9am-7pm, Sat/Sun 9am-5pm. **Information center** of Peneda-Gerês, Rodovia Nova, Quinta das Parretas, tel. 053-613166/7/8, tel. 613169, Mon-Fri 9am-12:30pm and 2pm-5:30pm. **Bus station**: Av. General N. de Matos. **Train station**: Lg. da Estação, at the end of Rua Andrade Corvo. **Market**: Tuesdays. **Club for Amateur Anglers**, R. dos Chãos 112. **Hospital**:

tel. 613614. **Automobile club** of Portugal, tel. 27051. **Post office**: Av. Maréchal Gomes da Costa. **BRAGANÇA: Tourist Office**: Av. Cidade de Zamora, tel. 381273, daily 9am-12:30pm and 2pm-6pm, winter: Mon-Fri 9am-12:30pm and 2pm-5pm. **Information office for the Park of Montezinho**: Salvador Nunes Teixeira, tel. 381234/381444, Fax: 381179. **Riding school**, França, tel. 381179. **CHAVES: Tourist Office**: R. de S. António 213 and Terreiro de Cavalaria, tel. 21029. **ESPOSENDE: Tourist Office**: Av. Marginal, tel. 961354. **Market**: fortnightly Mondays. **GUIMARÃES: Tourist Office**: Alameda São Damas, 9am-7pm, closed Sundays. Winter: 9am-12:30pm and 2pm-5:30pm, tel. 412450. Pr. de Santiago, only in summer: 10am-1pm and 3pm-6pm. **Hospital**: tel. 512612. **MIRANDA DO DOURO: Tourist Office**: Largo do Menino Jesus da Cartolinha. tel. 41122. **PENEDA-GERÊS NP: Information center**: Lindoso, Mezio, Bico de Pássaro. Quinta das Parretas, Braga. Terras do Bouro, Vidoeiro. Gerês-Vilar da Veiga. Montalegre, Rua do Reigoso. **Riding school/stables**: Vidoeiro. **PONTE DA BARCA: Tourist Office**: Lg. da Misericórdia, tel. 42899. **Market**: fortnightly Wednesdays. **PONTE DE LIMA: Tourist Office**: Pr. da República, Tel/Fax: 942335, 9am-12:30pm and 2:30pm-6pm, Sun 9:30am-12:30pm. **Riding school**: Club Equestre, Vale de Pereiras, Arcozelo, tel. 942466/ 941552. **Market**: fortnightly Mondays. **VALENÇA DO MINHO: Tourist Office**: Av. de Espanha, tel. 23374. **Market**: Wednesdays. **VIANA DO CASTELO: Tourist Office**: R. do Hospital Velho, tel. 22620/24971, Fax: 829798, 9am-12:30pm and 2:30pm-6pm, Sun 9am-12:30pm. **Cable car** to Sta. Luzia: Av. 25 de Abril hourly 9am-7pm. **Hospital**: Av. 25 de Abril, tel. 829081. **Post office**: Av. do Combatentes. **Market**: Fridays. **Car rental**: Avis, R. do Gontim, tel. 823994. Hertz, Av, Conde da Carreira, tel. 822250. **Train station**: at the end of Av. dos Combatentes. **Bus station**: Av. dos Combatentes. **Boat rides**: Passeio Fluvial (1/2 to 3 hours) José M. Brito Portela, R. Boa Vontade 16, Meadela, tel. 842290.

Festivals
BARCELOS: May 1-3, city festival *Festa das Cruzes*. **BRAGA**: Spectacular processions during Easter week. *S. João*, festival of the town's saint June 23-25. **GUIMARÃES**: *Gualteriana pilgrimage* on the first weekend in August. Wine harvest. August 5-8: town festival. **PONTE DE LIMA**: Aug 21-22: *Pilgrimage of Sr. do Perdidos*; July 18: *Pilgrimage of der Sta. Ma. Madalena*; around Sep 19, city festival. **VIANA DO CASTELO**: *Festas da Agonia*, Fri-Sun after Aug 15, procession on the sea, folk costumes.

FOOD AND WINE

Portuguese cuisine is simple peasant cooking that makes good use of the country's agricultural products, especially legumes, and pork. Every region of Portugal has its own set of delightful specialties, and locals even insist on the fact that there are differences from village to village. The best bet for travelers with a curious palate is to try the dishes marked *a la casa*, which means house-style.

On the Minho, a good meal begins with a *caldo verde*, a soup made of potatoes and the high-stem green cabbage that grows in just about every garden in northern Portugal. *Cozido minhoto* is a solid stew, and as dessert one should try the *arroz doce do Minho*, a sweet dish made of milk and rice.

Preceding pages: The port wine barrels used to be transported on Rabelo boats all the time. Cuba in the Alentejo is one of the centers of choral singing. Above: Delicious fish dishes. Right: Lamego is well known for its hams.

Tras-os-Montes is a dry area with cold winters, and as in many regions with harsher climates, heavier foods are part of the standard fare: onion soup, *caldo de cebola*; partridge broth, *caldo de perdriz*; or a "dry" soup, *sopa seca*, are just some of the warm-ups. Many inns offer game, such as rabbit, *coelho à trasmontana*, or turkey, *pavo*, usually with fresh mushrooms (*cogumelos*).

Cod, or *bacalhau*, is the home fish of Porto, and going through a menu in any restaurant in town, one gets the impression that lengthy life stories are behind some of the dishes: *Bacalhau à Gomes de Sá, Bacalhau à João do Buraco*, or *Bacalhau à Zé do Pipo*. Other specialties are a dish of rice and chicken, *arroz de frango*, or the cutlet named after a merciful priest, *bife à Padre Piedade*. *Tripas à moda do Porto*, tripe Porto style, is the town's most famous concoction. Its history goes back to the age of discoveries, when the local farmers were requested to salt and pickle their livestock for the sailors on their long journeys. En-

trails, of course, do not keep, so the people of Porto (known derogatorily as *tripeiros*, or "tripers," in Portugal) set about cooking them up in as many ways as possible.

In the Beira, the mountainous region around the Serra de Estrêla, one finds heavy soups such as *sopa da Beira*, *sopa serrana*, and *sopa de Mangualde*. In addition to the usual meat dishes and the *cabrito* or *leitão assado*, roasted goat or lamb, the local menus often include fish from the river. Every dish is accompanied by *batatas*, potatoes prepared in the most diverse ways. Other tasty morsels are the mountain cheese *Quejo da serra*, and the various sausages, *chouriço*, *morcelas*, or *farinheiras*.

Caracóis (snails), and shrimp or prawn soup (*sopa de camarão* or *de lagosta*) are particularly appreciated in the Ribatejo and the Estremadura. The main courses often include fish, also prepared as a stew named *caldeirada*, or – especially fine – a tripe stew steamed in wine, known as *cachola*.

Peasant cuisine is the rule in the Alentejo. *Açorda* is a traditional bread soup enriched with meat, eggs, or fish, depending on the area. *Migas* are similar, a kind of bread dumpling served with pork. *Gaspacho* is a cold vegetable soup made mostly of tomatoes and garlic that can be very refreshing, especially on hot summer days. Rabbit or lamb stews (*ensopado de coelho* or *borrego*) are also very popular here, as are river fish and sweet desserts. They have such promising – and intriguing – names as *barriga da freira* (sister's belly), or *papos de anjo* (angel's goitres).

Fish is the main dish on the Algarve coast and along the entire Atlantic seaboard, be it fresh shellfish, octopus (*polvo*), or small squids (*lulas*). Most restaurants have the catch of the day on their menus and a good stew known as *cataplana*. The desserts are reminiscent of the area's Arab heritage. They are filling and very sweet, and consist mostly of honey, almonds, sugar, and eggs, such as the famous *morgandinhos*.

900 Miles of Atlantic Coast, Fresh Fish Everywhere

All of Portugal is always well supplied with fresh fish. Even if you are not doing your own cooking, you should not miss out on a visit to the colorful and lively markets of Lisbon, Porto, or the smaller ports, to get a closer look at the wide variety on sale. The restaurants inland usually offer three or four different kinds, including *linguado*, sole, a kind of tasty swordfish called *peixe espada*, the excellent sea perch *pargo*, and *congrio*, or conger eel, which is unfortunately very bony.

Along the coast one finds a number of fish that don't even appear in the dictionary, but among the finest types that are known are the ray (*raia*), the turbot (*rodovalho*), and a kind of eel (*enguia*). Fresh-water fish are often eaten in the

north, notably trout (*trutas*), and the lamprey (*lampreia*), which is a regional specialty.

If there is a national dish, then it is the *bacalhau*, dried or pickled cod, whose history goes back to the Romans. It comes in countless variations. Good cooks like to boast that they have a recipe for every day of the year. The quality of the dish depends on how the fish was prepared, that is soaked and freed of excess salt. It is then fried, steamed, fried in batter, put in omelettes, filled, or diced into a sauce; in short, the cook's fantasy is the limit. In every establishment, no matter how simple and prosaic the menu, one can be sure of a good, hearty meal when ordering *bacalhau* in the style of the house.

Another safe recommendation is *cataplana*, already mentioned earlier. The word describes a cooking vessel of copper or aluminium in the shape of an old-fashioned hot-water bottle. It is used to prepare the best stews. A fish *cataplana* usually consists of various fish and op-

Above and above right: Fresh fish is available all over the place, and is often grilled on the spot. Right: Good cheer and smiles.

tionally crabs or mussels steamed in a tasty broth. There are other fish recipes that are also worth trying: devilfish with rice (*arroz de tamboril*) or noodles (*amassada de tamboril*) is highly recommended.

The wines of Portugal

The table wines of Portugal are unknown in much of Europe, and for no justifiable reason. Every restaurant usually has access to a good, dry house wine from the region. The price is always right, and the quality above average.

Vinho Verde, green wine, refers to the fruity, young wines that are grown in the northwestern part of the country between the Minho and the Douro, and are drunk at a year of age.

The Douro wines grow along the Douro River in the vineyards east of Mesão Frio. 40 percent of the famous port wine is grown there, while 60 percent of the vineyards are reserved for the excellent Douro table wines, the most fa-

mous of which comes from the house of Mateus near Vila Real.

The Dão wines in the Beira, grown in the area between the Dão and Mondego Rivers, are also to be recommended. Here one finds probably the best Portuguese red wine: dry, mild, with an intensive bouquet, and an interesting price tag. The white wines here are equally advisable. Of similar quality are the Bairrada wines in the adjoining region around Anadia and Caramulos, where monks first planted vines in the 10th century.

The western Alentejo has five smaller wine-growing regions that are struggling for recognition. These dry, hearty wines grown around Reguengos, Redondo, Portalegre, and Borba, and the strong white wines from Vidigueira might well find a coterie of fans.

Wine-growing has been a tradition in the Estremadura since the days of the Romans. Colares, Carcavelos, and Bucelasare are all officialy recognized for their vintage wines, but the vineyards between Arruda dos Vinhos and Óbidos produce

similarly good wines. The sand wines grown along the coast near Colares to the north of Lisbon have earned the most outstanding marks: kings drank them in Sintra, Mafra, and Queluz, and King João I is said to have presented his faithful Field Marshal Nuno Alvarez Pereira with, not a glass or bottle of this wine, but the entire tract of Land for his heroic deeds in the Battle of Aljubarrota. The wine is only drunk after being aged for at least seven to ten years, and is therefore one of the most expensive in Portugal.

The wine of Carcavelos, a small area that lies between Cascais and Oerias, also received royal honors. In 1752, King José I gave a barrel of it to the Chinese Emperor. And Wellington is also said to have preferred it to all other wines.

Because of the amount of sun that pours onto the grapes, the wines grown on the Algarve coast are dark and heavy,

yet they are also mild and not sweet. There is, however, one dessert wine well worth sampling: the muscat wine of Setúbal, which was already being imported to England in the 14th century.

Port

The most internationally famous Portuguese grape is that used in making port wine. It grows in the Douro region that begins about 60 miles (100 km) to the east of Porto near Mesão Frio and stretches all the way to the Spanish border.

Port wine is fermented from white or red grapes, and consists of a mixture of vines: Touriga Nacional and Francese, Tinta Ruriz and Amarela, Barroca. The bulk of the grapes are red, but port wine made from white grapes is gradually becoming more popular. During the fermenting process, a 70 percent brandy is added to the must to bring it up to 20 percent alcohol. Depending on the kind, port wine can be more or less sweet, ranging from an *extra dry* to a *very sweet.*

Above: Modern wine-making near Santa Marta de Penaguião. Right: The experts at work in a port wine cellar.

Ever since the Methuen Treaty of 1703, which guaranteed Portugal a most-favored status in trade with England, the British developed a taste for the Douro wines, and to help preserve them on their long journey, traders started adding brandy. This heavy, sweet wine was popular in England long before it developed a fan club in its native country. It was the British, too, who set up the first exporting companies in Portugal. They used to send port wine back to England on the same ships that had arrived carrying British textiles. Their names, Taylor's, Croft's, Sandeman, Graham's can be seen in big lettering in the vineyards and at the entrance of the big wine-cellars.

Because of marketing problems and competition, the Marquis de Pombal decreed a set of detailed trade rules in 1756, defining the borders of the wine-growing region and limiting it to 250,000 hectares, of which about 30,000 are cultivated. In addition he founded a cartel controlled by the owners of the estates in the region. The smaller cultivators, who were disadvantaged by these new laws, rose up in arms, but their rebellion was bloodily suppressed and many were put to death. That is how Europe's first strictly controlled special region came to be. To this day, 103 of the 335 boundary stones placed by Pombal, more than 6 feet (2 m) high, are still standing.

Besides the degree of sweetness, the wines are categorized according to how they have been stored, in barrels or in bottles. Most consist of a cut of several vintages in order to equalize the quality. Only the very expensive wines are single-year vintages that have undergone at least 12 years of barrel storage.

The towns where port wine is actually produced are marked by large balloon-shaped containers. Most of the grapes, however, are pressed to must and shipped to the cellars of Vila Nova da Gaia (opposite Porto on the Douro) just as the British did in the 18th century. Thus, the only relationship between Porto and port wine is in the name.

THE ART OF THE TILE

There's hardly a country in the world where art has taken on such a peculiar form of expression as in Portugal. Colorful, patterned, or painted tiles decorate walls, churches, palaces, stairwells, gardens, fountains, bars, restaurants, train stations and other public buildings, as well as the unique creations put up by returning foreign workers. Decorating with tiles is a 600-year-old tradition in Portugal, and there is no end in sight.

The Portuguese word for tile, *azulejo*, derives from the word *azul*, meaning blue. The reason is that most of the tiles in Portugal are painted in a brilliant blue color. Another etymology, which is in fact more probable, is in the Arabic word

Above and above right: 15th-century tiles in Sintra and Beja (the Monastery of Conceição) – early examples of the art of the tile in Portugal. Right: The influence of Delft tiles made itself felt at the end of the 16th century (Beja).

az-zulaij, which indicates a small polished stone or mosaic tile.

The earliest examples of tile art were introduced to the Iberian Peninsula by the Moors. They decorated the walls and floors of their mosques and palaces with strictly geometric patterns (according to the laws of Islam prohibiting pictorial representation) made up of countless little colored stones. This technique was further developed in the Middle Ages and later adopted by the Christians.

The oldest extant tiles in Portugal were imported from Seville in the 15th century by Manuel I for his palace in Sintra. In those days the motifs were still by and large geometrical, and the color most frequently used was green. The tiles were prepared using the so-called *corda seca* method, in which greased cords were placed between them to prevent the different paints from running into one another. The same effect could be achieved by drawing depressions between the tiles, which meant that the pattern appeared in relief.

Only few of these kinds of tiles still exist: for example, on the floor of the palace in Sintra, in the Jesus Monastery of Setúbal, in the Conceição Convent in Beja, in the old Cathedral of Coimbra, and in a palace near the town of Vila Fresca de Azeitão.

Tile production started in Lisbon in the 16th century. The Italian Francesco Niculoso introduced the fayence technique from his native Faenza, which used pre-kilned clay tiles covered with a white tin-based glazing on which one could paint. This naturally allowed for greater freedom of artistic expression, and new forms and motifs such as plants and animals began appearing. The São Roque Church in Lisbon has some beautiful samples of the art of this period. They date back to 1584 and were painted by Francisco de Matos.

Flemish tile painting, which was most probably influenced by Ming-dynasty porcelain imported from China, became known in Portugal around the end of the 16th century. Blue was from then on the dominant color used to paint the *azulejos* thanks to the popularity of the blue Delft tiles. The use of individually-painted tiles in monochromic, functional rooms such as kitchens or corridors also springs from the Dutch tradition. *Figuras avulsas*, that is, a single image such as an animal, a flower, or a ship often surrounded by some sort of border, were painted on the tiles. A kitchen decorated in this style can be seen in the Palaçio da Pimenta, which nowadays serves as the city museum of Lisbon.

In the 17th century, the Jesuit influence on architecture made itself felt with functional buildings and gigantic, thrifty hall churches. The popular thirst for pomp and glory was stilled by the use of *azulejos* and altars of carved and gilded wood. The importing of Flemish wall carpets had for the most part ceased after the Spanish wars of religion, and vast "*azulejo*-carpets" were created to fill the vacuum. Square sections of wall were filled with geometric patterns of blue, white, and yellow, and surrounded by an

225

ornamental frieze. The churches of Espirito Santo, Santo Antão, and São Mamede in Évora as well as the São Sebastião chapel of the Lumiar Palace in Lisbon, are excellent examples of this art form.

The economic upswing spawned by the discovery of gold in Brazil at the end of the 17th century was a boon to anyone working in the building sector at the time, and the country was soon flooded with *azulejo* paintings. Many Baroque churches were decorated with acres of tiles depicting iconographical motifs, the miracles and lives of the patron saints, often with little naive details. In their secular houses, the nobility preferred mythological scenes, and later pastoral motifs in the style of Watteau. Among the more splendid examples of this period are the works

Above: A typical "convite" figure in Faro. Right: In the 20th century many public places, such as train stations, were decorated with blue tile pictures (Aveiro).

in the Palace of the Fronteira Counts on the edge of Lisbon and in the São Vicente de Fora and Graça monasteries, which are also in Lisbon. The *convite* figures, life-size lackeys painted on tiles set in the walls in stairwells or to each side of entrances, also date from this period. These friendly pictures with their inviting gestures can be seen on townhouses and palaces to this day. Good examples of them are found in Lisbon at Rúa do Comércio 38, Rúa de São Paulo 220, and Rúa de São Boaventura 43.

Beginning in the 18th century, the tile painters ceased to be considered mere handymen, but rather artists in their own right, and their names started to become known. Some of the more famous ones were the father-and-son team Antonio and Policarpo de Oliveiras Bernardes, Nicolau de Freitas, Gabriel del Barco, Valentim de Almeida, Antonio Vital Rifarto, the Dutchman W. van der Kloet, and Antonio Pereira.

After the earthquake of 1755, which destroyed much of Lisbon, tile production had to be speeded up for the reconstruction work. The Royal Tile Manufacture of Rato was founded in 1767. This factory produce entire series of tiles with Rococo motifs (flower bouquets and garlands arranged symmetrically on the panels) during the reigns of José I and Maria I.

During the 19th century, production was industrialized, and the tiles proved more resistant to weathering. This meant that exteriors could also be tiled. Shops, restaurants, office buildings, even factories began covering their façades with tile paintings with advertisements or allegories. The decorations on the traditional beer house Cervejaria Trinidade in Lisbon and the houses on the Largo Rafael Bordalo Pinheiro date from this period.

The Romantics also had their influence on the art of tile painting. Rafael Bordalo Pinheiro, the caricaturist and artist with a

strong sense of the folkloristic, founded the ceramics factory of Caldas da Rainha in 1875. It produced masses of tiles with innumerable motifs thanks to Pinheiro's inexhaustible fantasy. Ceramics as a folk art now entered the drawing room of the growing bourgeoisie. By the way, Caldas holds an annual ceramics market every July.

At the beginning of the 20th century, Jorge Colaço decorated the palace of Buçaco, a job that kept him busy until his death in 1942. He was one of the main figures in the historicist movement, which was very popular. Some of the prime examples of these works are the train stations of Pinhão, Aveiro, and the São Bento station in Porto. At the same time, the Art Deco style created new uses for the tiles in the applied arts.

Since the 1950s, a new generation has been infusing its own, often unique brand of art into the tiles. Subway stations and blank walls of modern buildings were next on line for a covering. The best place to find specimens of this contemporary art is in the newer districts of Lisbon. The mural by María Keil on the stairway of the Avenida Infante Santo between houses Nr. 64 and 72 is one example. Others are the mural by João Abel Manta on Avenida Calouste Gulbenkian near the Amoreiras aqueduct, and the one by Julio Resende on the Palace of Justice. The new subway stations to the north of Amoreiras are also decorated with tiles: Colégio Militar station was done by Manuel Cargaleiro, Alto dos Moínhos by Júlio Pomar, Cidade Universitária by Vieira da Silva, and Laranjeiras by Sá Nogueira.

Two places in Portugal in particular leave a wonderful impression of the art of tile painting. The first is the Palace of Sintra, which was a royal residence since the 15th century: the successive annexes built over the centuries were beautifully decorated with tiles. The second is the collection in the Museu do Azulejo in the old Madre Deus Monastery in Lisbon, a museum that documents the complete history of this very special art form.

227

THE MANUELISTIC STYLE

Winding cords and knots of stone around altars and window and door frames never cease to amaze with their artistry. The Hieronymus Monastery and harbor tower of Belém, the unfinished chapel of Batalha, or the church of the Christ Monastery of Tomar all reveal examples of this type of ornamentation. The term "Manuelistic," which is commonly used to describe this decorative style, is not nearly as old as the style itself. It was first used in 1840 by a Brazilian scholar named van Varnhagen, who was seeking a word to describe the architectural period between the Gothic and the Renaissance, that is, from 1433 to 1521 during the reigns of Duarte, Afonso V, João II, and Manuel I. It is a very playful style used to decorate supporting parts, and represents a liberation from the strict codex of medieval form. The first steps in that direction were made under the influence of the French flamboyant style, which manneristically distorted the solemn Gothic. The Monastery of Batalha is a good example of this period.

The further development of Manuelism was spurred by the first voyages of discovery and the new high status of seafaring. The chronicles of Fernão Lopes and the writings of King Duarte reveal that this style had many facets and its own body of forms to rely upon. It is probably the only purely native movement in Portugal's architectural history.

The earliest buildings reveal definite Moorish elements. The draughtsmen of the Portuguese fortresses on the Moroccan coast obviously bathed in the local culture. Later, nautical elements such as knots, ropes, buoys, and coral entered the picture. The acme of the Manuelistic ornamental craze are the windows of Tomar, which can hardly be seen for all the decoration. In the hardly noticeable rose window above it all, the entire world of the style is revealed: The stone carvers caught the wind in the shape of a bulging sail held by ropes.

Besides decorating portals and windows, the Manuelists were also in the habit of applying their art to the supporting elements of vaulted arches. The groins were ramified many times over so that the vault ended up in star-shaped forms. Keystones were carved with the royal initials or symbolic figures. A frequent motif is the armillary sphere, which had represented the cosmos and its orbits since the days of Plato, and now symbolized the globe, the earth's rotation, and a means to direct ships to the "New World."

Motifs varied regionally. In the Alentejo, for example, one finds such agricultural elements as artichokes, acanthus leaves, or snakes. And instead of the seaman's rope, the carvers often depicted the Franciscan monks' sash. Yet monasteries and churches were not the only buildings to be endowed with Manuelistic decoration. Civilian and secular structures were also redone, such as the Town Halls of Viana do Castelo and Guimarães, as well as parts of the palace of Sintra and the ducal palace of Guimarães.

The Manuelist draughtsmen were known by name. Designer of many buildings was the Frenchman Boytaca, who was the court draughtsman for over 20 years. He designed the Jesus Monastery of Setúbal, the Cloister of Silence in the Santa Cruz Monastery of Coimbra, the church of Golegã, and the Hieronymus Monastery of Belém. Manuel Fernandes built the unfinished chapel of Batalha; the brothers Diogo and Francisco de Arruda did the church of Tomar, the harbor tower of Belém, and parts of the Royal Palace of Sintra. João de Castilho, a Basque, worked on the monastery of Belém after Boytaca's death.

Right: The Manuelistic cloister of the Hieronymus Monastery in Belém.

PORTUGUESE LITERATURE
From Courtly Love in the 12th Century to the Tribulations of Laborers in the 20th

The earliest known examples of Portuguese literature consist of short love poems. These *cantigas* recount the tale of some (generally unhappy) love, and are usually in the form of a conversation between the lover and her mother. Almost 2,000 of these medieval verses were printed in song anthologies about 200 years later.

The first poet to be known by name was Paio Soares de Paiva. He was born in 1141 during the time when Afonso I served as the first ruler of an independent Portugal. 100 years later, Dom Dinis was on the throne, known to all as the "poet king." He founded the University of Lisbon, and made a name for himself as a patron of the fine arts. The illegitimate son of Dom Dinis, Pedro, Count of Barcelos, was the last poet to be included in the anthology of the *cancioneiros*.

In 1385, after the Battle of Aljubarrota, and the accession to the throne of the Avis Dynasty, the need was felt for a national identity and historiography. Duarte I commissioned Fernão Lopes (1380-1460) to write a chronicle that would cover the history of the past century back to the reign of Pedro I. The author wrote a social study of the country, and added his own dramatic touch to certain episodes, such as the story of Inés de Castro and Leonor de Teles. This chronicle was a treasure trove for subsequent writers, like Camões or Herculano.

The art of book printing reached Portugal at the end of the 15th century. The first book was printed in Chaves in 1498. In the same year, Portuguese seamen had opened shipping lines all the way to Calcutta. It may seem a strange parallel, but the spreading of printed material proliferated as quickly as the discovery of new lands. Within the next 50 years, a time during which Portuguese ships sailed to China and Japan, nearly 1,200 titles were printed.

Gil Vicente (1456-1536) is one of the most significant personalities of this period. He began his career as a silversmith at the royal court, but he was soon given the task of organizing feasts and celebrations. He thus started writing and staging plays. A total of 44 pieces from his pen are known today, mostly popular plays with satirical overtones. Antonio Ribeiro Chiado, after whom the artists' quarter in Lisbon is named, followed Vicente's example. Berdardim Ribeiro (1482-1552) described his unhappy love for his cousin in *Historia de Menina e Moça*. At the same time, Francisco Sá de Miranda (1485-1558) introduced Italian poetry to Portugal.

The new geographical discoveries also inspired Luis Vaz de Camões (1524-1580): his *Lusiades* represented the most important national epic of Portugal. The work tells the story of Vasco da Gama's voyage of discovery to the Orient, and also manages to include the whole history and geography of Portugal. Camões also wrote plays and poems, and his life was in itself something of an adventure. He lost an eye during the conquest of Ceuta, and his love affair with Catalina de Athayde, who was married, earned him several years of banishment in the town of Constância.

The close relationship between French and Portuguese literature is revealed in the figure of the nun Mariana Alcoforado (1640-1723), whose *Lettres Portugaises*, a collection of love letters allegedly written in the Monastery of Beja to the Marquis de Chamilly, caused quite a controversy. Rainer Maria Rilke, the German poet, translated these missives, calling them the epitome of the love letter, and used them as proof that only women were capable of true love. In the meantime, however, there's evidence that they may have in fact been written by the French-

man Gabriel-Joseph Guillerague, who lived from 1639 to 1715.

Manuel Barbosa de Bocage (1756-1805) from Setúbal wrote romantic sonnets and poems. He was a student, a soldier, and an adventurer. He traveled to Brazil and Goa, lived for a while in Lisbon, and worked at the National Library. He is best known for his satirical works.

Portuguese literature in the Romantic Age was closely connected to the French Revolution and its ideals. Its most important exponents, Juan Bautista da Almeida Garret (1799-1854) and Alexandre Herculano (1810-1877), lived in exile, but returned to Porto to participate in the struggle against the besieging Miguelists. Camilo de Castelo Branco (1825-1890) was inspired to write his story *Amor de Perdiçao* by the life of his grandfather. He wrote it in 15 days while sitting out a one-year term in the prison of Porto for an illicit love affair.

In 1862, the students of Coimbra held a demonstration to protest against their university's archaic structures. They demanded "a sunbeam of freedom and progress, and a place at the great table of liberal promises." This was the seed of Lisbon's literary Round Table that began with the so-called generation of 1870. Censorship proved to be the downfall of this group of literati, but they did leave a very multifacetted picture of 19th-century Portugal to posterity. The sonnets of Antero de Quental (1842-1891), which are considered the most polished of this period, represent a reaction against the old-fashioned tenets of the Romantic movement. The novels of Eça de Queiroz (1845-1900) describe a society beset by decadence, and criticize the power of the clergy, the aristocracy, and the bourgeoisie. Manuel Guerra Junqueiro (1850-1923), who was influenced by French literature, was also considered a rebellious critic. In his *Death of Don Juan* he turned his acid pen against Romantic transfiguration; his *Age of the Eternal Father*

Right: Fernando Pessoa in bronze in front of his favorite café, "A Brasileira" in Lisbon.

struck at the rigidity of the church; his *Homeland* criticized provincial policy making; and in *The Simple Ones* he shot his arrows at progress and mechanization.

The 20th century opened with a retrospective on older values and the *saudade*, that basic melancholic stance that is considered so typical of the Portguese. Antonio Nobre (1867-1903) and J. Teixeira de Pascoaes (1877-1952) led the new *saudosista* movement with their philosophical poems of great musical quality.

Fernando Pessoa (1888-1935) is one of the great names in world literature. His works – philosophical poems about the true meaning of things – are in fact a kind of literary network. He was a lonely person, who never married and stayed away from social life, but he created a number of pseudonyms for himself: as Ricardo Reis he was a Latinist of the Horace school, as Alberto Caeiro he became a lyric realist, as Alvaro de Campos an engineer and poet, and he naturally also published under his own name, Pessoa.

Miguel Torga (1907-1995), who was born into a peasant family in Tras-os-Montes, worked in Brazil, and went through considerable existential trouble to finance his medical studies. He eludes any literary categorization: his work consists of newspaper articles, narratives, and poems describing the reality of the Portugal of his times. His most comprehensive work is his huge diary.

José Saramago is considered the most important contemporary poet in Portugal. He was born in 1922 in Azinhaga in the Ribatejo, and worked as a translator, publisher, and journalist. His fame rests-squarely on his lyric works, his plays, and novels, which give a lively and accurate picture of the history of the Portuguese people over the centuries. Some of his most important novels include: *Hope in the Alentejo, The Memorial, The Year in which Ricardo Reis Died, The Stone Raft*, and *The Siege of Lisbon*. His latest work is a tourist guide with pictures in which he described his own country with great feeling.

SAUDADE AND FADO

King Duarte, "The Eloquent," already used the word *saudade* in the 14th century in his *O leal conselheiro*. It describes a feeling of sadness that springs from the heart. And in the 16th century, Bernardim Ribeiro gave a vivid portrayal of this inner search in the tale of a nobleman who rides along the beach until he sees an abandoned boat. He gets off his horse, climbs into the boat, and rows off to sea.

Longing, unfulfilled love, melancholy, the thirst for distant lands, are all feelings that one finds in poetry the world over. The Portuguese, however, say that this basic melancholic attitude in literature, music, the fine arts, and even in every day life, is a national trait. One generation of 19th-century poets in Porto even created the *saudosismo* movement.

The *saudade* was cloaked in music in Coimbra. Students got into this mood

Above and right: Fado – music of feeling, melancholy, longing.

during the 19th century, and the fado of Coimbra was born. They wrote melancholic songs about first – and unrequited – love, and set their lyrics in the framework of the romantic locations in their own city, such as the Cathedral.

Another variation of the fado is sung in the harbor districts of Lisbon. It originated with the seamen who put their longings to music, mixing in Arabic, Brazilian, and folk elements. This style was especially popular in the outskirts of the large city, and was connected with the social problems of the 19th century. The people, mainly the poor, living their ragged lives between the tavern, prostitution, and absolutist suppression on the one hand, and an elitist culture on the other, found a means of expression in this music. Fado, according to the words of the anthropologist and *fadista* Joaquím País, is "night, pain, loneliness, the tragedy of life, passing each other by, but also solidarity, empathy, tenderness." Alfredo Marceneiro sings one of the most famous fados of Lisbon, *A casa das Mariquinhas*, which describes a moving farewell at the doors of a bordello. And it was in fact a gypsy woman named María Severa, who in spite of a short life and career made the Lisbon fado popular in the mid-19th century. A well-known fado establishment has been named after her.

The fado moved up in society at the beginning of the 20th century. Its promotion to the concert hall occured thanks mainly the the grande dame of the fado, Amalia Rodrigues, who was born in 1921. She has been singing since the 1940s, always dressed in black, with her inimitable, serious manner, her penetrating and clear voice that can fill any room, and accompanied only by the twelve-string Portuguese guitar. Rodrigues spread the fame of the fado into every corner of Portugal, and paved its way to the stages that had previously only invited the great voices of classical music. In the 1960s she appeared on the great stages of the in-

ternational music scene, such as Lincoln Center in New York and the Olympia in Paris, and the fado suddenly became a symbol of Portuguese culture. The opponents of the Salazar regime classified it as one of the three Fs that served as a popular narcotic: Fado, Fátima, and Football.

José Afonso was one of the people who opposed the idea of the fado as a silly folk phenomenon. He was a student born in 1929 to a simple family. He began his career as a fado singer in Coimbra, but soon developed his own particular style, with songs depicting the social realities of the Portuguese people and their everyday lives. He called the songs ballads. Even his music had an individual touch: he adapted the folk music of the Alentejo, and musical elements from Brazil and Africa, where he had spent his childhood. His lyrics, which originated in the labor movement, not only brought him great popularity, but also the reputation of being an agitator. Music cassettes with pirate recordings of his concert appearances traded hands under the counter

in the student haunts of Coimbra. Afonso also landed in jail several times. It's hardly coincidental that the broadcasting of his song *Grândola, vila morena* on April 25, 1974 signalled the beginning of the "Carnation Revolution," which led to the overthrow of the Salazar regime. When José Afonso died in 1987, he left behind an extensive body of songs that have conceded none of their topical quality. They form the basis of Portugal's contemporary folk movement.

The music of Amalia Rodrigues and José Afonso has set standards that have made it difficult for the younger generation of musicians to overcome. The new, beautiful voices of the fado, such as Dulce Pontes or Misia, do prove, however, that it was possible to be inspired by the old masters while still maintaining an individual style. The sustained instrumental music of the group *Madredeus* directed by the poet Pedro Ayres and accompanied by the voice of Teressa Salgueiro has achieved cult status in Portugal.

233

POUSADAS, PAÇOS, AND SOLARES
Alternatives to Hotels

Vacationing in Portugal is a lot more than the standard travel brochure can ever hope to project. Anyone looking for sun and sea only will find the appropriate supply of large hotels in the usual catalogues, but that means hunkering in some highly touristic enclave along the coast with accommodations in the standard, uniform, international style. If you are looking for something more unusual, something individual, then you might choose private accommodations in an apartment or a small house, available throughout the country at reasonable prices, and usually integrated into the day-to-day life of the Portuguese people. Local tourist offices have information on

Above: The fortress of Palmela is a Pousada these days. Right: The Quinta de Pomarchão in Arcozelo, a former estate that welcomes guests today.

this type of accommodation. The various categories of inns are also an attractive possibility. Should you be traveling through the country without previous bookings – which is possible except around Easter and Ascension Day in August –, then stop at *albergarias* or *estalagems*. They are usually pleasant and friendly, and done up in a rustic style.

Living like Dom Dinis

If you would rather play it safe, however, and have some extra cash, then you might want to tap into the *Pousadas* network, but previous booking is imperative. These "country inns" consist of about 40 luxury hotels set in beautiful landscapes and usually in exclusively tasteful buildings. The concept behind the Pousadas was concisely formulated by their founder in 1942: "The Pousadas strive to be innocent, gentle poems of the Portuguese landscape..."

Many of the hotels have been arranged in restored and modernized historic buildings, and many of them are of considerable importance. It is a special privilege to spend the night in the palace of King Dinis in Vila Nova de Cerveira, in one of the monastic cells of the Cloister of Santa Marinha near Guimarães, in the fortress palace of Estremoz, in the Lóios Monastery of Évora, or in one of the nine rooms of the Renaissance palace in the fortress of bidos. In the past few years, some historic buildings have been added to the Pousada chain that successfully integrate old structures with modern creature comforts, as in the fortresses of Crato and Alvito, the Franciscan Monastery of Beja, and the servants, quarters (with kitchen) of the castle of Queluz.

Other hotels belonging to the chain are modern buildings, but they usually stand in especially pretty settings. Some of them have been conceived as points of departure for hunting jaunts, such as the Pousada Santa María of Marvão, São Mi-

guel in Sousel, or the Pousada of the Baron von Forrester in Alijó in the valley of the Douro. Even if you are not staying in one of these hotels, you can still enjoy the setting while having a cup of coffee.

Manors of the Landed Gentry

Turismo Rural, Turismo de Habitaçao Rural, or *Agroturismo*, are the official terms referring to accommodations in the country, ideal for longer stays, or families with children.

The rooms are often located in romantic old palaces once belonging to the gentry, the so-called *paços, hunting lodges, casas do caçador*, or manor houses, *solares*, which have been redesigned for use as vacation apartments. In some of them breakfast with home-made butter and honey is brought by a neat chambermaid, others have a park and horses for the benefit of guests. Many rent out bicycles, all of them have gardens and frequently a swimming pool. The owners sometimes live in one of the

tracts of the building, and are open to communicating with guests. Another variation on the same theme is life in a farmhouse in the middle of a vineyard, in an old mill, or in a hunting hut at the edge of a forest. Booking ahead is advisable, especially during the summer and the period around Easter.

In the north, in Portugal's green region around the Lima River, one member of the local gentry became the organizer of the local administration of these vacation homes. The area has a particularly high concentration of old mansions thanks to a historic quirk of fate. About 80 *solares* are open to the public, divided into various classes and prices: they range from aristocratic villas (*casas antigas*), estates (*quintas* and *herdades*), to country houses (*casas rústicas*). They are either large and majestic, or comfortable with fireplace, with or without a swimming pool, with or without tennis courts, but every one has been carefully chosen and cared for, and is therefore special in its own way.

NATURE AND HIKING

Hikers are for the most part aesthetes, that is why **landscape protection areas** have been earmarked in certain areas threatened by a heavy influx of tourists. Among these are the park-like surroundings of Cascais and Sintra, the Serra do Açor east of Coimbra, the fossil coast along the Costa da Caparica, and the entire cliff region of the southwestern Alentejo and the western Algarve.

Nature protection areas are even more restricted in places with a particularly delicate ecosystem: the dunes of São Jacinto, the estuary of the Tejo and Sado, the marshlands Castro Marim, the wetlands along the Mondego, or the Mediterranean bush of Malcata near the Spanish border. These spots have no hiking trails, and they should be left out of any ordinary excursions. Unless you are an enthusiastic bird watcher, or an expert in shells or orchids, you should simply avoid the places.

The **Peneda-Gerês National Park** extends along Portugal's northern border on both sides of the Lima River. The best places to begin exploration of the Park are Castro Laboreiro, Arcos de Valdevez, Lindoso, Caldas de Gerês, and, way to the east and seldom visited, Montalegre. There are few signposted hiking trails that cross this beautiful mountainous region with its many lakes and rivers that are very inviting to take a refreshing swim, but most towns and villages are connected by paths that are pleasant to walk on. Among them are, for example, the five-hour hike from Cabril to Paradela, and the road from the border post of Portela do Homem to the now-inoperative tungsten mine at the foot of the Altar de Cabrões, the highest peak of the Park at 5,029 feet (1,538 m).

Right: Hiking through Portugal, a great way to meet and communicate with people.

The nature park of **Montezinho** is probably the most beautiful in Portugal. The gentle landscape of meadows, clean streams, and unspoiled villages at the lower altitudes becomes wilder as one climbs up slopes covered in oaks, pines, bush, and shrubbery. About two dozen old mills still stand here. Day tours are possible if you are based in Vinhais or Bragança.

The **Serra de Alvão** lies to the north of Vila Real. It has many villages that have hardly changed for centuries, and where traditional handicrafts such as hemp weaving and the production of black pottery are still performed. Few trails lead into the wooded slopes that offer hikers a great deal of pristine nature and beautiful views.

The **Nature Park of Serra de Estrêla** comprises almost the entire mountain range with its manifold rock formations and numerous excursion spots. Round trips lasting from one to three days can be made from Manteigas and Gouveia. They lead through the entire range of landscapes, from the green valley of the Alva to the bizarre region around Penhas Douradas. Genuine mountain climbing is also an option here, for example up to the 6,517 feet (1,993 m) summit of the Torre. An excellent hiking map of the Park is on sale in many shops.

The **Serras de Aire et Candeeiros** are two mountain ranges lying south of Porto do Mós and Fátima. They hardly reach an altitude of 2,289 feet (700 m), and consist of delightful pasturelands divided by fieldstone walls. The sights here include the stalagtite caves near Alvados and the salt marshes of Fonte da Bica.

The **Serra da Arrábida** climbs out of the sea to the west of Setúbal. It is a small range covered in Mediterranean bush. The single road crossing it is usually jammed with visitors, but the moment one leaves it, one is in total solitude. Every turn in the road seems to offer a new and more splendid view of the Sado

estuary. Both the ascent from the little vacation spots around Vila Fresca de Azeitão on the northern side and the descent to the sandy bays on the southern side are recommended hikes.

The **Serra de São Mamede** lies in the northeastern Alentejo between the pretty towns of Castelo de Vide, Marvão, Portalegre, and Arronches. Barring a few cork oak groves, it offers a fairly barren landscape, but is most beautiful in spring when whatever vegetation grows is green and the streams are filled with sparkling water.

The **Serra do Caramulo**, which adjoins the wonderful park-like countryside around Buçaco, has not officially been declared a nature park, but it is nevertheless worth a hike. The same applies to the **Serra do Marão** to the north of the Douro between Mesão Frio and Vila Real. It offers vineyards, clean brooks and rivers, very inviting villages, and excellent regional cuisine. To the south of the Douro behind Lamego lies the **Serra de Montemuro**. Using Castro Daire as a

base, one can go on tours lasting up to five hours on color-coded paths that lead to old water mills, swimming holes on the river, little Romanesque churches, stone crosses (the famous *cruceiros*), wonderful lookout platforms, and legion villages where locals still engage in traditional handicrafts.

Even those visiting the touristically heavily built-up Algarve should have no problem finding some natural settings to explore on foot, so don't forget to pack hiking boots. Numerous trails offering breathtaking views have been carved along or on top of the steep cliffs by the sea, especially between Lagos and Salema. Paths near Alte, Benafim, and Salir traverse the pine forests that lie at the foot of the coastal mountains. The **Serra de Monchique** has a number of round-trip hikes, for example from Monchique to the spa of Caldas de Monchique, up to the breezy summit of the Picota or the Foia – the highest point in this serra at 2,949 feet (902 m) –, and to the town of Pé do Frio.

TOURADA
Bullfighting Made in Portugal

In the Middle Ages, the knights used to prove their valor by fighting the wild bulls that roamed all over the Iberian Peninsula in those days. In the 16th century, the nobles made it their privilege to saddle their horses and prove their bravery and skill by killing a bull with a single stab. They were accompanied at all times by helpers on foot, the *peões de brega*, who would direct the bull toward their master by waving a cloth or their hands, or assist in a precarious situation.

When the Bourbons acceded to the Spanish throne in 1701, this cruel game, which cost the life of many a nobleman, was prohibited. Bullfighting then became the people's form of entertainment, and because commoners generally did not own horses, fighting the bull became a "pedestrian" activity.

But in Portugal, bullfighting continued to be an equestrian sport, and even today, the best horseback fighters, who even show up in Spain now and again, are from Portugal. Once again it was the Marquis de Pombal who, in the 18th century, stepped in to regulate a spectacle that often took on absurd aspects. Ever since then, the *tourada* is carried out according to some very specific rules. A flurry of trumpets and a procession of the participants dressed in festive clothing opens the fight. Several *toureiros* irritate the bull by waving their *capas*, and the *cavaleiro* plants his *farpas* – a spear equipped with a barb – into the bull's neck. After that comes the *tercio de muleta*, which consists of one of two acts: either the *matador* holds a red cloth and works the bull alone, performing various passes that each have a name, and demonstrating his skill at dominating the animal; or the *cavaleiro* exhibits his ability

Right: The audience expects elegance and daring from the matador.

on horseback, the high school of riding, and performs a variety of *sortes*.

The function of the old *peões*, the foot helpers, became a spectacle of its own, the *forçados*, which, together with the *pega*, formed a specifically Portuguese form of bullfighting. Eight unprotected men confront the bull. The aim of the game is to get together and hold the *live* bull down. The most courageous of the men allows himself to be taken onto the bull's horns to get a grip of the animal's neck. The *forçados* groups usually appear in the *campinos* costumes of the cattlemen of the Ribatejo.

Serious bullfighting in Spanish style was particularly popular at the turn of the 20th century. Some of the great personalities of the time were João Nuncio and Simão da Veiga. The Bullfighting Museum in the Campo Pequeno has many documents relating to this period. Since 1932, killing a bull before spectators is forbidden. The spectacle has since lost much of its public interest. Discussions of the pros and cons do, however, flare up every now and then, because the bulls, who are very weakened by the fight, are killed after leaving the arena anyway.

In Lisbon, the first bullfights were held on the Rossio. The first official bullfighting arenas were not built until the 19th century. The one in the Campo Pequeno, the country's largest, was constructed in 1892 in neo-Mudejar style like the great Spanish arenas. Bullfights are held there in summer on Sundays and Thursdays.

Enthusiasm for bullfighting is waning these days. Most arenas are located in the large towns, in tourist areas, along the lower course of the Tejo, in Montijo, Cartaxo, and Coruche, where most of the breeders have their farms. Most people in these areas live from the *toiros de lide*, and an one finds an expert public. The bullfights held in the seaside resorts on Saturdays – for example in Lagos, Quarteira, and Albufeira – are usually mere spectacles to wow the tourists.

TRAVEL PREPARATIONS

Climate

The weather in summer is generally warm or quite hot. However, in mountainous regions it can become quite cool at night. In the north it even rains every now and then, even during the height of summer, so you are advised to bring along a sweater and a light rain coat or parka. Expect frequent rainfall in the north in winter, freezing temperatures in the mountains, windy weather in Lisbon (average temperature during the winter months is 13 °C), and mild early spring weather along the Algarve coast.

Customs

The standard customs regulations for most European countries apply to Portugal: for people over 17 years of age, 200 cigarettes or 100 cigarillos or 50 cigars or 250 grams of tobacco (300, 150, 75, and 400 grams for EU citizens); 1 liter of spirits (22 percent alcohol upwards) and 2 liters of wine (1.5 liters and 5 liters respectively for EU citizens); 50 grams of perfume and a quarter liter of Cologne (75 grams and 3/8 liter respectively for EU citizens). Items such as computers, cameras, videos, sports apparatus, hunting rifles, fishing rods, radios, and so on, can be brought along without charge. Other items totaling a value of 7,500 Escudos (106,000 Escudos for EU citizens) can also be imported free.

If traveling with animals, you will need a certificate of good health that shows that the pet was vaccinated against rabies during the previous year, and no less than one month before entering Portugal.

Medication

Portuguese pharmacies are well supplied. All standard medication is available, though it often has a different name than what you might know from home. If you have a chronic illness, bring as much medicine as you will need (customs allow this), and keep one package separately just in case you need more. The pharmacist will then be able to provide you with the equivalent drug.

Photographic Material

Films, batteries, video tape are readily available in all cities and larger towns. Out in the country, however, you might run into some trouble finding the right film. It is usually excessively expensive and the expiration date is often overdue. It is therefore advisable to bring along your own material from home.

Passport and IDs

Citizens from the European Community, Switzerland, and Malta, can travel to Portugal with their ID cards. A stay of 90 days is automatically granted. Citizens from other countries need a valid passport. Members of the Commonwealth and Latin American countries are also granted a stay of 90 days (180 days for Brazilians), otherwise it's 60 days. If traveling by car through Europe, you will find that the borders are quite literally open. Keep a photocopy of your passport or ID in your luggage just in case you lose the original document.

TRAVEL TO PORTUGAL

By Plane

Lisbon, Porto, and Faro on the Portuguese mainland have international airports. Lisbon and Porto catch most of the regular flights by major airlines; Faro is used mostly by charter companies. The Portuguese airlines TAP, LAR, and Portugalia often offer special fares.

By Car

If traveling from central Europe, count on two days driving. If spending the night in Spain, you would be well advised not to leave anything in your car overnight. Don't forget that many highways, notably in France, require substantial tolls.

By Train

Again, if traveling from central Europe, count on a long ride (36 hours from Germany). Trains run over Geneva-Barcelona-Madrid, and you will have to put up with at least two changes. A train connects Paris and Lisbon daily with auto-rail service as well.

TRAVEL IN PORTUGAL

By Plane

There are daily flights from Porto and Lisbon to Faro and the other Portuguese islands (Madeira and the Azores), as well as regular flights between the islands themselves. Portugal's main cities are also connected by shuttle flights.

Airlines in Lisbon: **TAP-Air Portugal**, Praça Marquês de Pombal 3, tel. (01) 57-50-20 und 53-88-52.

Airport information in Lisbon:
tel. (01) 80-20-60 und 80-45-00; **Portugalia**, tel. (01) 848-47-59; **TAP Air Portugal**, (01) 848-91-82, **LAR Linhas Aéreas Regionais**, tel. (01) 848-06-37.

Airport shuttle in Lisbon:
Linha Verde (green line) takes about 30 minutes from the airport (6 mi / 10 km) to the Rossio and to Praça do Commercio. In addition there are the lines Nr. 8, 22, 44, and 45 from the airport to the center of town.

Taxis wait in line at the exit of the airport.
Airlines at the Pedras Rubras airport (about 5 mi / 8 km north of Porto): TAP – Air Portugal, Praça Mouzinho de Albuquerque 105, tel. 69-98-41.

Airport shuttle in Faro: Line Nr. 18 goes out to the airport.

By Bicycle

Special cycling roads are for the most part unknown in Portugal., but there are countless smaller roads that are perfect for an excursion by bike. Even though bicycles are a common means of transportation in Portugal, you should be careful of the automobile drivers, who tend to go at high speeds on narrow roads, overtake in blind curves, etc... Most cities have bicycle rentals. The local tourist office can be of assistance. Should you be spending a *turismo rural* vacation, you might find bicycles for rent at your place of stay.

By Bus

The bus company *Rodoviária Nacional* has stations in all major towns. Portugal's cities are connected by bus several times a day. Local bus companies extend the service to smaller towns and villages in ther district several times a day. Their bus stations are not, however, always the same as those of the *Rodoviária Nacional*. Time of departure in the smaller towns are sometimes not signposted. The most reliable information can be had at the local cafés or in a nearby store.

By Car

The traffic regulations are pretty much the same as in the rest of Europe, and they are posted at the border crossings. Driving under the influence (0.5 per mille) results in heavy penalties. Speed in townships is limited to 60 kph, on main roads to 90 kph, and on highways to 120 kph. Children under the age of 12 must sit in the back seat. If your license is less than a year old, you will mave to limit your speed to 90 kph on the highways.

Beware! Overtaking even with traffic coming on the opposite lane is often done if the break-down lane is wide enough. If driving slowly you will be expected to make way for the faster car. This practice, however, is illegal. Also, on some three-lane roads, the central lane is used to overtake for traffic in both directions.

Main roads are laid out according to a somewhat confusing system. Many of them are also so new that they cannot be found on the usual maps. A toll highway, the A-1 (*Auto-Estrada*) connects Lisbon and Porto. Major routes (*Itinerário Principal = IP*) and other connecting routes (*Itinerário Complementario = IC*) are generally signposted. They are being built up into 3- and 4-lane roads. The IP-1 crosses from north to south in the west, the IP-2 runs along the Spanish border. Most of the other routes connect from west to east. As for road maps, one of the best is the Michelin number 437 at a scale of 1:400,000. It is very detailed. The newest roads, however, are found on the tourist maps of the tourist office (scale 1:600,000). All IP and IC routes and National/Nature Parks are well marked.

Rental Cars

There are rental agencies in all the major towns. The renter must be at least 21 years old. An international driver's license is not absolutely necessary. Renting a car is often cheaper while booking your flight in your home country.

By Train

The Portuguese railway company has been actively expanding its network and adding express trains to its program (notably Lisbon-Porto). Some routes have been put out of service, such as the last segment along the Douro beyond Pocinho. Traveling through the country by train is one way of getting in touch with the people and their everyday lives, but it is not restful. Using the train around Lisbon, Faro, and Porto, on the other hand, is practical and pleasant. Users over 65 years of age can travel at half price. Autorail trains commute between Porto and Lisbon, Lisbon and Guarda, and between Porto/Lisbon and Faro.

PRACTICAL TIPS

Banks

Banks are usually open between 9am and 3pm. Identification is necessary when changing money. They usually take a changer's fee of 1000 $ ($ is the usual sign for the Portuguese escudo). Not all banks cash Eurochecks (max. 30,000 $). Most automatic tellers accept Visa, Mastercard, and EC cards. They usually have indications in several languages, and using your PIN number, you can take out as much money as your account allows. The machines often give a receit.

Border Controls

Thanks to the European Community, controls at the borders are limited to spot-checking of vehicles. A number of new border crossings have been opened in the past few years that are not necessarily indicated on the available maps.

Break-downs and Accidents

The Automobile Club of Portugal (ACP) has a network that pretty much covers the entire country with fair efficiency. It is also affiliated with most foreign automobile clubs, so if driving to Portugal, check with your home automobile club.

The emergency number of the ACP (24-hour service) is 01-942-50-95.

In the case of an accident or breakdown on the highway, go to the nearest orange emergency telephone (little arrows along the side plank point in the right direction, and ring for help. You will have to give directions. Otherwise call 115 for all emergencies.

Business Hours

Shops usually open from 9am to 1pm and from 3pm to 6 or 7 pm; and only in the morning on Saturdays. Shopping malls generally stay open all day and until 10 or 11pm. Museums and other noteworthy sights are by and large open from 10am to 12:30pm and from 2pm to 5pm, in summer sometimes until 6pm in order to accommodate the heavier crowds. Mondays they stay closed.

Clothing

The Portuguese habits should be respected at all times, especially when it comes to visiting churches or places of pilgrimage during masses or events:

avoid wearing shorts, mini skirts, or revealing T-shirts and tank tops. Skinny dipping is not common except on some Algarve beaches. Topless bathing is accepted on beaches frequented by tourists.

Crime

The most common crime is petty larceny, a sad fact throughout Europe. One should always make sure one's car is empty when parked in Lisbon or Porto. That includes removal of the radio/cassette player. Beware of pickpockets, too, especially in crowded places such as train stations, tourist markets, and the like. You should not leave things lying about without supervision in camping sites or on the beach. Make note of the number of your credit cards or check card and checks, and inform your bank immediately in the event they should be stolen.

Currency

The Portuguese currency is the escudo, which is abbreviated to $. Coins come in denominations of 1, 2, 5, 10, 20, 50, 100, 200, 500, and bills in denominations of 1,000, 2,00, 5,000 and 10,000. Import of currency is unlimited, export is limited to 100,000. In case of larger transfers (for buying land or making a bank deposit), consult the Portuguese consulate in your home country. Major credit cards (Visa, Mastercard, American Express) are accepted throughout the country.

Drinking Water

Tap water throughout Portugal can be drunk, but it is fairly well chlorinated in some places. Mineral water in bottles (*agua mineral*) without carbonation comes from natural springs and is available all over the place.

Eating

Finding an inexpensive restaurant in Portugal is not a problem. Breakfast (considered a light meal) is usually served between 8am and 10am, lunch between noon and 3pm, and dinner from 7pm onward. Every restaurant is required to serve a tourist menu that is usually cheap and includes something to drink. In addition to the meal, it is customary to serve bread, butter, and an assortment of patés or a cheese. Each of these tidbits is charged separately, so you may end up with a higher bill than you calculated. If you would rather forego these dishes – the main meal being usually quite filling – tell the waiter while he is serving them.

Electricity

Portugal runs on 220 volts, and uses standard Continental European plugs.

Gas Stations

The supply network for drivers covers the entire country, and unleaded gasoline can be found increasingly even in the more remote places. The stations along the highway are open all night. Those along the major roads usually close at midnight, those in smaller towns at 8pm. Diesel: *gasoleo*; super: *super*; normal: *normal*; lead-free: *sim chumbo*.

Handicapped Service

Only few hotels and sights have been properly arranged for the handicapped (fortresses, monasteries, museums), and public buildings are not at all handicapped-friendly.

Markets

Every major town has a covered market that is open every day, and offers vegetables, fruit, meat, and fish. They are usually open during normal business hours, though in the smaller towns they might close for the afternoon. The periodic village markets, that generally last a week or two weeks (in smaller villages), are the right place to purchase household articles, textiles, and clothing. You will also find regional handicrafts, homemade products such as honey, jams, and cheese.

Medical Care / Emergencies

Medical care in Portugal is good, and guaranteed throughout the country. Hospitals have ambulance service that is for the most part free of charge in the case of an emergency. The Algarve coast has a number of foreign doctors (German, British), and several private clinics. For more information, consult the local tourist office or your receptionist. The medical emergency number is 115.

Museums

Museums in Portugal are by and large state-run, but there are a number of private ones as well. Regional and local museums are legion. Almost all are closed on Mondays, and stick to the usual opening hours during the rest of the week. Small towns often have a regional or community museum (*museu municipal*) giving an overview of local history beginning with Roman tombstones, and ending with the collection of snuff-boxes of the museum's sponsor. The most interesting items are often buried in a lot of fluff. Most museums only take visitors through in groups or with a guide.

National holidays

National holidays are on January 1 (New Year's Day); April 25 (the day of the"Carnation Revolution"); Good Friday; May 1; Corpus Christi; June 6 (day of the death of Luis de Camoooes); June 10 (national holiday); August 15 (the Ascencion); October 5 (Republic Day); November 1 (All Saints' Day); December 1 (Independence Day); December 8 (Immaculada, the day of the Immaculate Conception); December 25 (Christmas): Furthermore, many areas and towns have their own festivals and feast days.

National Parks

Portugal has one national park and a whole range of nature parks and nature conservation areas. The **Serviço Nacional de Parques, Reservas e Conserva-** çao de Naturaleza, R. Ferreira Lapa 29, 1100 Lisbon. The parks all have information centers located in the nearest larger town. They offer brochures giving details on hiking paths, the local fauna and flora, special teaching itineraries, and the like. These offices are also responsible for renting out cabins for four to ten people, where one can stay for a few days or even weeks at a relatively low rate.

Pharmacies

Pharmacies (*farmácia*) are open during normal business hours. Many drugs are available without the prescription required in other countries, for example, antibiotics. The nearest emergency pharmacy is usually indicated.

Post Offices

The *correio* is open 8:30am-6pm weekdays in larger towns, otherwise 9am-12:30pm and 2:30pm-6pm. Post offices close weekends. Stamps are sold in places that have a red horse as an emblem. Public phones out in the provinces are marked with a sign saying CCT.

Press

International newspapers and magazines are available in most large towns and tourist areas. The papers arrive on the day of printing in Lisbon, but you will have to put up with at least a day's delay out in the country.

Shopping

Portugal is by and large cheaper than the rest of Europe. Wages in the textile industry are quite low, and such wares (bed linen, towels, etc) are inexpensive in comparison to elsewhere, especially along the border. On the other hand, finding good wine or port at a reasonable price is not that easy. Purchasing from a cooperative is cheaper than from a private dealer. Pottery is available throughout Portugal at a reasonable price. It makes for a good and practical souvenir.

Sports

Fishing is very popular throughout Portugal. Sea fishing is done along the beach and along the steep cliffs. Fishing in lakes requires a special permit. For more information get in touch with the local tourist office, or call the fishing federation of Portugal (FPPD) in Lisbon, tel. (01) 356-3147.

Golf: There are about 30 golf courses in Portugal. 17 of those are along the Algarve coast, eight are around Lisbon, the rest are around Porto, near Peniche, Rio Maior, Viseu, and Ponte de Lima. Membership in the local club is not usually needed if you would like to play a round.

Hunting: Many inland areas have been advertising for their good hunting. There are special hunting lodges out in the country (see pp. 237 and 247 below). Hunting permits are available for the northern half of the country from the **Comissiâo Venatoria Regional do Norte**, Rua dos Poveiros 56, 4000 Porto, and for the southern part from the **Comissiâo Venatoria Regional do Sul**, Av. Jólico Dinis 26, 1000 Lisbon.

Riding: There are numerous riding centers around the larger towns and along the Algarve coast. These *centros hipicos* offer horses for excursions and lessons. The manors used by *Turismo rural* frequently have stables.

Sailing: The Atlantic coast is a great sailing challenge, but one should be experienced, or at least check with the local weather station before heading out to sea. The Algarve coast has many yacht harbors, but they are not cheap. The best harbors along the western coast are around Lisbon, Sétubal, and Estoril.

Surfing and **Windsurfing**: There are a number of windsurfing schools on the Algarve, and the best and strongest winds are around Sagres. The best surfing waves are along the western coast where the Atlantic breaks in huge swells. Surfers and swimmers are warned about the powerful currents that can be lethal!

Telephone and Fax

Telephoning to and from Portugal can be done directly, and that from every public phone. The easiest way of phoning is by arming yourself with a telephone card (*crediphone*) which is available at the post office. They come in two sizes: 50 and 120 units. Coin-operated phones only take coins of up to 50 $.

The international code for Portugal is 00351. To dial a number in Portugal from abroad you then leave the first 0 out of the number in Portugal. The international codes from portugal are: United States and Canada 001; England 0044; Australia 0061; New Zealand 0064.

Time

Since March 31, 1996, Portugals's clocks have been set to Western European Time (Greenwich Mean Time, GMT), as the country lies at the extreme western end of the Greenwich Mean Time Zone. The switch from winter to summer time is the same as in the rest of Europe.

Tips

Service Charges are included in the price. Nevertheless, it is common practice to round up the sum to the nearest hundred. In the better establishments, one usually leaves about 10 percent, depending on the service naturally.

Toilets

Public toilets are frequent in Portugal, and they are generally kept clean. The sign pointing the way says *Sanitarios*. The ladies' room is marked *mulheres* or *senhoras*, the men's room *homems* or *cabalheiros*.

Tourist Information

Just about every town and village has a tourist office (*posto do turismo*). They share the same business hours as most shops. In larger towns they do stay open during the lunch hour, and in tourist spots they close at 8 or 9pm in summer. City maps and information about local hotels or other accommodations are given for free. Furthermore, the entire country has been artificially divided up into touristic regions that have nothing to do with the normal administrative districts of the land. These regions have such names as the"Blue Coast" or the"Golden Plain," and they have their own tourist information centers in their main town. You will find the address and phone numbers of the regional tourist offices listed at the end of each chapter in this book dealing with that region.

ACCOMMODATIONS

Camping

Camping sites in Portugal are for the most part well tended to. The *Roteiro Campista*, a camping guide that is updated every year, can be purchased throughout the country. It gives a detailed description of every site, and grants them one to four stars, depending on the quality. Most sites have hook-ups for campers/mobile homes, and some even rent out little inexpensive bungalows. Many of the camping sites belong to private organizations, the most important ones being ORBITUR and INATEL. Membership is not a must to use these sites.

Hotels

Hotels come in all varieties from one to five stars. There is no official body that grants these stars, so they can only be taken as a vague point of reference. The official hotel guide is incomplete and gives no prices.

Other categories are: *albergaria*, a country hotel; *estalagem*, a quality inn; *residencial*, a residence, hotel without restaurant; *pensão*, bed-and-breakfast; *casa de hóspedes*, guest house, a simple bed-and-breakfast; *dormidas*, a sleeping place.

Reservations

If traveling to the seaside in Portugal during the summer season and around Easter, you would be well advised to make reservations in advance. The same applies to taking up accommodations in Pousadas or in country manors (*turismo rural*). If planning a round rip in Portugal, it is enough to make a phone call a few days before your arrival.

Many hotels are in the meantime equipped with fax machines. This is probably the best way of getting your message through loud and clear without being transferred from one office to the next and speaking with people whose command of the English language might be rudimentary at best.

Youth Hostels

There are youth hostels in Alcoutim, Areie Branca, Aveiro, Braga, Coimbra, Esposende, Faro, Lagos, Leira, Lisbon, Mira, the Peneda-Gerês National Park, Ovar, Porto, Portalegre, Portimaaao, Praia da Areia Branca, Serra da Estrêla, Santarém, Sintra, Setúbal, Vila Nova de Ceveira, Vila Real, Vila Real de Santo António. An international youth hostel pass is required.

Pousadas

Pousadas are the state-run luxury hotels. For brochures and reservations write or call: **Pousadas de Portugal**, Av. Sta. Joana a Princesa 10, 1700 Lisbon, tel. (01) 848-1221/848-9078/848-4602. Fax: (01) 805-5846/848-4349.

All tourist offices have a list of the Pousadas with the updated prices according to the season.

Turismo Rural or holidays in the country

Accommodations are in old noble manors, town villas, small castles, estates, and the like. The addresses usually have no street number, but rather refer to a small village, or some place out in the country. The nearest larger town is used as a postal address.

Official categories:

Turismo de Habitação (TH): a room in a manor, noble or historic residence.

Turismo rural (TR): room or apartment in an estate or other rural setting.

Agro-turismo (AT): room or apartment in a farmhouse or partly working estate.

A complete catalogue (*Guia Oficial do Turismo Rural*) is on sale at the **Direcçâo-Geral do Turismo**, Av. António Augusto de Aguiar 86, 1000 Lisbon, tel. (01) 57-50-86, Fax: 55-69-17.

The regional union of renters **TURI-HAB** runs about 80 establishments of varying quality in the north of the country: **Associação do Turismo de Habitação**, Praça da República, 4990 Ponte de Lima, tel. (058) 74-16-72/74-28-27/94-27-29; Fax: (058) 74-14-44.

PRIVETUR: **Associaçâo Portuguesa do Turismo de Habitaçâo**, Largo das Pereiras, 4990 Ponte de Lima, Tel/Fax: (058) 74-14-93.

ADDRESSES

Embassies and Consulates in Portugal
AUSTRALIA: Av. da Liberdade, 244-2. e 4., 1200 Lisbon, tel. (01) 52-33-50, 52-34-21. **CANADA**: Av. da Liberdade, 144-156-4, 1200 Lisbon, tel. (01) 347-48-92. **GREAT BRITAIN**: Rua S. Domingos à Lapa, 37, 1200 Lisbon, tel. (01) 396-1191, 396-11-47. **IRELAND**: Rua da Imprensa à Estrela 1-4, 1200 Lisbon, tel. (01) 60-45-19, 396- 15-69. **U.S.A.**: Av. das Forças Armadas, 1600 Lisbon, tel. (01) 726-66-00.

Portuguese Tourist Offices Abroad
CANADA: 60 Bloor Street West, Suite 1005, Toronto, Ontario M4W 3B8, tel. (1) 416-921-7376, Fax: (1) 416-921-13-53. **GREAT BRITAIN**: 22-25a Sackville Street, 2nd Floor, London WIX IDE, tel. (44) 171-494-1441, Fax: (44) 171-494-1868. **IRELAND**: 54, Dawson Street, Dublin 2, tel. (353) 670-9133/34. Fax: (353) 670-9141. **U.S.A.**: 590 Fifth Avenue, 4th Floor, New York, N.Y. 10036-4704, tel. (1) 212-354-4403/4, Fax: (1) 212- 494-1868.

GLOSSARY

Albufeira . . . . Lagoon
Alcáçova . . . . Arab fortress
Alfarje Wooden ceiling in Moorish style
Alminha . . . . Cross by the road
Anta . . . . Dolmen, megalith
Barragem . . . . Storage lake
Cruceiro . . . . Stone cross by the road
Chafariz . . . . Baroque fountain
Chromleche . . . . Cromlech, Stone-Age cultic place
Espigueiro Wooden or granite corncrib
Igreja Matriz . . . . Community church
Manuelino . . . . . . Very ornamented Renaissance style
Menhir . . . . Menhir
Mozarabes . . . . Christians who lived in Moorish Spain
Mudéjar . . . . Moorish building style after the Reconquista
Padrão . . . . Memorial column
Pelourinho . . . . Pillory
Pousada . . . Inn in the country, chain of luxury hotels
Quinta . . . . . Country manor, estate
Reconquista . . . . . . Re-conquering from the Moors
Sé . . . . Cathedral
Solar . . . . Nobleman's palace
Talha dourada . . Gilded woodcarving, late Baroque

Basic vocabulary
Tourist office . . . . *posto do turismo*
Post office . . . . *correio*
Doctor . . . . *médico*
Toilets . . . . *sanitarios*
Man . . . . *homem*
Woman . . . . *senhora, mulher*
Postal stamp . . . . *selo*
yes / no . . . . *sim / nâo*
Thank you (as a man) . . . . *obrigado*

Thank you (as a woman)	*obrigada*
Please	*por favor*
Hello	*bom día*
Good afternoon	*boa tarde*
Good night	*boa noite*
Excuse me	*desculpe*
right / left	*dereita / esquerda*
with / without	*com / sem*
a lot / a little	*moito / pouco*
more / less	*mais / menos*
big / small	*grande / pequeno*
hot / cold	*quente / frio*
good / bad	*bom / mau*
white / black	*branco / preto*
cheap / expensive	*caro / barato*
open / closed	*aberto / fechado*
pull / push	*puxe / empurre*
I don't understand	*não comprendo*
Where is...?	*onde é...?*
How much is...?	*quanto custa?*
Street	*rua, carrer*
Square	*praça, largo*
City district	*bairro*
Bus/train stop	*paragem*
Junk store, antiques	*velharias*
Lookout platform	*miradouro*
Bullfight	*tourada*
Disco	*boite*
Money exchange	*cambio*
Gas station	*gasolineira*
Unleaded	*sem chumbo*
Diesel	*gasoleo*

Days of the week

Monday	*segunda feira* (2ª)
Tuesday	*terceira feira* (3ª)
Wednesday	*cuarta feira* (4ª)
Thursday	*quinta feira* (5ª)
Friday	*sexta feira* (6ª)
Saturday	*sábado*
Sunday	*domingo*

Numbers

One	*um*
Two	*dois*
Three	*três*
Four	*quatro*
Five	*cinco*
Six	*seis*
Seven	*sete*
Eight	*oito*
Nine	*nove*
Ten	*dez*
Eleven	*onze*
Twelve	*doze*
Twenty	*vinte*
Hundred	*cem*
Thousand	*mil*

In the restaurant

Menu	*ementa*
Tourist menu	*ementa turística*
Daily special	*prato do día*
Breakfast	*pequeno almoço*
Lunch	*almoço*
Dinner	*jantar*
The bill	*conta*
Snacks	*petiscos*
House style	*a la casa*
Bread	*pão*
Water	*agua*
Butter	*manteiga*
Sugar	*açucar*
Lemon	*limão*
Oil	*oleo*
Garlic	*alho*
Salt	*sal*
Broth / Soup	*caldo / sopa*
Ham	*presunto*
Olives	*azeitonas*
Rice	*arroz*
Egg	*ovo*
Noodles	*massa*
Potatoes	*batatas*
Cheese	*queijo*
Fried	*assado*
Grilled	*grelhado*
Boiled	*cozido*
In batter	*frito*
Meat	*carne*
Pork	*porco*
Beef	*bife, vaca*
Veal	*vitela*
Lamb	*borrego, anho*
Suckling pig	*leitão*
Rabbit	*coelho*
Poultry	*aves*
Chicken	*frango*
Turkey	*peru*
Fish	*peixe*
Steinbutt	*rodavalho*

Tuna . . . . *atum*
Makerel . . . . *cavala*
Cod, dried cod . . . . *bacalhau*
Salmon . . . . *salmão*
Eel . . . . *engula, enguia*
Ray . . . . *raia*
Sole . . . . *linguado*
Calamares . . . . *lula*
Octopus . . . . *polvo*
Sea eel . . . . *peixe espada*
Lamprey . . . . *lampreia*
Perch . . . . *pescada*
Trout . . . . *truta*
Vegetables . . . . *legumes*
Fruit . . . . *frutas*
Salad . . . . *salada*
Dessert . . . . *postre*
Drinks . . . . *bebidas*
Glass . . . . *vaso*
Bottle . . . . *garrafa*
Red / white wine . *vinho tinto / branco*
House wine . . . . *vinho da casa*
Beer . . . . *cerveja*
Mineral water . . . . . *agua mineral*
Juice . . . . *sumo*
Milk . . . . *leite*
Tea . . . . *chá*

AUTHORS

Dr. **Sabine Tzschaschel**, Project Editor of the two Nelles Guides *Spain North* and *Spain South* and author of numerous travel pieces, studied geography in Munich and taught for many years at the university there. She has focussed much attention on the cultural and economic aspects of Portugal and Spain. She lived for many years in Madrid as a free-lance writer, and works nowadays at the Geographical Institute in Leipzig.

Dr. **Gabriel Calvo**, who hails from Spain, is a professor of literature and author of screenplays. He studied in Bilbao and Madrid, and taught in Cadiz, Sevilla, Nürnberg, and Bayreuth. He is a free-lance journalist who divides his time between Germany and Madrid. His studies of the cultural connections on the Iberian Peninsula have led him on many trips through Spain and Portugal. His profound essays on culture and history already enriched the Nelles Guides *Spain North* and *Spain South*.

PHOTOGRAPHERS

Archiv für Kunst und Geschichte Berlin 22, 24, 26, 28
Begsteiger, A. M. 8/9, 108, 113, 154
Calvo, Gabriel 14, 16, 18, 19, 20, 29, 30, 40, 48R, 50, 56, 62/63, 67, 70, 71, 75, 80/81, 82, 89, 91, 92, 97, 114, 116, 122, 126, 127, 128R, 129, 130, 131, 132, 134, 135, 145, 151, 152, 164, 166, 169, 177, 178, 188, 190, 192, 196/197, 207, 211, 216/217, 218, 219, 221, 224R, 225, 226, 227
Castor, Dietlind 237
Day, Roger 235
Ender, Klaus 17, 115
Event Horizons 72
Fischer, Peter 34/35, 36/37, 38, 41, 48L, 51, 53, 57, 58, 220L, 231
Galikowski, Elisabeth 21, 66, 73, 149, 167, 233
Gassner, Andreas cover, 69, 86, 93, 98, 120/121, 144, 175, 179, 182/183, 189, 191, 193, 208, 210, 223
Gruschwitz, Bernd 160, 224L, 229
Haafke, Udo 109
Hackenberg, Klaus (Mainbild) 10/11
ICEP, Portuguese Tourist- and Trade office 239
Rein, Udo 25, 45, 49, 94, 102/103, 112
Riethmüller, Robert 12/13, 46
Rudolph, Walter 104
Scheibner, Johann 31, 33, 44, 47, 52, 76, 234
Skupy-Pesek, Jitka 128L, 220R
Stankiewicz, Thomas 232
Stuhler, Werner 23, 110, 148, 158/159
Wackenhut, Jürgen 111, 133, 138/139, 140, 146, 165, 168, 174, 176, 184, 198, 200, 201, 202, 203, 206, 209, 214/215, 222

Explore the World

AVAILABLE TITLES

Australia
Bali / Lombok
Berlin and Potsdam
Brittany
California
 Las Vegas, Reno,
 Baja California
Cambodia / Laos
Canada
 Ontario, Québec,
 Atlantic Provinces
Caribbean
 The Greater Antilles,
 Bermuda, Bahamas
Caribbean
 The Lesser Antilles
China
Corsica
Crete
Cyprus
Egypt
Florida
Greece - *The Mainland*
Hawaii
Hungary
India
 Northern, Northeastern
 and Central India

India
 Southern India
Indonesia
 Sumatra, Java, Bali,
 Lombok, Sulawesi
Ireland
Israel - with Excursions
 to Jordan
Kenya
London, England and Wales
Malaysia
Mexico
Morocco
Moscow / St Petersburg
Munich
 Excursions to Castels,
 Lakes & Mountains
Nepal
New York - *City and State*
New Zealand
Paris
Philippines
Portugal
Prague / Czech Republic
Provence
Rome
South Africa
Spain - *North*

Spain
 Mediterranean Coast,
 Southern Spain,
 Balearic Islands
Sri Lanka
Thailand
Turkey
Tuscany
U.S.A.
 The East, Midwest and
 South
U.S.A.
 The West, Rockies and
 Texas
Vietnam

Nelles Guides – authorative, informed and informative.
Allways up-to-date, extensivley illustrated, and with first-rate relief maps.
256 pages, appr. 150 color photos, appr. 25 maps

Explore the World

AVAILABLE TITLES

Afghanistan 1 : 1,5 M
Australia 1 : 4 M
Bangkok - *Greater Bangkok,*
  Bangkok City 1 : 75 Th / 1 : 15 Th
Burma - Myanmar 1 : 1,5 M
Caribbean Islands 1 *Bermuda,*
  Bahamas, Greater Antilles
  1 : 2,5 M
Caribbean Islands 2 *Lesser Antilles*
  1 : 2,5 M
Central America 1 : 1,75 M
Crete - Kreta 1 : 200 Th
China 1 - *Northeastern* 1 : 1,5 M
China 2 - *Northern* 1 : 1,5 M
China 3 - *Central* 1 : 1,5 M
China 4 - *Southern* 1 : 1,5 M
Egypt 1 : 2,5 M / 1 : 750 Th
Hawaiian Islands
  1 : 330 Th / 1 : 125 Th
Hawaiian Islands 1 *Kauai* 1 : 125 Th
Hawaiian Islands 2 *Honolulu*
  - *Oahu* 1 : 125 Th
Hawaiian Islands 3 *Maui - Molokai*
  - *Lanai* 1 : 125 Th
Hawaiian Islands 4 *Hawaii, The*
  Big Island 1 : 330 Th / 1 : 125 Th
Himalaya 1 : 1,5 M
Hong Kong 1 : 22,5 Th
Indian Subcontinent 1 : 4 M

India 1 - *Northern* 1 : 1,5 M
India 2 - *Western* 1 : 1,5 M
India 3 - *Eastern* 1 : 1,5 M
India 4 - *Southern* 1 : 1,5 M
India 5 - *Northeastern - Bangladesh*
  1 : 1,5 M
Indonesia 1 : 4 M
Indonesia 1 *Sumatra* 1 : 1,5 M
Indonesia 2 *Java + Nusa*
Tenggara
  1 : 1,5 M
Indonesia 3 *Bali* 1 : 180 Th
Indonesia 4 *Kalimantan* 1 : 1,5 M
Indonesia 5 *Java + Bali* 1 : 650 Th
Indonesia 6 *Sulawesi* 1 : 1,5 M
Indonesia 7 *Irian Jaya + Maluku*
  1 : 1,5 M
Jakarta 1 : 22,5 Th
Japan 1 : 1,5 M
Kenya 1 : 1,1 M
Korea 1 : 1,5 M
Malaysia 1 : 1,5 M
West Malaysia 1 : 650 Th
Manila 1 : 17,5 Th
Mexico 1 : 2,5 M
Nepal 1 : 500 Th / 1 : 1,5 M
Trekking Map *Khumbu Himal /*
  Solu Khumbu 1 : 75 Th
New Zealand 1 : 1,25 M
Pakistan 1 : 1,5 M
Philippines 1 : 1,5 M

Singapore 1 : 22,5 Th
Southeast Asia 1 : 4 M
Sri Lanka 1 : 450 Th
Tanzania - Rwanda, Burundi
  1 : 1,5 M
Thailand 1 : 1,5 M
Taiwan 1 : 400 Th
Vietnam, Laos, Cambodia
  1 : 1,5 M

FORTHCOMING

Colombia - Ecuador 1 : 2,5 M
Trekking Map *Kathmandu Valley /*
  Helambu, Langtang 1 : 75 Th
Venezuela - Guyana, Suriname,
  French Guiana 1 : 2,5 M

Nelles Maps in european top quality!
Relief mapping, kilometer charts and tourist attractions.
Allways up-to-date!